Nuffield
HOME ECONOMICS

THE BASIC COURSE

BEDFORDSHIRE EDUCATION SERVICE
STRATTON SCHOOL
BIGGLESWADE, BEDFORDSHIRE

The pupil to whom this book is issued must enter his or her name and the other details on the first vacant line.

NAMES OF PREVIOUS OWNERS MUST NOT BE DELETED

Date	Name and Initials	Form	Condition A, B or C

Each pupil is responsible for the books issued and at the end of a year must return them. In case of loss the value of the book must be refunded.

Organizers, Nuffield Home Economics 1977—81:
Harry Falukner and Sharon M. Mansell
General Editors, *The Basic Course:*
Harry Faulkner and Sharon M. Mansell
Consultant General Editor, from 1981: Marie Edwards

FOOD SCIENCE

Editor	Sharon M. Mansell
Authors	Denise Bowen
	Joy Grossman
	Ralph Hancock
	Barbara Lake
	Sharon M. Mansell
	Helen J. Maunder

NUTRITION

Editors	Sharon M. Mansell
	Jenny Salmon
Author	Jenny Salmon

FIBRES AND FABRICS

Editors	Sharon M. Mansell
	A. Ridley
Author	A. Ridley

PEOPLE AND HOMES

Editor	Harry Faulkner
Authors	Harry Faulkner
	Mike Lyth

The Nuffield-Chelsea Curriculum Trust would like to thank the following who acted as consultants or who took part in the early stages of planning this book:

Dr Geoffrey Bevan,
Lever Brothers Ltd

Michael K. Bowker

Mary Chinnery

Margaret Chitty

Gwen Conacher,
Electricity Council

Dr R.C. Hardwick,
National Vegetable Research Station

Colin Harrison

Edgar Howard

Eva Mitchell

Dr P.K. Mitchell

Maureen Sawbridge,
Shirley Institute

Betty Tuckley

Don Withnall

The Trust would also like to thank Nottingham Educational Supplies Ltd, 17 Ludlow Hill Road, Melton Road, West Bridgford, Nottingham NG2 6HD for their help in developing the Nuffield Fibres and Fabrics Pack associated with the work in this book and in *Fibres and Fabrics*.

Nuffield
HOME ECONOMICS
The Basic Course

Published for the Nuffield-Chelsea Curriculum Trust by Hutchinson Education

Hutchinson & Co. (Publishers) Ltd

An imprint of the Hutchinson Publishing Group

17–21 Conway Street, London W1P 6JD

Hutchinson Publishing Group (Australia) Pty Ltd
16–22 Church Street, Hawthorn,
Melbourne, Victoria 3122

Hutchinson Group (NZ) Ltd
32–34 View Road, PO Box 40-086, Glenfield, Auckland 10

Hutchinson Group (SA) (Pty) Ltd
PO Box 337, Bergvlei 2012, South Africa

First published 1982
Reprinted with corrections 1982, 1983, 1985

© Nuffield-Chelsea Curriculum Trust 1982

All rights reserved. No part of this publication may be reproduced, stored in a retrieval system, or transmitted in any form or by any means — electronic, mechanical, photocopying, or otherwise — without the prior permission of the copyright owner.

British Library Cataloguing in Publication Data
Nuffield home economics.
  The basic course
  1. Home economics
  I. Nuffield-Chelsea Curriculum Trust
  640   TX167

ISBN 0 09 145601 0

Design and art direction by Ivan and Robin Dodd

Printed in Great Britian by Anchor Brendon Ltd, Tiptree, Essex

CONTENTS

Food science

Chapter 1 What has science got to do with food? *page 2*
Chapter 2 Preparing food *8*
Chapter 3 Using cookers *14*
Chapter 4 Cooking *20*
Chapter 5 How does cooking change food? *26*
Chapter 6 Measuring and mixing *34*
Chapter 7 Keeping food *40*

Nutrition

Chapter 8 Food in different countries *page 46*
Chapter 9 What is in our food? *52*
Chapter 10 Energy *58*
Chapter 11 Food choices *64*
Chapter 12 Digestion *72*
Chapter 13 Food and its effect on health *78*
Chapter 14 Choosing a nutritious diet *84*
Chapter 15 Solving nutrition problems *90*

Fibres and fabrics

Chapter 16 The importance of fabrics *page 94*
Chapter 17 Fabric structure and properties *100*
Chapter 18 Yarns *106*
Chapter 19 Textile fibres *112*
Chapter 20 Fabrics and colour *118*
Chapter 21 Fabrics for clothing *124*
Chapter 22 Soiling and cleaning *130*

People and homes

Chapter 23 Homes and houses *page 138*
Chapter 24 Windows, walls, and roofs *144*
Chapter 25 The materials game *150*
Chapter 26 Electricity: what it costs *154*
Chapter 27 Electricity: making it safe *160*
Chapter 28 Electricity: saving work *166*
Chapter 29 Lighting for living *170*
Chapter 30 Home heating and energy *178*

Index *page 184*

ACKNOWLEDGEMENTS

Paul Almasy: 8.1f.
Ginnie Atkinson: 8.8.
Australian Information Service, London: 19.2.
Barnaby's Picture Library: 8.9, 8.10, 16.1, 16.2, 16.3, 16.5, 16.8, 21.3, 22.1.
BBC Copyright Photo: 13.7.
Birds Eye Wall's Ltd: 2.4, 11.11.
Anthony Blake Photo Library: 4.13, 5.1a, b, c, d, 6.1, 6.6.
Nigel Bloxham Photography: 15.4.
Dr Brian Bracegirdle: 7.3.
Bob Bray: 11.6, 11.7, 11.8, 14.1, 15.6, 26.1.
British Egg Information Service: 5.9.
British Gas: 3.1a, 3.14, 4.2, 4.4b, 4.14.
British Launderers' Research Association: 22.9a.
British Library: 22.4.
British Steel Corporation: 21.6b.
British Sugar Bureau: 1.4.
British Transport Hotels Ltd: 3.2.
Canadian High Commission: 11.2, 24.7, 24.9.
J. Allan Cash Ltd: 1.3, 11.1, 11.3, 14.8, 16.6, 19.2, 23.4, 23.5.
Cement and Concrete Association: 24.6.
Central Electricity Generating Board: 30.9.
Chelsea College Audio Visual Service Unit: 3.12, 6.11, 6.12, 7.6a, b, 9.1, 9.2, 9.3, 10.5, 10.8, 10.11, 11.10, 19.4, 26.3, 26.4, 26.5, 26.6, 27.2, 27.5, 27.6, 28.4, 29.6, 29.14b.
Commonwealth Mycological Institute (D.W. Fry): 7.2.
Compix: 23.8.
R.J. Corbin: 5.15.
Courtaulds Ltd: 16.7, 16.9, 17.1, 17.5, 17.7, 17.12, 21.7b, 21.8.
T I Creda Ltd: 3.1c, 3.11, 4.5.
Design Council: 29.9.
Ivan Dodd: 23.9.
Dunlop Ltd: 13.12, 16.4, 16.5, 21.13.
Du Pont (U.K.) Ltd: 19.9, 21.6a.
Electricity Council: 3.7.
Essex County Council, Planning Department: 24.3, 24.4.
Evening Standard, London, (14.2.74): 12.10.
Flour Advisory Bureau: 5.8, 5.10, 5.12.
Ford of Britain: 16.1.
GEOSLIDES (Peter Corrigan): 14.2.
By courtesy of the Government Chemist, Department of Industry, Crown copyright reserved: 9.6.
Dr T.H. Grenby, Guy's Hospital, London: 13.8.
H.J. Heinz Co. Ltd: 1.10, 1.11, 1.12, 1.14.

Home Laundering Consultative Council: 22.14, 22.15, 22.16.
ICI Fibres: 18.16.
ILEA Learning Materials Service: 13.13, 14.3.
International Institute for Cotton: 19.2.
Japan Information Centre, London: 8.1d.
Journal of the Royal College of Physicians of London: vol. 10, no.3, p.213—275, fig.2: 13.6a.
Kentucky Fried Chicken (Great Britain) Ltd: 2.2.
Keystone Press Agency Ltd: 11.13, 13.3.
Frank Kitson: 4.4a, 11.12, 18.3, 18.7, 21.2a, b, 23.7, 24.2.
Lisa Konrad: 21.5b.
E.D. Lacey: 14.7.
Raymond Leng: 21.5a.
Lever Brothers Ltd: 22.2.
MacQuitty International Collection: 23.3.
Mansell Collection Ltd: 20.7, 30.1.
J.R. Mansell: 8.7.
Marks and Spencer Ltd: 19.5, 19.6.
Milk Marketing Board: 14.1, 14.2.
Ministry of Defence: 20.3.
Dr P.K. Mitchell: 23.6.
Motor Cycle Weekly: 16.7.
Myson Marketing Services Ltd: 30.2.
NASA/Barnaby's Picture Library: 16.7.
Nairn Floors Ltd: 25.4.
National Vegetable Research Station: 1.1.
OXFAM: 8.2, 13.11.
PACE: 12.4, 13.1.
Potato Marketing Board: 5.5.
Press Association Photos: 16.4, 17.15.
Prestige Group Ltd: 4.15, 28.5.
Provincial Sports Photography: 18.9, 18.10, 21.9.
Ranks Hovis McDougall Ltd: 6.2
Ransomes Sims and Jefferies Ltd: 17.4.
Rijksmuseum Vincent van Gogh, Amsterdam: 29.2.
Rotaflex Home Lighting: 29.11.
Royal Society for the Prevention of Accidents: 22.19.
J. Sainsbury Ltd: 9.7.
St Bartholomew's Hospital Medical School, London: 15.3.
St Helier Hospital, Carshalton, Surrey: 14.6a, b.
Jenny Salmon: 11.9.
Crown copyright: Science Museum, London: 3.1d.
Lent to Science Museum, London by R. and A. Main Ltd: 3.1b.
Doug Scott: 21.4.
Scottish Tourist Board: 11.5.
Shirley Institute: 17.2, 17.3, 18.8, 19.2, 19.3.
Scientific and Technical (Mail

Order) Ltd: 18.11.
Sketchley Cleaners: 22.17.
Slimming Magazine: 10.1.
Space Frontiers Ltd: 23.2.
John Stickland: 24.5.
Surrey County Council Media Resources Centre: 8.1a, b, c, e.
Syndication International Ltd: 16.4.
Thames Valley Police: 20.4.
Thompson and Morgan (Ipswich) Ltd: 1.2.
Thorn Domestic Appliances (Electrical) Ltd: 2.13, 26.2, 27.12, 28.5.
Thorn Lighting Ltd: 29.1, 29.10.
T I Tower Housewares: 4.10.
Anthony Tucker: 30.13.
UNESCO Courier (January 1979): 8.4.
UNICEF Photo: 23.1.
Victoria and Albert Museum, Crown copyright: 20.1.
Western Americana Picture Library: 28.1.
Wicanders (Great Britain) Ltd: 25.4.
Wolsey: 21.7a.
World Health Organization: 13.4.
Yachting Monthly: 16.3.
Figure 1.8 is adapted from Stobart, T. (1970) *The International Wine and Food Society's guide to herbs, spices and flavourings.* George Rainbird.
Figures 3.5 and 3.6 are from Birds Eye Wall's Ltd.
Figures 12.6, 12.7, 12.8, and 12.9 are from Rowett, H.G.Q. (1973) *Basic anatomy and physiology.* John Murray. Second edition.
Figure 24.8 is adapted from Oliver, P. (ed.) (1971) *Shelter in Africa.* Barry & Jenkins.

Cartoons by Robin Dodd and Christine Roche.
Cover illustration by Rory Kee.
Tables by Nina Konrad.
Other illustrations and diagrams by Michael Copus, Robin Dodd, Roger Limbrick, Rodney Paull, and Technical Print.

Food science is about where food comes from, and ways of making it more enjoyable to eat and easy to use. It tells you how to make sure that food is fit to eat and that it keeps well. It is also about discovering new sources of food and making the best use of those foods already available.

Food science will help you to understand the way food behaves when you prepare it, mix, cook, freeze, or process it in other ways. So it will help you to choose your ingredients and make best use of them. You will also learn about cooking and processing methods to help you to make delicious meals every time.

Food science

Chapter 1 What has science got to do with food? *page 2*

Chapter 2 Preparing food *8*

Chapter 3 Using cookers *14*

Chapter 4 Cooking *20*

Chapter 5 How does cooking change food? *26*

Chapter 6 Measuring and mixing *34*

Chapter 7 Keeping food *40*

CHAPTER 1
What has science got to do with food?

1.1
WHAT GOES INTO A CAN OF BEANS?

'I only want a simple snack — just open a can of beans.' But a can of beans is not as simple as you might think. One popular brand of beans has these ingredients (listed — by law — in order of the amounts present): beans, tomatoes, sugar, salt, food starch, spirit vinegar, spices.

First of all, let's see where these ingredients come from.

Figure 1.1
*Navy beans.
Beans like these do not grow in this country because the climate is not warm enough. They are called 'navy' or 'pea' beans, and come from the U.S.A. (Michigan) and Canada (Ontario), and also from Eastern Europe and from Chile.*

Figure 1.2
Italian tomatoes.

Tomatoes used in baked beans have to be imported too. For the sauce, tomatoes with a rich colour and flavour are needed. The long, plum-shaped variety which grows in the Mediterranean countries is used. These tomatoes are imported mainly from Italy after being canned whole or made into purée (paste).

Figure 1.3
Sugar cane is a gigantic variety of grass. It can grow to a height of 5 metres (16 feet).

Figure 1.4
The sugar beet looks rather like a parsnip, and stores sugar in its root. An average sugar beet weighs about one kilogram and gives about 14 teaspoons of sugar.

Figure 1.5
Salt is mined or obtained by drying sea water (evaporation). Most salt used in England comes from Cheshire.

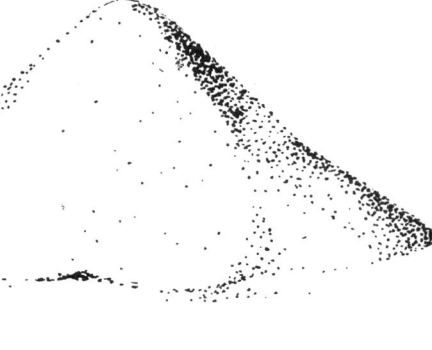

Figure 1.6
Maize is imported from America. Cornflour is the starch from ground maize ('sweet corn'). Many plants store their sugar by changing it into starch.

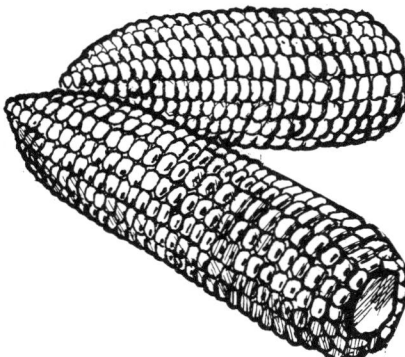

Figure 1.7
Vinegar is made from alcohol. It is generally made from malt (grain which has begun to germinate) or from wine.

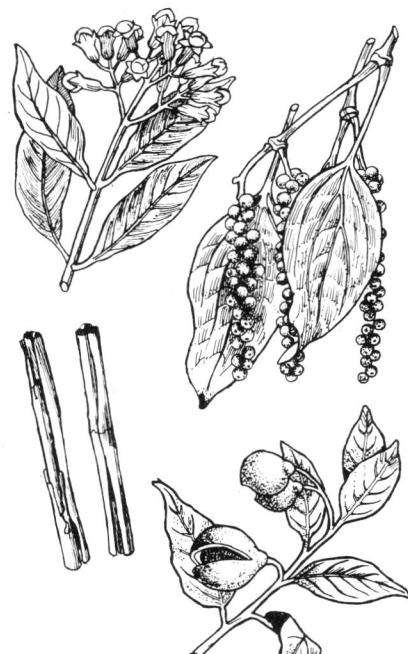

Figure 1.8
Spices in baked beans may include pepper, cinnamon, nutmeg, and cloves. Many of the spices we use come from Zanzibar, Indonesia, and the West Indies.

Sugar is made from the sap (juice) of sugar cane grown in hot wet areas of the world such as the Caribbean, west, east, and central Africa, Mauritius, and the Philippines. Or it may be made out of sugar beet grown in cooler climates, such as Britain, Denmark, and the Netherlands. Sugar is extracted from the stalks of sugar cane by crushing them. Sugar is washed out of sugar beet by slicing the roots and soaking them in hot water. Both types of sugar juice are then evaporated to drive off the water and form crystals.

Green leaves of plants use the energy of the sun to combine carbon dioxide from the air with water to make sugar. This process is called photosynthesis. Some of the sugar is used for growth and the rest is stored in the plant. Sugar beet and sugar cane store more sugar than most plants, and have become our main source of this food.

Q 1
a Which ingredient is present in the greatest amount in baked beans?
b Which ingredients are present in the smallest amount?

Q 2
Can you suggest why both sugar and salt are added?

Q 3
Can you list ten British foods that really do come from Britain?

You might have thought that baked beans were a typical British food. In one sense they are — over a million cans a day are sold in Britain. But as you have seen, each mouthful of beans has ingredients from several different parts of the world! About 80 000 tonnes of navy beans have to be imported into Britain each year to make baked beans, at a cost of more than £25 million.

Canned beans can be made ready to eat in a few minutes. This is why they are called a 'convenience food'. They are a 'processed food' because they are given a lot of treatment before you buy them. They are also a 'preserved food' because they keep in good condition for a long time in the can.

Q 4
List three other convenience foods, three other processed foods, and three other ways of preserving food. (The convenience foods may be processed or preserved too, but try to list different things in each case.)

Q 5
Suggest three reasons why baked beans are so popular.

Q 6
a What amount of baked beans does your school kitchen use in one week?
b Work out the average weekly amount of baked beans eaten by people in your school.

Q 7
Why is sugar imported when sugar beet can be grown in Britain?

3

1.2 WORKING ON THE BEANS

You can see that your can of beans is not as simple as you would think at first. But the story has only just begun.

The navy beans are grown in huge fields, and harvested by enormous machines.

Q 8
Why is this done on such a large scale?

The tomatoes, sugar cane, and all the other plants have to be grown and harvested too. The cans are made out of steel sheet.

When you open a can of beans you take a lot for granted. You assume that the contents will be perfectly cooked, safe, and good to eat. When you buy another tin you will expect the beans to taste the same as in the previous one. You will also expect the beans to look right, and that there will be just the right mixture of beans and sauce. You probably do not stop to think how the raw materials were processed.

All the ingredients and processes are carefully controlled and tested at each stage during the manufacture of foodstuffs. This is called 'quality control'.

When raw navy beans arrive at the factory they are small, hard, white, and oval-shaped. Each bean goes through many separate sorting processes.

Most of the processes are automatically carried out by machines. Each batch of beans is first inspected by eye. Then the beans are blown with air to clean off dust and dirt. They are graded for size, so that they will all cook at the same rate. Then each bean is scanned by an 'electronic eye'. Any dark or discoloured beans are rejected.

Figure 1.9

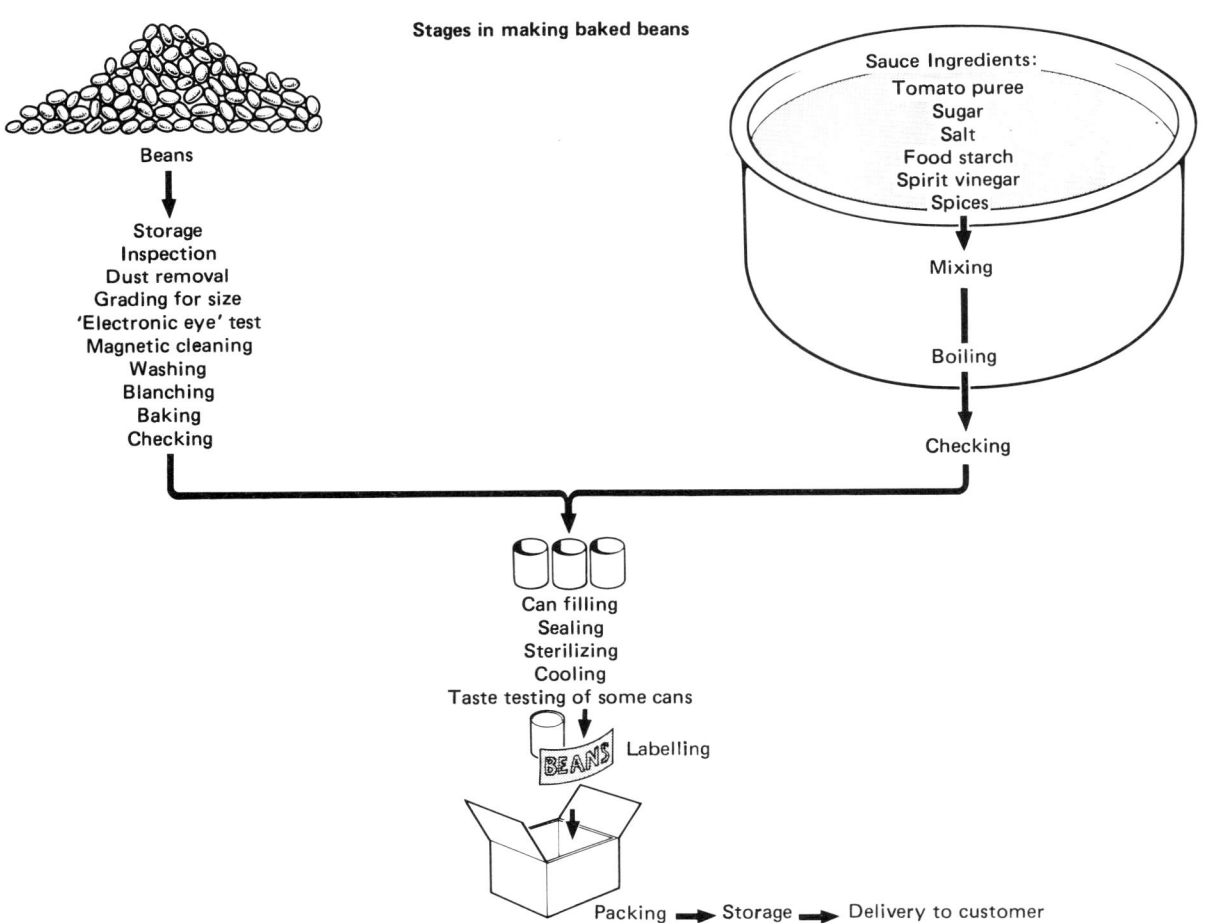

Figure 1.10
The 'electronic eyes' which examine every bean.

The beans then pass under magnets to remove any chips of steel which may have been picked up from the harvesting machinery, and then any stones or grit are removed by washing. Finally they are ready for cooking.

Q 9
How many sorting processes have the beans passed through at this stage?

Q 10
Why does it matter to grade the beans for size?

After blanching (cooking for a short time in hot water) the beans are baked. (Some manufacturers do not bake the beans — they say it makes no difference. But then — by law — they are not allowed to give them the traditional name of 'baked beans'.)

Figure 1.11
A can-filling machine.

The beans are measured into cans and covered with a measured amount of sauce in a machine like the one in figure 1.11.

Next, the cans are sealed and heated at a high temperature to kill off harmful micro-organisms (germs). After cooking they are finished off with attractive, brightly coloured labels.

Q 11
Why are the beans sealed in a can and then heated?

A final check is always made by opening some of the cans for the most important test — which just cannot be done by machines — the taste test.

Figure 1.12
The taste panel.

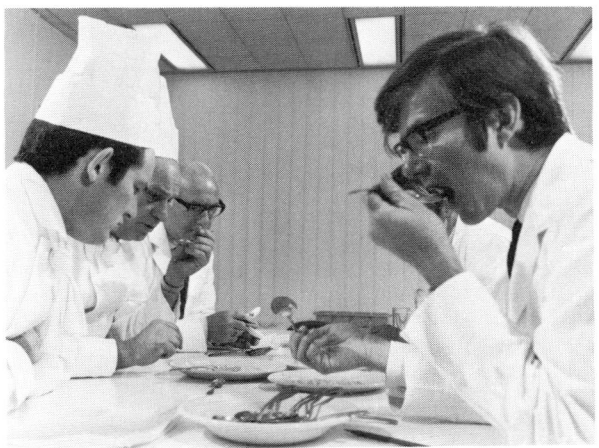

The cans are packed into cartons and sent all over the country. The whole process has taken months and involved hundreds of people directly. Hundreds of food scientists and technologists have also done work in the past, breeding better types of navy bean and tomato plant, thinking up economic and efficient ways of growing, harvesting, and processing them, designing and building canning works, and so on. Plant research is still going on, and scientists are trying to breed a navy bean plant that can grow in this country.

Q 12
Why might Britain want to grow her own beans for baking?

1.3 TRADITIONAL BEANS

Cook your own baked beans
Try this recipe. See if you prefer it to the canned kind.

Beans need to be soaked in water overnight and then cooked for a long time. To save you the time, this has already been done for you.

YOU WILL NEED:

100 g haricot or other dried beans (partly cooked)
½ a 379-g (standard) can Italian tomatoes
½ a 15-ml (table) spoonful chopped onion
(or ½ a 5-ml (tea) spoonful dried onion)
½ a 15-ml (table) spoonful dark brown sugar
½ a 15-ml (table) spoonful vinegar
¼ of a 5-ml (tea) spoonful cornflour
¼ of a 5-ml (tea) spoonful salt
1/8 of a 5-ml (tea) spoonful fresh ground black pepper
Pinch each of: powdered cinnamon, nutmeg, and cloves
Water
2 saucers
250-ml single-portion ovenproof dish
Baking sheet
Vegetable knife
Chopping board
Small basin
Cling film
Oven gloves
15-ml (table) spoon
5-ml (tea) spoon

1 Turn on the oven at 200 °C (400 °F, gas mark 6).

2 Put a 5 ml (tea) spoonful of beans onto a saucer to eat later. Cover with cling film.

3 Chop the tomatoes and onions finely.

4 Put the beans, tomatoes, onion, salt, pepper, and spices into the ovenproof dish.

5 Put the cornflour into the basin. Add a 15-ml (table) spoonful of water, and blend (mix) with a teaspoon until the mixture is smooth. Pour this over the other ingredients in the dish. Add more water if necessary, so that it comes almost to the top of the mixture. Sprinkle the sugar evenly over the top.

6 Stand the dish on the baking sheet and bake in the oven for 45 minutes. Remove the dish with oven gloves — it will be very hot.

7 Spread out a 5-ml (tea) spoonful of beans from the dish on a saucer, and leave to cool. Eat the 'sauceless' beans you saved earlier. Then try the ones you have cooked, and compare the flavours.

Q 13
Describe the difference in flavour, and say which you prefer.

Q 14
Was the flavour worth the time and effort? (Remember there was all that soaking and cooking before you began.)

8 Now compare your beans with those that your friends have made and with some canned baked beans. Make a table for your results as below.

9 Take a 5-ml (tea) spoonful sample of each lot of beans. Look at each sample, then smell it, and taste it. Write a few words describing each sample in your table — 'dark', 'salty', 'burnt', and so on.

10 Give 4 marks for the sample you liked best, 3 marks for the next best, and so on.

Beans made by:	Myself	(Name)	(Name)	Canned beans
Appearance				
Smell				
Taste				
Order of preference				

Figure 1.13

Q 15
List the reasons why you thought one sample was the best.

11 Compare your ideas, and your answer to the last question, with those of your friends.

Q 16
You all followed the same recipe. Did your results differ? Why might this have been?

To be able to get the same results every time, a cook in a manufacturer's test kitchen measures every single ingredient much more carefully

Figure 1.14
An advertisement for 'Heinz' beans from 1900.

than you were able to. He must know to the last pinch of salt what makes the tomato sauce taste the way it does. Even a tiny mistake in the amount of salt matters, for if the dish goes into production that mistake may be repeated a million times.

Q 17
How would you measure a pinch of salt?

Q 18
Work out the total cost of the ingredients you used. Is it more or less than the price of a 454 g (1 lb) sized can of beans? Why?

Beans around the world
Read this section while the beans are cooking. If you are not certain where the different countries are, use a map to check. Look up other recipes using different kinds of beans.

Beans have been an important food in different countries since ancient times. Because they are easy to grow, store, and transport, they are a food which can always be available.

1 Boston (U.S.A.): the original baked bean recipe was invented here, long before anyone thought of putting them into cans.

2 Ontario (Canada) and . . .

3 Michigan (U.S.A.): navy beans are grown here. They have this name because they were eaten on ships.

4 Mexico: dried beans are an important part of the national diet. 'Chili con carne' is a hot, peppery stew made of beans and chunks of beef.

5 Britain: 'butter' beans are a British speciality.

6 France: 'French' green beans are tiny, and you eat the pod as well. Dried 'haricot' beans make the traditional 'cassoulet', a rich baked bean dish with pork, goose, and duck.

7 Italy: a typical Italian bean dish is 'tonno con fagioli' — tuna fish with haricot beans in olive oil.

8 Greece: Greeks eat 'fassoulia', a version of baked beans in tomato sauce.

9 Egypt: 'ful' (dried brown beans) are very popular and have been since the time of the Pharoahs.

10 Kenya: tiny green 'bobby' beans are grown for export, and make a wintertime luxury for Britain.

11 India: lentils, peas, and chickpeas largely take the place of beans in the national diet.

12 China: bean sprouts are grown from 'mung' beans.

In this chapter you have learned something about the way the food industry works, and how food quality is controlled. Ingredients from different parts of the world are often combined to form popular foods found in every supermarket. In the next chapter you will learn about the food industry and some of the ways in which people's eating habits have changed.

CHAPTER 2
Preparing food

2.1
FOODS YOU EAT

Do you ever think about the sort of food you eat? Try to remember the foods you have eaten since yesterday morning. Make a list.

Q 1
How many extra snacks did you eat?

Of course, to get a better idea of all the sorts of foods you eat, you would need to keep a record of everything you ate for at least a week. You could try to keep a diary. Do you eat different foods on weekdays from weekends? How often do you eat chips in one week?

Foods which are bought prepared and ready to eat, or partly prepared, are called convenience foods. You can see how the sales of some frozen foods have increased in the chart below.

Q 2
Look at the list of foods you have eaten since yesterday.
a Tick the foods you ate which were bought ready to eat, *e.g.* fish and chips.
b Put a cross by those foods which were bought partly prepared, *e.g.* fish fingers.
c Put a circle by the foods which were home-made from scratch (without using canned or frozen ingredients).

Q 3
Since yesterday, how many people in your class have only eaten foods which were all home-made?

Q 4
Look at figure 2.1.
a Which type of frozen food were people eating most of in 1973?
b Which type is still the most popular in 1978?
c Which frozen products have shown the least change? Can you suggest a reason for this?
d Which type of food has shown the biggest increase in popularity?

Figure 2.1
The amount of some frozen foods eaten in the United Kingdom (in grams per person per week).

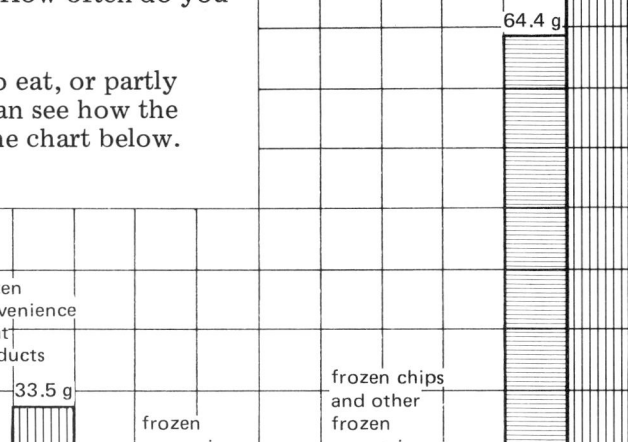

More people are also eating away from home. Takeaway foods have become very popular.

Q 5
How many different types of takeaway food have you eaten in the past week?

Q 6
Why do you think convenience foods are so popular these days?

Figure 2.2

Figure 2.3

A century ago, few convenience foods existed and women had to spend more time running the home, shopping, and preparing and cooking food. Today, many women go out to work as well as run the home. Shopping tends to be done less frequently, because many convenience foods can be stored for some time. After a busy day's work, family meals must be quick to prepare to save time and effort. Choices have to be made about how best to use time, money, equipment, and food. Each family will have different priorities.

Table 2.1
The number of women at work.

	Total women at work (millions)	Working married women (millions)	Working single women (millions)	Percentage of everyone working
1972	9.12	5.89	3.22	36.5 %
1975	9.78	6.60	3.18	38.0 %
1978	10.27	6.96	3.31	39.1 %
1981 (estimated)	10.57	7.13	3.44	39.5 %
1986 (estimated)	11.17	7.70	3.47	40.2 %

Q 7
a In table 2.1, how many women are estimated to be working in 1981?
b Is the number of women increasing or decreasing compared with 1972?

Q 8
Why do you think this is happening?

Q 9
a Look at table 2.1. Is it estimated that more married or single women are working in 1981?
b Look at the column showing the total number of women at work in 1981. What percentage is this of everyone working?
c How do you think this might affect food choices?

2.2 PREPARING MEALS

Most of the food you eat must first be cut up or processed in some way before it is cooked.

Q 10
List ten foods which can either be eaten raw or which do not have to be prepared before you eat them.

Many people enjoy cooking and trying out different recipes. But it can take a lot of time. Most of the work is still done by women, even though they may have been out at work as well. Other members of the family can help. Table 2.2 shows the results of one survey. This is how often some people said they tried to cook a meal.

	11—16-year-olds (%)	Husbands (%)
Every day	4	3
2—6 times a week	21	17
Once a week	22	11
Once a month	12	9
Less often	15	18
Never	26	42

Base (for figures on 11—16-year-olds): households with 11—16-year-olds; (for figures on husbands): households with a husband.

Table 2.2
How often do teenagers and husbands cook a meal?

Q 11
a How often do you and your father cook a meal at home?
b Why do you suppose so many teenagers and husbands never cook?

If you have to cook for yourselves, one way of saving time is to eat takeaway foods. Another way is to buy partly prepared foods. With foods such as fish cakes, much of the work has already been done for you. But this means that you may pay more than if you bought fresh foods and prepared them yourselves.

To save time and help save money many homes now have small appliances such as food mixers, liquidizers, and toasters. These speed up cooking.

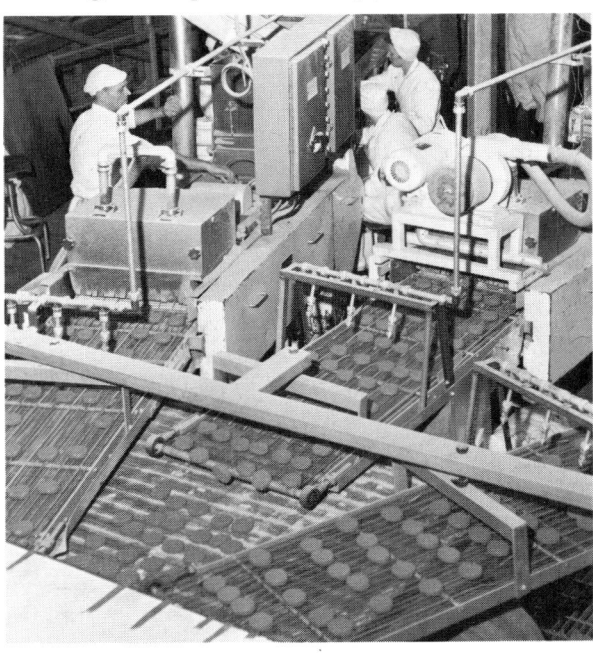

Figure 2.4
The large-scale production of fish cakes.

2.3 MAKING COLESLAW

Is it worth the time and effort to make your own coleslaw at home? Find out how much coleslaw costs to buy ready-made. Try these two different ways of making it to see which is the fastest. Time yourself with a stopwatch.

YOU WILL NEED:
½ onion
½ white cabbage
1 carrot
Mayonnaise (or plain yoghurt)

Vegetable knife
Grater
Chopping board
Wooden spoon
Blender
Strainer
Stopwatch

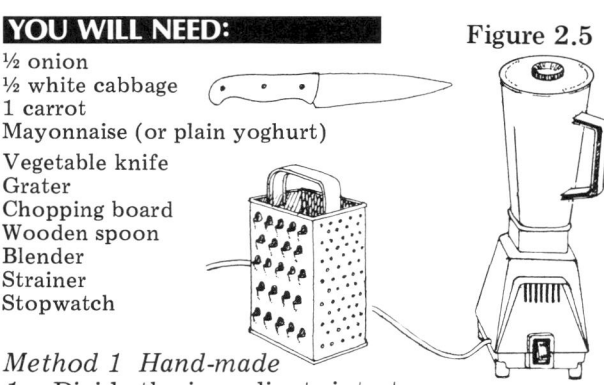

Figure 2.5

Method 1 Hand-made
1 Divide the ingredients into two equal portions.

2 Shred one lump of cabbage and onion finely with the knife (or grate them).

3 Grate one piece of carrot.

4 Mix the cabbage, onion, and carrot with the mayonnaise (or yoghurt).

10

5 Note the time taken.

6 Work out the cost.

Method 2 Using a blender

1 Chop the other pieces of carrot, cabbage, and onion roughly with the knife.

2 Put the vegetables in the blender. Just cover them with cold water and put the lid on.

3 Switch on the blender for a *few* seconds to shred the vegetables.

4 Strain the water off the vegetables and mix them with the mayonnaise (or yoghurt).

5 Note the time taken and work out the cost.

6 Record your results in a table like this.

	Hand-made coleslaw	Blender coleslaw	Shop-bought coleslaw
Cost (pence)			
Time (minutes, seconds)			

Figure 2.6

Q 12
Which way of making coleslaw was quickest?

Q 13
When you buy a tub of coleslaw, what extra costs has the manufacturer had to include in working out how much to charge you?

Q 14
Why may shop-bought food sometimes be as cheap as you can make it for yourself?

One of the good things about preparing your own food is that you can decide which ingredients you want to use. With shop-bought foods you often have less choice.

2.4 USING DIFFERENT GADGETS

The choice of equipment you have will depend on how often you cook, the number of people you are cooking for, the amount of money you have to spend, storage space, and whether you really need it.

Look at this recipe for lemon chiffon.

Ingredients
3 eggs (separated)
75 g sugar
Grated rind of 1 lemon
Juice of 1 lemon

Q 15
List the tools you think you would use to make this recipe.

2.4a Separating an egg

How quickly can you separate the yolk of an egg from its white? There are a number of ways of doing this. Try them: use just the shell, an egg-cup, or a separator.

YOU WILL NEED:
3 same-size eggs
Saucer and egg cup
Egg separator
4 small basins
Knife
Stopwatch

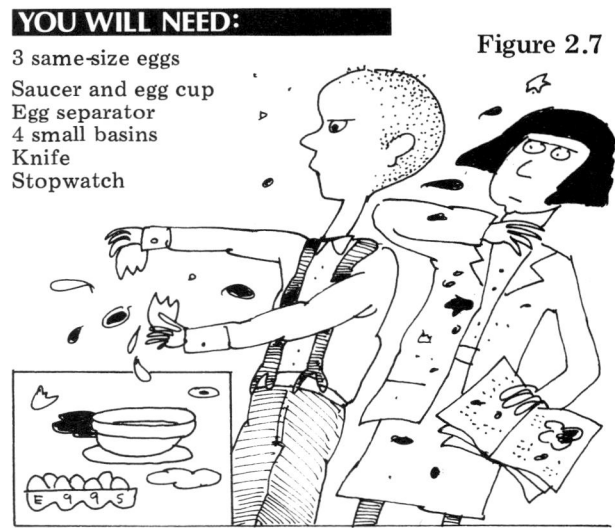
Figure 2.7

Take care not to break the egg yolks as you work. Note the time you take for each method.

Make a table of your results.

Method	Time (seconds)
using shell	
using egg cup	
using separator	

Figure 2.8

Q 16
Which was the easiest method?

Q 17
Which way of separating the egg saved most time?

2.4b
Grating

Lemon rind (the zest) is full of flavour. But the white pith tastes bitter. Grating takes off thin layers of food. Graters have holes of different sizes. Each size is intended to grate differently. The bigger the hole, the coarser the cut.

Q 18
Look at a grater. Which size hole should you use to grate the rind of a lemon to be sure that you will not get any of the bitter tasting white pith underneath?

2.4c
Squeezing lemons

Is it worth buying a lemon squeezer to extract juice?

Try these two different ways and find out. To help decide the choice, time each and record the amount of juice you get.

YOU WILL NEED:

Lemon
Lemon squeezer
Vegetable knife
Chopping board
5-ml (tea) spoon and
2 bowls *or* 2 test-tubes
Stopwatch

Figure 2.9

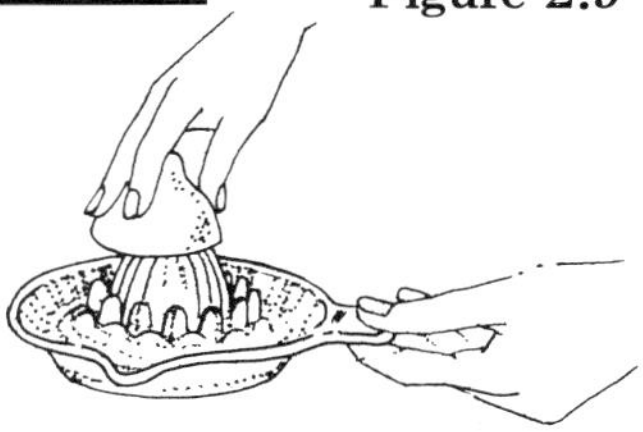

1   Cut the lemon as nearly as possible into two identical halves.

2   Squeeze the lemon juice from one half using only your fingers.

3   Use a lemon squeezer for the other half.

4   Measure the amount of juice you get with each method.

5   Record your results in a table like the one below.

Figure 2.10

	By hand	Lemon squeezer
Amount of juice (ml)		
Time (seconds)		

Q 19
Which method gave most juice?

Q 20
Which method was quicker?

2.4d
Whisking

Knives, forks, balloon whisks, rotary hand whisks, electric blenders, or electric mixers can all be used for whisking air into mixtures. The choice really depends upon the amount and kind of food to be whisked, how often you need to whisk foods, and the time and effort it will take. This activity helps you to decide whether the cost of the tool is worth it.

Try beating egg whites to compare a balloon whisk with a rotary hand whisk and an electric whisk.

YOU WILL NEED:

3 egg whites (same volume)
Balloon whisk and measuring jug
Rotary hand whisk and measuring jug
Electric whisk and measuring jug
Stopwatch

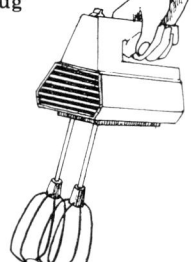

Figure 2.11

1   Notice the structure and colour of the egg whites before you begin.

2   Put the egg whites into the measuring jugs.

3   Using the three different whisks, beat each egg white until it forms stiff peaks.

4   Note the time taken using each whisk.

5   Measure the volume of the whisked egg.

6   Record your results in a table like the one in figure 2.12.

Q 21
Which whisk gave the fastest results?

	Time taken (seconds)	Volume (mL)	Colour Before/After	Structure Before/After
Balloon whisk				
Rotary hand whisk				
Electric whisk				

Figure 2.12

Q 22
Which gave the biggest volume of egg white?

Q 23
Would this have been a fair comparison if eggs were used of a different
a grade
b age
c colour?

You have now prepared all the ingredients for lemon chiffon. Your teacher will tell you how to finish making the recipe.

2.4e
Food processors

Food processors are designed to do a wide range of jobs with much fewer special attachments than the ordinary mixer. They can mix, chop, slice, shred, knead, liquidize, blend, and mince.

Figure 2.13
A food processor.

Figure 2.14 is a table of different food preparation processes. Some tools can do more of these tasks than others.

Copy the table into your book. For each piece of equipment listed, tick the columns for the process you think it will do. The more ticks a tool has the more useful it is likely to be.

You will have seen from these activities that it is not just the cooking but the preparation of food that takes up your time. Choosing the right equipment helps you to make the best use of time and money.

Figure 2.14

Tools	Food preparation processes							
	Cutting	Peeling	Separating	Juice extracting	Whisking	Straining	Grating	Mixing
Peeler								
Knife								
Fork								
Spoon								
Hand whisk								
Lemon squeezer								
Strainer								
Electric whisk								
Blender								
Food processor								

CHAPTER 3
Using cookers

3.1
COOKER DESIGN

The best cooker is the one that suits your needs and your home. You don't have to buy the most expensive cooker in the showroom to cook delicious food. You can get just as good results from quite a cheap one.

You can see how cooker design has changed by comparing the pictures below.

Figure 3.1

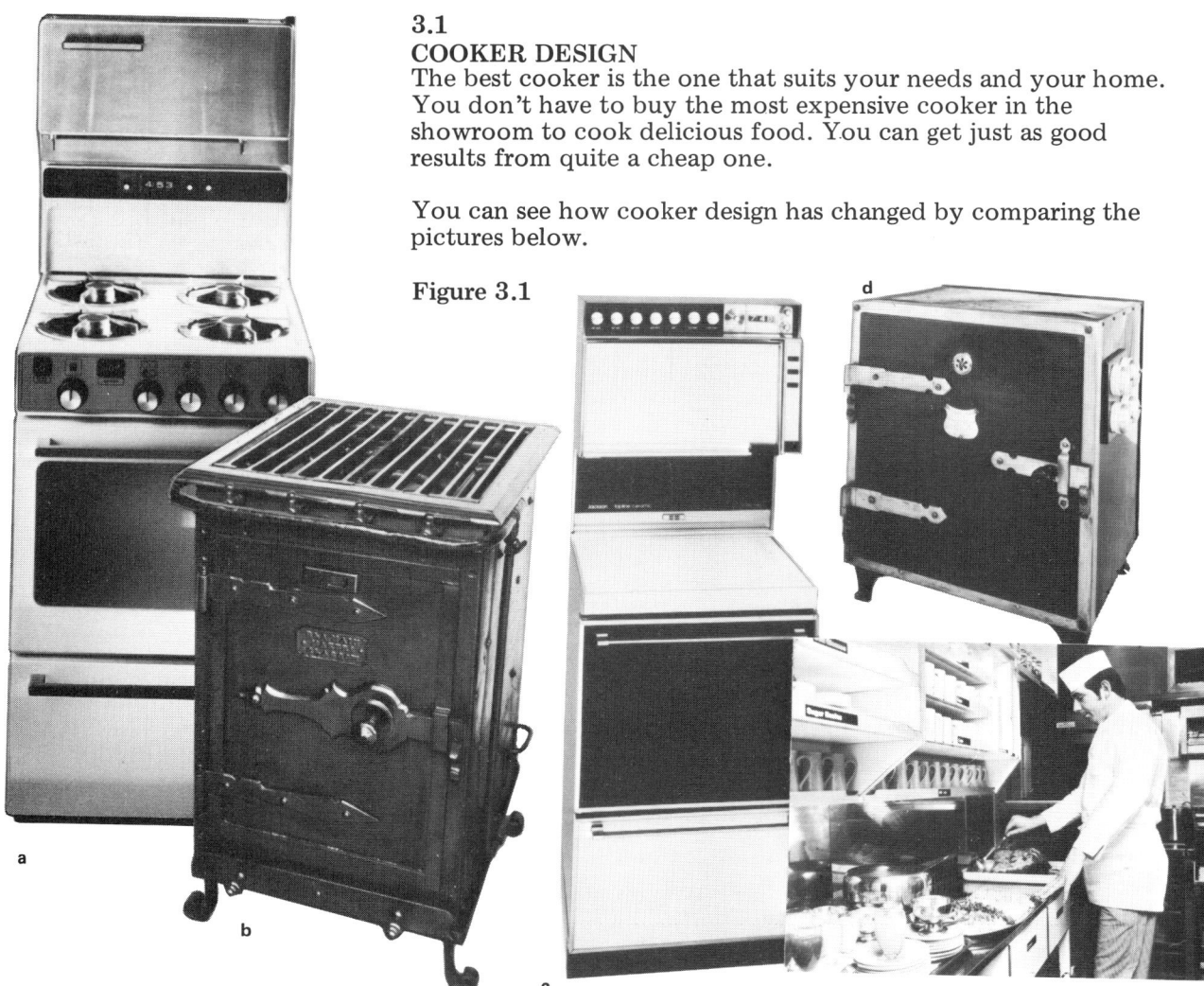

Figure 3.2
The 'kitchen' in a high speed train.

Use worksheet M6 to compare the design features of cookers in the home economics room and at home.

Cookers are designed to do the six basic cooking processes: baking, boiling, grilling, frying, roasting, and stewing. Each method of cooking is suitable for different kinds of food.

Q 1
Complete the table below with the name of a food which can be cooked by each process, and the part of the cooker used.

Figure 3.3

	Baking	Boiling	Grilling	Frying	Roasting	Stewing
Food			Toasted cheese			
Part of cooker used			Grill			

Figure 3.4

3.2
COOKING ECONOMICALLY

There are several ways that different parts of the cooker can be used to make the same meal. Here are some figures supplied by the fuel industries' appliance testing laboratories. To find the most economical way of cooking a standard meal for two people (lamb chops, tomatoes, peas, and carrots) they cooked it in three ways and measured how much electricity or gas were used each time. These tests were done under ideal laboratory conditions. You would probably not get the same figures if you tried it yourself, but you would still be able to see the difference. Gas is costed in *therms*. Electricity is costed in *units*. (See *People and homes* Chapter 26.)

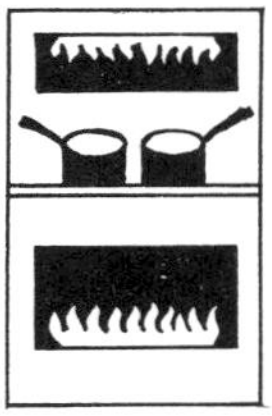

	Electricity	Gas
Method 1		
Chops *oven*	1.27 units	0.027 therms
Tomatoes *grill*	0.27 units	0.014 therms
Carrots *ring 1*	0.34 units	0.005 therms
Peas *ring 2*	0.25 units	0.004 therms
	2.13 units	0.050 therms
Method 2		
Chops and tomatoes *grill*	0.74 units	0.028 therms
Peas and carrots (together) *ring 1*	0.53 units	0.005 therms
	1.27 units	0.033 therms
Method 3		
Chops and tomatoes (fried together) *ring 1*	0.28 units	0.007 therms
Peas and carrots (together) *ring 2*	0.53 units	0.005 therms
	0.81 units	0.012 therms

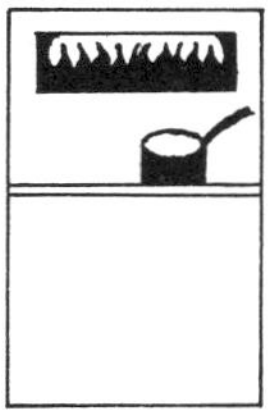

Q 2
Which method used
a least electricity
b least gas?

Q 3
Ask your teacher how much a therm of gas and a unit of electricity cost. Work out the cost of each method. (Are you surprised how little it costs to cook a hot meal?)

Q 4
Imagine what the three different meals would look like.
a What differences might grilling, frying, or baking make to the chops and tomatoes?
b Is it worth using the oven?

3.3
CHANGING COOKING HABITS

In Chapter 2 you saw how our food and eating habits have changed. This affects the way people cook too.

Figures 3.5 and 3.6 show you some changes in the way people used their cookers between 1967 and 1976. The figures are taken from two surveys.

Figure 3.5
How often do you use the oven?

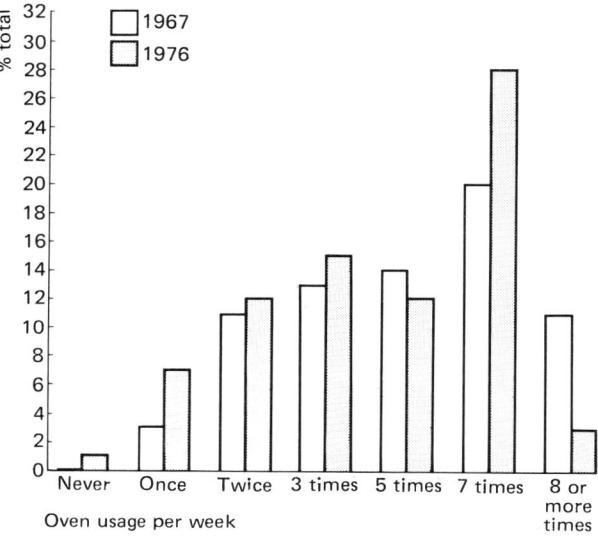

Oven usage per week

Figure 3.6
How often do you use the grill?

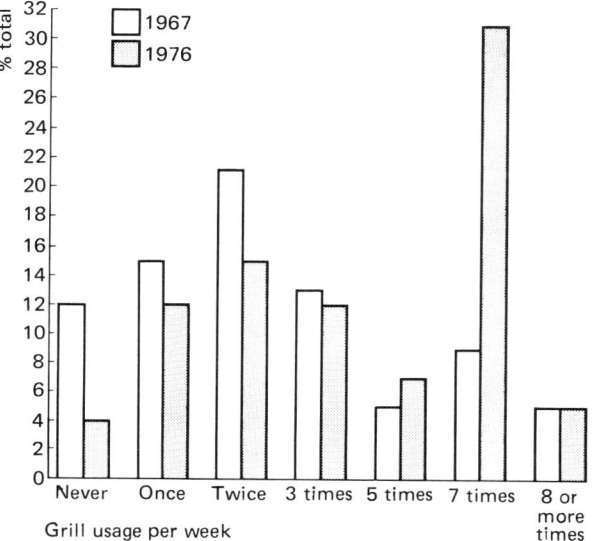

Grill usage per week

Q 5
In figure 3.5, were people using their ovens more or less in 1976 than in 1967?

Q 6
a In figure 3.6, were people using their grills more or less in 1976 than in 1967?
b Why do you think this is?

Q 7
How often each week are the grill and oven used in your home?

3.4
MAKING A CHOICE: GRILLS

Grilling cooks food at a high temperature, so it is a fast method of cooking. Grills have toasting areas of different sizes. To save fuel, many cookers have dual-controlled grills. Only half need be used for small quantities of food.

There are other small electric appliances designed to 'grill' foods too. Compare the cost of using a toaster and contact grill with the grill of a cooker.

Figure 3.7

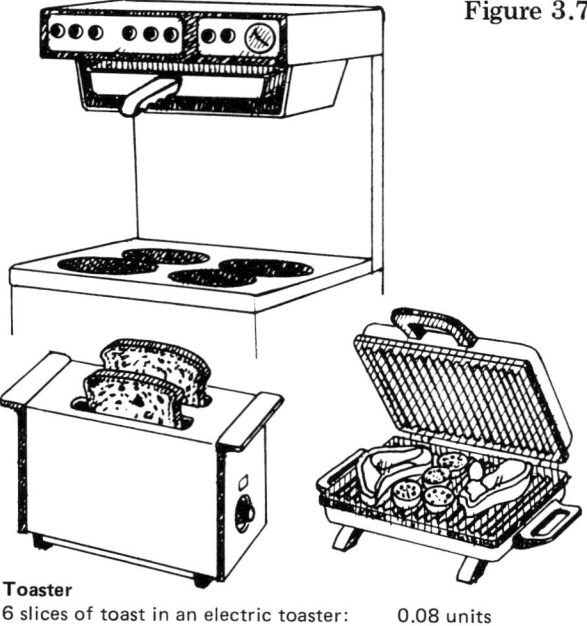

Toaster
6 slices of toast in an electric toaster: 0.08 units
6 slices of toast in an electric cooker grill: 0.33 units

Contact grill
A mixed grill for 2 people in a contact grill: 0.23 units
A mixed grill for 2 people in an electric cooker grill: 0.67 units

Q 8
Which way of making toast uses least energy?

Small electrical appliances such as the contact grill certainly save time and money when cooking small quantities of food.

But one advantage of using the cooker grill is that greater quantities of food can be cooked at the same time. It all depends on the number of people you are catering for.

3.5
MAKING A CHOICE: BOILING WATER

You frequently boil water to make coffee or tea, or to cook vegetables. Some ways are quicker and easier than others. Does a gas burner, an electric boiling-ring, or an electric kettle boil water fastest?

YOU WILL NEED:
Water
Gas and electric rings
2 15-cm (6-inch) aluminium saucepans (same make, identical size, with flat base and well-fitting lid)
Electric kettle
Measuring jug
Thermometer
Stopwatch

1 See how long it takes to boil a litre of water. Compare using a gas cooker, an electric cooker, and an electric kettle.

Q 9
What would you need to do to make sure that this is a fair test? (Here are some things to think about: the size of the saucepans, the size of the rings, and whether you have the lid on or not.)

Figure 3.8

2 Write down your results in a table like the one below.

Figure 3.9

Appliance	Time to boil 1 litre of water
Gas burner	
Electric ring	
Electric kettle	

Q 10
Which is the quickest way to boil water? Why?

Q 11
Did the water take longer to boil on the gas or electric ring? Can you suggest why?

3.6
USING DIFFERENT OVEN TEMPERATURES

Cooking large family meals, Sunday lunch, or Christmas dinner will be the times when the oven is used most. Different foods cook best at different temperatures — see worksheet M7. Thermostat settings for ordinary ovens (not fan ovens) refer to the *middle* of the oven. It is warmer above the middle of the oven and cooler below it. This is because hot air rises — see Chapter 4. By using these different temperatures, food needing different thermostat settings can be cooked together in the oven at the same time. So a large meal can be cooked quite economically.

Figure 3.10

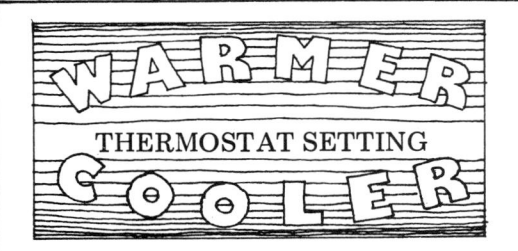

Check the temperature on different shelf positions when the regulo is set at thermostat setting 4 or 180 °C (350 °F). Use either temperature labels stuck onto a baking sheet or oven thermometers. The shelf positions are counted from the top downwards. (Check the baseplate too.)

17

Q 12
a What temperature was recorded on the oven baseplate?
b Would it be possible to cook at this temperature?

Some foods can be cooked just as well either by using a lower temperature for a longer time, or a higher temperature for a shorter time.

Look at worksheet M7. Meat can be roasted from 160 °C to 220 °C (325 °F to 425 °F), thermostat setting 3 to 7.

Q 13
Use a recipe book to list three puddings and three vegetables which could be cooked at the same time as meat.

3.7
TESTING DIFFERENT TEMPERATURES

All new types of cooker are checked at gas and electric appliance testing centres before you buy them. They are checked for safety and to make sure that they cook properly and match the design specification set by the cooker manufacturer. In other words, the cooker must do the job for which it is designed — and be safe. Many tests are carried out and a report is sent to the cooker manufacturer. Any faults are put right before more cookers of that type are made.

Figure 3.12
These tags show that the cookers have been checked for safety.

Figure 3.11
Testing electric cookers for safety.

Foods are cooked in the ovens to test oven performance. To make a fair test, the foods are deliberately not considered as foods, but just as standard materials for testing cookers. The aim is simply to see what happens to the food mixture when it is cooked.

These three tests measure temperature, cooking time, and evenness of cooking (judged by browning).

Scones need to be cooked in a hot oven if they are to rise properly. Because of their small size they cook quickly. They are used to test thermostat setting 7, 220 °C (425 °F).

Small cakes cook for a longer time than scones. They are cooked in paper cases at thermostat setting 5, 190 °C (375 °F).

Victoria sandwiches cook in two tins, with no baking sheet. They take longer to cook than small cakes. They are cooked at thermostat setting 4, 180 °C (350 °F).

You can try temperature-test cooking for yourself.

YOU WILL NEED:

Ingredients for scones *or* small cakes *or* Victoria sandwich
Ruler
Watch or clock
B.S.I. shade card

1 Working in groups, make the scones, small cakes, or Victoria sandwich using the recipes and methods your teacher suggests.

2 Compare the results for each test food.

3 Measure the height of rise of each scone or small cake or Victoria sandwich.

4 To measure the height more carefully you could cut down through the middle. This would also show you how it is cooked inside.

5 To get the average height of rise on each shelf, add each measurement together and divide by the total number of scones or cakes.

6 Use the shade chart to work out the average browning shade of the tray of scones and small cakes.

7 Make a table of your results like this.

	Scones	Small cakes	Victoria sandwich
Cooking time (minutes, seconds)			
Average height of rise (mm)			
Average browning			

Figure 3.13

Q 14
a Would the height rise of one scone or cake be a fair test of the height of rising for the whole tray?
b Give reasons for your answer.

Q 15
Were the results different in the gas or electric cookers?

Figure 3.14
A home economist at British Gas Research Laboratories using food as standard materials to test cookers for efficiency.

CHAPTER 4

Cooking

4.1
WHAT AFFECTS COOKING TIME?

Cooking time varies. It depends upon the type of food, its size, the method of cooking, and the temperature at which the food is cooked. To cook food at any temperature, high or low, you need to get heat into it. The food usually gets heat from the hot air, water, steam, or fat surrounding it. But in grilling and microwave cooking, food is heated by *radiation* (rays) and not by the air surrounding it.

Figure 4.1
Methods of cooking.

Q 1
The table opposite shows some different methods of cooking. Copy out the table in your notebooks and fill in the columns. In the second column, write down the material you think takes heat to the food: 'air', 'water', 'steam', 'fat', or 'none of these'. In the last column give two examples of foods cooked in this way.

Cooking process	Material carrying heat to the food	Examples of foods cooked this way
Baking		
Boiling		
Grilling		
Frying		
Roasting		
Stewing		
Poaching		
Pressure cooking		
Microwave cookery		

4.2
GETTING HEAT TO THE FOOD

Heat is a form of *energy*. You can't see, touch, or taste heat. But you know that it exists because of the way it affects you and the way it changes things. Heat can make things melt, boil, catch fire, dry out (evaporate), change colour, get bigger (expand), get smaller, or change things into something else.

Whatever type of cooker you use, gas, electric, or solid fuel, heat travels from the electric element or burner to the food by *conduction*, *convection*, or *radiation*. In some cooking methods, heat travels by more than one of these ways.

4.3
GRILLING

How does heat get to food under the grill?

YOU WILL NEED:

Slice of white bread
2 strips of kitchen foil,
10 cm × 2 cm (4 inches × ½ inch)
Candle
Matches
Tongs
Grill pan and rack
Oven gloves

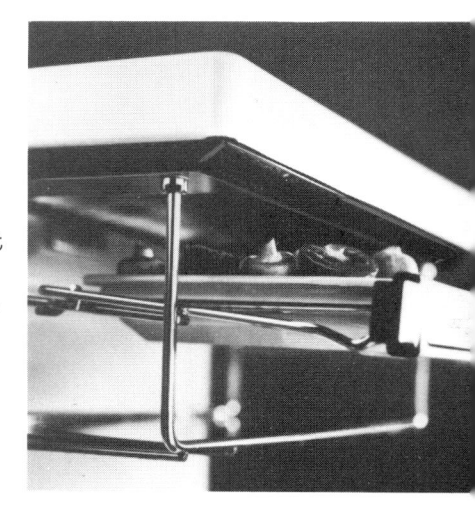

Figure 4.2

Figure 4.3

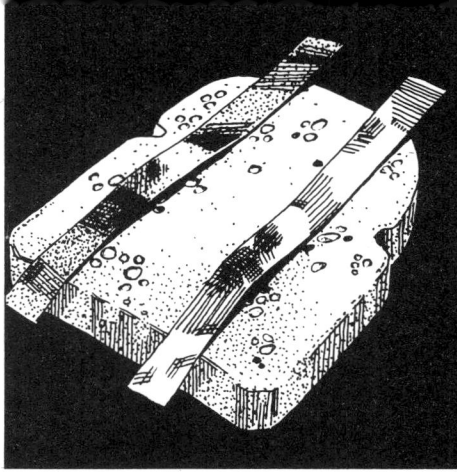

1 Hold one strip of foil with tongs in a smoky candle flame to blacken it.

2 Switch the grill on to heat it up.

3 Toast the bread as shown in figure 4.3 with the strips of foil on top.

Q 2
Look at the patch of bread that was under the shiny foil. Why do you think that this was not toasted?

Energy from the grill beams in rays, a bit like sunshine, onto the bread. The rays turn to heat as they strike the bread and toast it. The shiny strips of foil reflect (bounce back) the rays like a mirror and stop them getting to the bread. Because rays travel in straight lines they cannot bend round the back of the bread to toast it. So food only has one surface exposed to the heat and must be turned over to cook the other side.

Q 3
a What was the bread like under the blackened foil?
b Why do you think this got slightly toasted?

The blackened foil absorbs (soaks up) the energy rays from the grill, gets hot, and sends out its own energy rays. These also turn to heat as they hit the bread underneath and toast it.

Figure 4.4

Radiation is energy in the form of rays. Hot objects radiate energy. The hotter the object the more energy it radiates. When a grill is made red-hot it radiates a lot of energy and so it cooks the food quickly. This is how a toaster works too. If the food is grilled in thick pieces it takes longer for the heat to reach the centre of the food and cook it. So unless you lower the grill pan and turn the heat down, the intense radiation burns the outside of thick slices of food before the inside is cooked.

Q 4
Why must you toast bread first, when you make Welsh Rarebit or toasted cheese?

Q 5
Why must kebabs (foods grilled on a skewer) be turned as they cook?

Microwaves are rays rather like those coming from the grill. They only turn to heat when they hit water molecules. Microwaves pass straight through paper, glass, or plastic containers without making them hot. But they bounce back off metals, so metal dishes cannot be used for cooking food. If food inside has water in it the microwaves will turn to heat.

Microwave energy makes the molecules of water in food vibrate (jiggle) at very high speed. This cooks foods at high speeds and saves energy.

Figure 4.5
A microwave oven.

4.4 COOKING UTENSILS

Cooking dishes and pans which let heat through easily don't waste fuel which is meant to heat the food inside them. This next test shows you some differences between three pudding basins. Take care, you will be using boiling water. ⚠

Which basin lets heat through most quickly — plastic, glass, or foil?

YOU WILL NEED:
Water
3 pudding basins to hold 250 ml water (about ½ pint), 1 each of boilable plastic, glass, and foil — as near the same shape and size as possible
3 saucepans, same shape and size, same metal *or* 1 large one
3 100 °C thermometers
Stopwatch or timer
Measuring jug
Oven gloves
Graph paper

1 Measure 250 ml (½ pint) cold water into each basin.

2 Half fill the saucepan with cold water and stand the basins in it as in figure 4.6.

Figure 4.6
Use 3 saucepans or one large one.

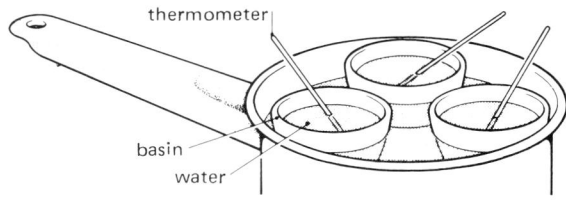

3 Take the temperature of the water in the basins and saucepan and note it down.

4 Turn the gas burner or ring full on. Keep it full on throughout the heating stage of the test.

5 Note the temperature of the water in the basins every minute, until one reaches 40 °C. Turn off the heat. Note the temperature of the water in the saucepan when the water in one of the basins has reached 40 °C.

6 Using oven gloves, carefully lift out the basins of hot water.

7 Take the temperature of the water in each basin every minute over the next 15 minutes.

8 Make two tables of your results like the ones in figure 4.7. Use them to draw a graph showing the rates of heating up and cooling down of the water in the basins (see figure 4.8). Draw the line for each basin on the same graph but in a different colour. Compare how easily heat passes through the basins.

Q 6
In which basin did the water heat up fastest?

Q 7
When the temperature of the water in each basin reached 40 °C, what was the temperature of the water in the pan in each case?

Q 8
In which basin did the water cool down fastest?

Figure 4.7

Heating up	
Basin	Water temperature, at times in minutes 0 1 2 3 4 5 6 7 8 9 10 11 12 13 14 15
Plastic	
Glass	
Foil	

Cooling down	
Basin	Water temperature, at times in minutes 0 1 2 3 4 5 6 7 8 9 10 11 12 13 14 15
Plastic	
Glass	
Foil	

Figure 4.8
Draw a graph like this to record your results.

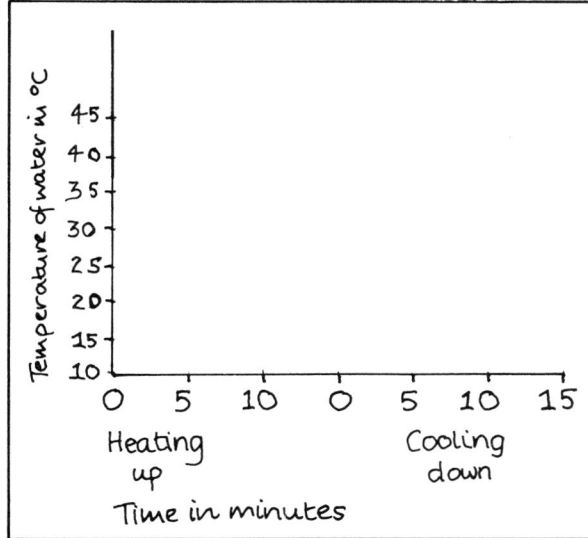

Q 9
Which basin do you think heat passes through
a most easily?
b least easily?

Remember that because the basins you used were not exactly the same in size, shape, and thickness you cannot say definitely whether foil, plastic, or glass lets heat through best. But you can say which *basin* did.

Heat flows in things from places of high temperature to places of low temperature. Materials are built up from tiny particles called atoms or molecules (molecules are groups of atoms).

In solids (*e.g.* metals, wood, china) molecules jiggle about but still fit closely together in a pattern. See figure 4.9.

Figure 4.9
Models of a solid, a liquid, and a gas.

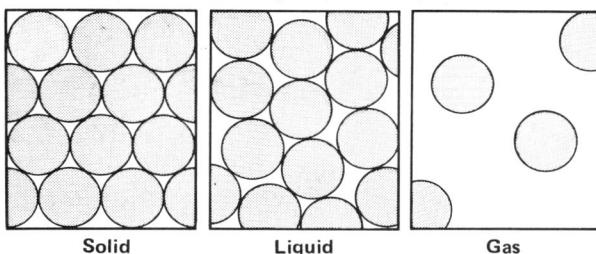

Solid   Liquid   Gas

In *conduction*, when things are heated, the molecules nearest the heat pick up some energy and start to jiggle about faster. These, in turn, pass on their energy to other molecules nearby, making them jiggle faster too. Heat is passed in turn from one molecule to another right through the material.

Q 10
a Does heat travel most easily by conduction through solids, liquids, or gases?
b Why do you think this is?

Good conductors are things which let heat pass through them easily. Metals like copper and aluminium are very good, so they are used for cooking pots and pans. Poor conductors do not let heat pass through them easily. They are useful as insulators for heat-proof knobs and handles on cookery equipment. Plastics, glass, and wood are some examples.

Metals are much better conductors than other materials because of their 'free electrons'. These are thousands of times smaller than atoms. They whiz about in the spaces between atoms, and carry energy quickly.

Air is a bad conductor of heat because the molecules are spaced a long way apart. (See figure 4.9.)

Figure 4.10
'Hot pans'.

These stainless steel saucepans can have a special plastic case to keep food hot without using fuel. The air gap between the plastic case and the saucepan acts as a bad conductor of heat, so that the loss of heat is slowed down. Because the air is trapped it cannot escape in convection currents.

4.5
BOILING, BAKING...

How does heat get through liquids and air?

YOU WILL NEED:

Used tea-leaves
Water
500-ml glass beaker
Frying pan
Oven gloves
Wooden spoon
Thermometer
Watch or timer
Cooker

Figure 4.11

1 Half fill the beaker with cold water and sprinkle in the tea-leaves.

2 Stand the beaker in the frying pan, and pour about 3 cm (about 1 inch) water into the frying pan. Heat slowly.

3 Watch carefully. After about 2 minutes, note the temperature of the water at the top and bottom of the beaker.

Q 11
What was the first thing you saw happening in the water?

Q 12
Was the water the same temperature at the top and bottom of the beaker?

Q 13
What happened to the tea-leaves?

Q 14
If you stir the water what happens to
a the tea-leaves?
b the temperature of the water?

Q 15
Turn up the heat. Do the tea-leaves move faster or slower now? What is the temperature?

Q 16
Turn the heat off. How long is it before the tea-leaves stop moving? What is the temperature of the water now?

As heat was conducted through the metal pan and glass beaker, water at the bottom of the beaker got hot first. It expanded and became less dense (got lighter for its size), and floated to the top. The denser cold water sank to the bottom. Then it got hot in turn and began to rise.

These moving streams of hot water rising and cold water sinking are called convection currents. Heat travels by convection currents in water and other liquids. You saw the tea-leaves move by convection currents in the beaker of water.

The hotter the water, the faster the convection currents move.

Figure 4.12
When poaching eggs, convection currents must move very slowly. Otherwise the white will break up before it has time to cook.

Figure 4.13

In boiling, stewing, poaching, and frying, heat travels through the pan first by conduction, then to the food by convection currents. Heat also travels partly by conduction in the molecules of liquid.

In baking and roasting, food is heated in the oven mainly by convection currents in hot air. Because the molecules are further apart in air, heat cannot travel so easily, so foods take longer to cook.

Q 17
Compare the time taken to boil potatoes with the time taken to cook them as baked jacket potatoes.

Because of convection currents the hottest air collects at the top of an *ordinary* oven. So foods cook at *different* temperatures on different shelves.

In a *fan oven*, the hot air is circulated more evenly round the oven so convection currents are less important. Foods cook at the *same temperature* on different shelves.

Figure 4.14
Foods can be cooked at different temperatures at the same time in an ordinary oven.

Figure 4.15
In a slow cooker, convection currents move very slowly. Heat also travels by conduction.

Convection currents cannot happen in solids, because their molecules are so tightly packed that they cannot move. But in baking, heat is conducted from the metal cooker walls and shelves and passes through the dish to heat the food. Food also cooks by radiation in the oven.

CHAPTER 5
How does cooking change food?

5.1 COOKING CHANGES FOOD

Cooking changes food in different ways. Some foods become harder when cooked, others softer. Some foods melt; others become firm and solid. They may absorb (take in) water, become moist and swell up, or water and other substances may evaporate so that they dry and shrink. Foods may change colour as they cook. (Do you know what colour raw prawns are?) Nearly always the taste changes too.

Figure 5.1a
Boiled gammon (bacon), potatoes, carrots, and onions.

Figure 5.1b
Lemon meringue pie.

Figure 5.1c
Steamed sponge pudding.

Figure 5.2

Change	Foods which change like this as they cook
soften	potato butter
harden	
melt	
take in water	
swell up	
lose water	
shrink	
go brown	
go yellow	
go white	
lose flavour	
gain flavour	

Q 1
Look at the foods in the photographs. Try to think how each of these foods changes as it cooks. Make a table like the one in figure 5.2.

Q 2
What other changes could be added to this list?

To understand why foods change as they cook, you need to take a closer look at what they are made of.

5.2
WHAT IS IN FOOD?
Foods are mixtures of several different ingredients. You will have realized this from reading recipes. Use worksheet M21 to compare the water and fat content of rice, spaghetti, eggs, sausages, haricot beans, and potatoes when they are raw and when they are cooked.

Figure 5.1d
Risotto.

Q 3
What do you think happens to the water and fat content of these foods as they cook? Discuss your ideas with your teacher.

5.3
THE EFFECT OF HEAT ON FOOD
Foods are a complicated mixture of different things, so it is often very difficult to explain the changes which happen when they cook. Use worksheet M11 to get a better idea of some of these changes. You will investigate some of the changes which happen to protein, sugar, starch, fibre, fat, and water. By looking at these different changes you will be able to spot what happens to the foods you cook.

5.4 SIZE OF FOOD

For food to be completely cooked, heat has to reach its *centre*. Heat travels through the *surface* of food from the outside.

Q 4
Is there a link between the *size* of food and the cooking time?

You could compare large and small potatoes boiled together in the same pan after 5 minutes and 10 minutes. Cut them open to see.

Q 5
All the foods shown in figure 5.1a on the previous page are boiled.
a What is the cooking time for each food? (Use a recipe book to check.)
b Apart from size, what else might affect cooking time?

Foods cook more *quickly* when cut into *smaller* pieces. (And they also cool down more quickly when put on a plate.)

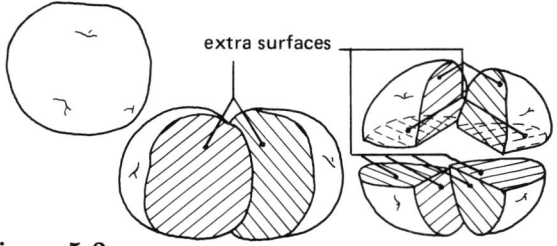

Figure 5.3
Each cut you make increases the surface area of the food.

Cutting up food helps food to cook more quickly for two reasons:
One: the *bigger* the *surface area*, the *more* heat can pass through.
Two: the *smaller* the size of food, the *less* distance heat has to travel to reach the centre.

Figure 5.4

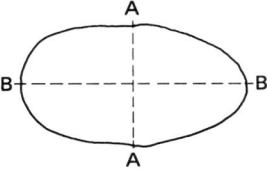

Q 6
If you wanted to cook this potato more quickly, which way would you make the cut? Through line AA or BB?

Figure 5.5
If potatoes are all the same size they should cook at the same speed.

Q 7
The shape of food is important in baking too. Look at figure 5.6. In which shaped tin is the mixture likely to cook *a* fastest *b* slowest? Why?

Figure 5.6
A selection of baking tins.

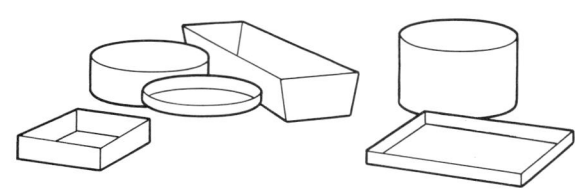

5.5 COOKING BREAD, CAKES, AND PASTRIES

To get a light open texture, raising agents must be added to the mixture of ingredients. Tiny bubbles of gas form and are trapped in the mixture. During cooking, the gas bubbles expand, stretch the mixture, and make it rise. See figure 5.7.

Figure 5.7
Gas bubbles expand on heating and make mixtures rise.

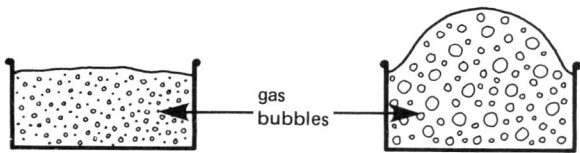

Gas bubbles can be formed from air, steam, and carbon dioxide.

Air bubbles are trapped when mixtures are beaten, whisked, or creamed.

Steam is given off when water in food is heated. This water can be naturally present in the food, or added as an ingredient.

Carbon dioxide is formed by the action of either heat or an acid on bicarbonate of soda. Yeast cells also produce carbon dioxide when they are given food (sugar), water, and a suitable temperature.

Figure 5.9
Soufflé: what is the raising agent here?

Figure 5.10
Most types of bread contain yeast.

Figure 5.8
Soda bread: bicarbonate of soda is the raising agent.

See how raising agents give off bubbles of gas for yourself.

YOU WILL NEED:

Warm water
15 g fresh yeast
1½ 5-ml (tea) spoons sugar
Freshly prepared lime water
3 labels
3 boiling-tubes with stoppers and double-bend delivery tubes
3 beakers
3 test-tubes and rack
Stopwatch

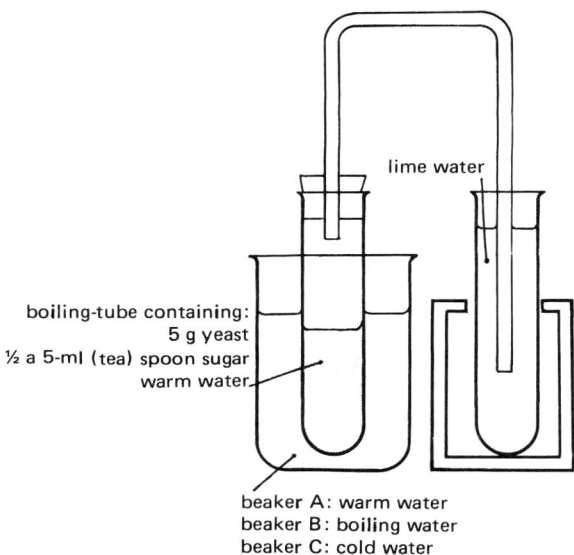

Figure 5.11
Set up three sets of apparatus like this.

1 Put lime water into the 3 test-tubes.

2 Put 5 g yeast and ½ a 5-ml (tea) spoon sugar into each boiling-tube.

3 Fill each boiling-tube full with warm water, and put the stopper on. Label them A, B, and C.

4 Put boiling-tube A in a beaker of warm water at 40 °C. Put B into boiling water. Leave C in cold water.

5 Compare the rate of bubbling. (Use the stopwatch.)

Q 8
a What happens to the lime water in each test-tube?
b How long does this take to happen in each case?

Q 9
What is the gas produced by the yeast?

You could test baking powders in a similar way.

For a bread or cake mixture to rise, it must be able to trap the gas as it forms.

In the making of bread, a protein is formed called *gluten*. This acts like a balloon or bubble gum and holds the gas in the mixture. See for yourself what gluten is like. First you will need to separate it from the rest of the flour.

You will need:
100 g hard flour
Pinch of salt
About 2 15-ml tablespoons of water
Basin
Nylon sieve
Baking sheet
Worksheet M19

1 Mix the flour, salt, and water together in the basin to form a stiff dough.

2 Knead the dough ball in your fingers for about 3 minutes.

3 Cut the dough ball in half. Shape into two balls.

4 Put one ball aside to compare with the other one later.

5 Cover the other dough ball with cold water, and soak it for 20 minutes.

6 Work the dough ball with your fingers to wash out the flour.

7 Test the water for starch. (See worksheet M19. Don't get iodine in your eyes!) ⚠

8 Go on washing the ball until the water runs clear.

9 Test the ball for starch.

10 Compare this gluten ball with the other dough ball.

11 Bake both balls on a sheet at 200 °C (400 °F), regulo 6.

12 Compare the size and texture of each ball.

30

Figure 5.12
Different kinds of flour.

How does flour vary? Repeat the experiment, using different kinds of flour.

Q 10
Which flour would not be suitable for making bread?

5.6 COOKING ONIONS

How does cooking change onions?

YOU WILL NEED:

2 onions	Saucepan
Vegetable knife	Water
Chopping board	Measuring jug
	3 saucers

1   Peel and chop the onions as shown below. Divide them into three portions.

Figure 5.13

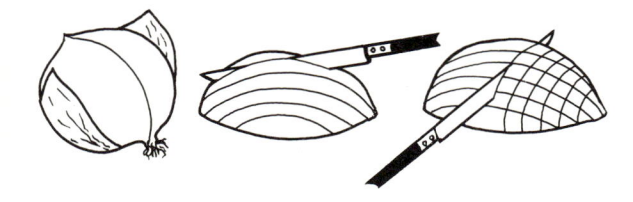

Q 11
Is the onion smell stronger or weaker now that it is cut up?

Q 12
What do you notice happening on the cut surfaces?

2   Put one portion onto a saucer and label it as the control ('sample A').

3   Boil the second portion in 1 cup (about 225 ml) salted water for 1 minute only. Strain the liquid into a cup, put the vegetable onto a saucer and label as 'sample B'.

4   Do the same to the next sample, but boil for 5 minutes. This is 'sample C'.

5   Compare the colour, flavour, and texture of the raw and cooked samples.

6   Compare the volume, colour, and flavour of the cooking water from samples B and C.

7   Make tables of your results like the ones below. Discuss your observations with your teacher.

Figure 5.14

Vegetable	Volume	Colour	Flavour
Sample A			
Sample B			
Sample C			

Cooking water	Volume	Colour	Flavour
Sample B			
Sample C			

5.7 COOKING GREEN VEGETABLES

Compare the colour and texture of green vegetables cooked in different ways.

YOU WILL NEED:

50 g cabbage (or other leaf vegetable)	4 400-ml beakers (or small pans)
Pinch bicarbonate of soda	Vegetable knife
1 5-ml (tea) spoon vinegar	Chopping board
Pinch salt	Watch or timer
pH papers	Worksheet M12

1 Chop the vegetable. Mix the inner and outer leaves together. Divide it into 4 small samples; keep 1 of them as the control ('sample A').

2 Measure out equal volumes of water as follows:

for sample B   Tap water, plus a pinch of salt;
for sample C   As B, plus a pinch of bicarbonate of soda;
for sample D   As B, plus a teaspoon of vinegar.

3 Measure the pH of each one. If you are not sure how to do this, see worksheet M12.

4 Cook the samples of green vegetable for equal lengths of time.

5 Compare the colour and texture of each sample with the raw sample (A). Look at the cooking water.

Q 13
Which of the cooked samples *looks* most appetizing?

Q 14
Is the *texture* noticeably different in any of the samples? (Try pinching the vegetable between your fingers, then taste it.)

Q 15
Is tap water a different pH from the cooking water in samples C and D?

5.8
VITAMIN C IN VEGETABLES

Vegetables have nutrients and other chemicals dissolved in water inside their cells. One nutrient is vitamin C. This is in many vegetables, including cabbage, Brussels sprouts, and cauliflower.

You can test for vitamin C using a blue dye. For the test to work the vitamin C must be released from the cells to mix with the dye.

Does water wash vitamin C out of raw vegetables and cooked vegetables?

What effect does heat have on the cell walls of vegetables?

Figure 5.15
Sources of vitamin C: cauliflower (above), cabbage (below), and Brussels sprouts (opposite).

YOU WILL NEED:
2 similar-sized Brussels sprouts (or two similar-sized cauliflower florets)
Blue dye solution in a dropper bottle
Colourless vinegar (ethanoic acid)
2 100-ml graduated beakers
2 test-tubes in a rack
Watch-glass
5-ml graduated syringe
1 gauze
5-ml (tea) spoon

1 Trim the sprouts (or florets). Put one in each beaker with 50 ml water. Leave one of them to stand.

2 Cook the other one. If you haven't got a Bunsen burner, stand the beaker on a gauze, over the cooker ring. Use the watch-glass as a lid. Don't let the beaker boil dry! ⚠

3 When the sprout is cooked, add 2 teaspoonfuls of vinegar. Let it cool!

Testing the washing water
1 Add 2 teaspoonfuls of vinegar to the raw sprout's beaker. Wash out the syringe and use it to put 2 ml of this water into a test-tube.

2 Add a drop of blue dye. If it turns pink then colourless, go on adding drops until you get a pink colour which lasts. Count the number of drops. Care! The blue dye (DCPIP) is poisonous. ⚠

3 Repeat the test to check your result, and write the number of drops in your note book.

Testing the cooking water
1 Add water to the beaker to make it up to 50 ml again. Then use the syringe to measure 2 ml cooking water into a test-tube.

2 Add a drop of blue dye. If it goes pink, then colourless, the water contains vitamin C.

3 Count the number of drops of dye which will go colourless. Stop when the pink colour stays even when you rock the tube to and fro. Write down the number of drops in your note book.

4 Repeat the test, using another 2 ml of the cooking water in a clean test-tube. Write down this number of drops in your note book too.

The *more* dye turning colourless, the *more* vitamin C has come out of the sprout into the cooking water.

Q 16
a Which water contained more vitamin C: the cooking water, or the soaking water?
b Where did the vitamin C come from?

Q 17
Which words would finish this sentence? Vitamin C is washed out of sprouts because heating makes the cell walls . . . .

Q 18
a What do you think would happen if you chopped a sprout into tiny bits and soaked it in some cold water?
b How could you check your answer?

Figure 5.16

Cooking losses in perspective
Look at the food tables on worksheet M21. Compare the figures for raw and cooked fruits and vegetables. Cooking can lead to a loss of vitamin C, but usually more cooked food can be eaten than raw — so you may not be so badly off after all.

CHAPTER 6

Measuring and mixing

6.1
HOW CAN FOODS BE VARIED?

Brandy snaps are crunchy and sweet. Their crispness depends on the proportions of the ingredients and the temperature and length of cooking. Other foods can vary quite a lot too, as you will have discovered for yourself. Are the variations in the dishes you cook always intentional?

To find some reasons why foods vary, try experimenting with these ingredients for chocolate sauce. Work with a partner; it will be quicker.

YOU WILL NEED:

	Pupil 1	Pupil 2
Cornflour (maize flour):	10 g	20 g
Cocoa powder:	10 g	10 g
Silver top milk:	200 ml	200 ml
Granulated sugar:	20 g	20 g
Butter:	5 g	5 g
Vanilla essence:	3 drops	3 drops
	¼-pint serving boat	¼-pint mould

Each pupil

1-pint measuring jug
1-pint saucepan
Wooden spoon
1-pint mixing bowl
Tablespoon
Large bowl with ice and water mixture
Cooker

1 Make the chocolate sauce mixtures by the 'one-stage method' or 'blending method'. Use a recipe book to check how to do this.

2 Pour the mixtures into prepared moulds or serving boats. Cool them quickly in iced water.

3 Compare the results of your experiments.

Figure 6.1
Can you name the foods in the picture?

Different *consistencies* (thickness or thinness) of sauce mixtures are produced by varying the proportion of the *thickening agent* (in this case cornflour) to the liquid.

Recipes tell you *which* ingredients to use and *how much* of them to take. Following the instructions carefully helps to make sure that the right changes happen during cooking. You will be able to rely on getting the result you wanted and the ingredients will not be wasted.

Q 1
a Were the *same ingredients* used for both recipes?
b Were the *same amounts* used? If not, which ones varied?
c What effect did this have on the finished dishes?

Q 2
What else could be varied in a chocolate sauce mixture?

Q 3
Find out what ingredients are used in a tube of bought chocolate sauce. Are the ingredients the same as the ones you used?

Q 4
How does the food manufacturer make sure that he gets reliable results each time?

Q 5
List as many reasons as you can why there are small differences between home-made Victoria sandwich cakes.

Figure 6.2
Flour, fat, and yeast are mixed together in large quantities for bread production.

Using a well-tried recipe helps to make certain that food will turn out all right. But cooking can be an art as well as a science. By varying the basic recipe and changing the ingredients for decoration or flavouring, or assembling it differently, interesting new dishes can be made, based on the same recipe proportions.

Figure 6.3

6.2 COMPOSITION OF FOODS: RECIPE BUILDING

Shortcrust pastry is a traditional standard recipe based on flour, fat, and water. As its name suggests, the pastry should be crisp or 'short' when cooked. The proportion and kind of fat affects the crispness. It is used to make a variety of sweet and savoury dishes.

The basic proportions are:
½ as much fat as flour and
about 1 5-ml (tea) spoon of water to every 25 g (1 oz) of flour.

Q 6
Why should the amount of water be varied?

By how much can the amount of water be varied and still produce an acceptable result?

To make a fair test, only vary the water. Make sure that each pastry is made in exactly the same way.

YOU WILL NEED:

Controlled ingredients (ingredients which stay the same)

100 g plain flour
½ level 5-ml (tea) spoon salt
25 g lard
25 g hard margarine

Variable ingredients (ingredients which change)

Cold water
Mix 1: 1 5-ml (tea) spoon
Mix 2: 2 5-ml (tea) spoons
Mix 3: 4 5-ml (tea) spoons
Mix 4: 6 5-ml (tea) spoons
Mix 5: 8 5-ml (tea) spoons

Mixing bowl
Sieve
15-ml (table) spoon
5-ml (tea) spoon
Palette knife
Rolling pin

1 Use a recipe book to check the method for making the pastry.

2 Vary the quantity of water used for mixing the pastry dough as suggested above.

3 Roll out each mix of pastry. Use guides to make sure that they are the same thickness.

4 Cut at least 3 squares, about 5 cm × 5 cm, from each mix of dough.

Figure 6.4

Figure 6.6
A well-known way of using pastry.

5 Put onto a baking sheet. Cook for 12 to 15 minutes at 200 °C (400 °F). Cook yours for the *same time* as the others in the group. Use the *same shelf position*.

6 Cool the pastry and compare the results. Make a table like the *first* one below (figure 6.4). (Suggest a way to measure crumbliness.)

100 g pastry made with cold water using:	How easy was it to handle?	How crumbly was it?	Which was the best?
Mix 1: 1 spoonful			
Mix 2: 2 spoonfuls			
Mix 3: 4 spoonfuls			
Mix 4: 6 spoonfuls			
Mix 5: 8 spoonfuls			

100 g pastry made with:	How crumbly was it?	Taste	Colour	Which was the best?
Mix 1: 50 g lard				
Mix 2: 50 g hard block margarine				
Mix 3: 25 g lard and 25 g hard block margarine				
Mix 4: 50 g butter				
Mix 5: 50 g soft tub margarine				

Figure 6.5

Q 7
a Which pastry was hard and tough?
b Which was difficult to bind?
c Which mixtures were nice to eat?

Does it matter very much if the ingredients themselves are changed? Try experimenting with shortcrust pastry again, but this time changing the fat used.

YOU WILL NEED:

Controlled ingredients (ingredients which stay the same)
100 g plain flour and
1 level 5-ml (tea) spoon salt sieved together
4 or 5 5-ml (tea) spoons very cold water
(use the same amount for each test)

Variable ingredients (ingredients which change)

Mix 1: 50 g lard
Mix 2: 50 g hard block margarine
Mix 3: 25 g lard and
  25 g hard block margarine
Mix 4: 50 g butter
Mix 5: 50 g soft tub margarine

Cooking equipment as before.

1 Prepare and cook the pastry as before.

2 Copy and complete the table (figure 6.5), and compare your results.

Q 8
a Which fat, or fats, gave the best crumbliness?
b Which fat gave the pastry with the palest colour? Why?
c Which property of pastry is the most important one?
d Name three other fats you could include in this experiment.

Q 9
List five other ingredients which could be used in the recipe to change the taste and texture of the pastry.

Now you can begin to see how important it is to follow recipes. With a tested, standard recipe you can be sure that the proportions of ingredients will give a good result.

6.3 WAYS OF MEASURING

To follow a recipe, you have to measure the weight of solid foods and measure the volume of liquids. This makes sure the ingredients are correctly balanced. Otherwise, the finished dish may be quite different from what you expect. Some ingredients are difficult to measure, and accuracy can be a problem. For example, syrup, treacle, and honey are sticky to handle. They can be weighed or measured by volume.

Q 10
a How many different sorts of measuring equipment can you pick out from the recipes in section 6.1?
b What other important units, used in cooking, are not quoted in the recipes? (List the metric units and the imperial units separately.)

Q 11
a How would you measure 25 g of butter from a block weighing 250 g without weighing?
b Can volumes be estimated as easily as weights?

Old recipes use pounds or ounces for weights, fluid ounces, gills, or pints for volume, and the Fahrenheit scale for temperature measurement. In very old recipes, unfamiliar units of measurement are sometimes quoted.

Figure 6.7

Mince Pyes (1795)

A pound and a half of beef, a pound and three qrs. of suet, cut in pieces. and a little black pepper and salt. Let it stew a little in a "stew pan", then poure it out in a Mugg Pott, and let it stand till quite cold, then chope it small and put to it a dram of cloves, one dram of mace, pounded fine, a pound and a half of apples cut small, one pound and a qr of good soft sugare a pound of currants, one pound of raisins cut small. the pill of three lemons cut small and the juce. If not sharpe enough put in a little verges, a pint of Elden wine, mix it well to geather and then put it down in a pott. when your mixture ripens put in brandy to your taste.

37

You may need to change an old recipe to metric units if your measuring equipment is up to date. Nomograms are useful for conversions. Simple ones are shown in figure 6.8. Use a ruler to help you do the conversion.

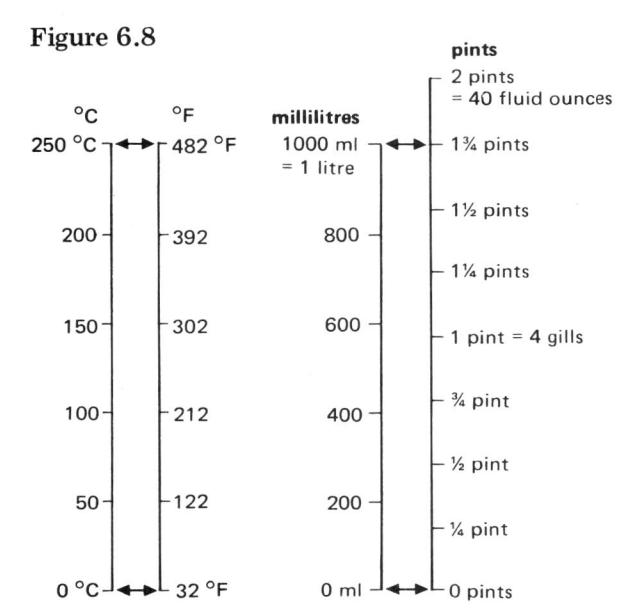

Figure 6.8

Q 12
How many millilitres (ml) make
a 1 pint
b 1 gill?

Q 13
Cooking at 200 °C is the same as using regulo 6. What is the equivalent Fahrenheit temperature?

Q 14
Why is 0 °C the same as 32 °F on the nomogram?

How much do cup measurements differ?

Cups are handy measures to use at home. American and Continental recipes use them a lot. But cups (and coffee mugs) are different sizes.

YOU WILL NEED:

½ lb flour or rice
Teacup
Coffee mug (or breakfast cup)
15-ml (table) spoon
Balance

1 Weigh the teacup and note the weight.

2 Spoon the flour (or rice) gently into the cup and level off.

3 Weigh the teacup and flour (or rice) and record the weight.

4 Repeat the experiment using the other cup or mug and record your results like this.

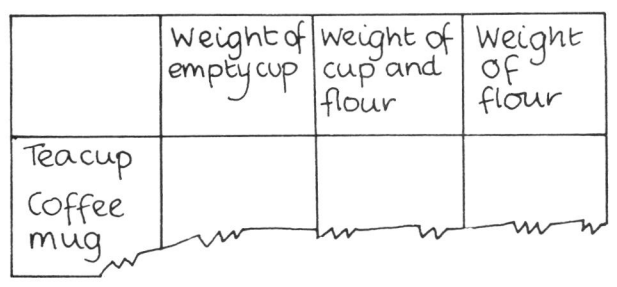

Figure 6.9

Q 15
Which container held
a the most flour (or rice)
b the least flour (or rice)?

Q 16
Would the difference affect a recipe very much?

Some kinds of the same foods pack together more closely than the others. The same cup will hold a bigger weight of the more dense ones. Sugars give a good example of this. Look at figure 6.10.

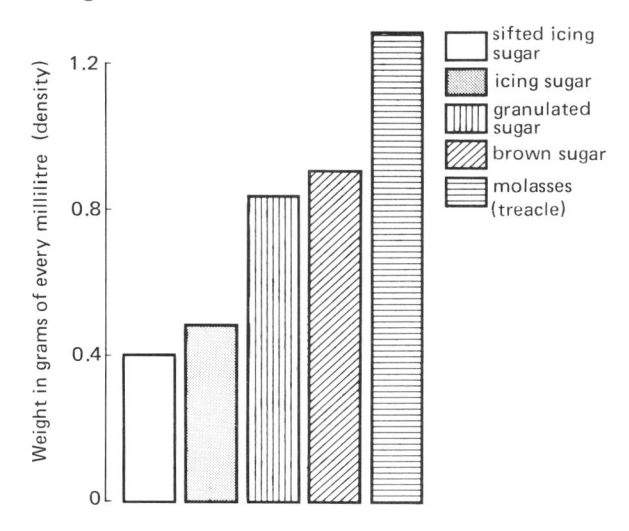

Figure 6.10
Comparing the density of sugars.

So the same cup would give roughly twice the weight of brown sugar compared with icing sugar. This could make a lot of difference when measuring out the ingredients for a cake.

Standard measures are very useful. The standard British cup holds 250 ml (or just under half a pint).

Q 17
a Work out the weight of granulated sugar which this measure would hold.
b Why does sieving (sifting) change the density of powdered ingredients?

6.4 CHOICE OF MEASURING EQUIPMENT

Figure 6.11
Equipment for weighing and measuring.

Figure 6.12
Teaspoons can vary enormously in shape and size — but sometimes they hold the same amount!

Which equipment do you use when you cook? Probably not a chemical balance. They weigh accurately to a hundredth of a gram or less. As you saw with the pastry mix, food ingredients don't need to be weighed to such fine limits. Cheaper and faster weighing is done using kitchen balances. These are specially designed for convenient use in the kitchen. Spoons make very handy measures too.

Q 18
Name as many spoon measures as you can.

Q 19
Why are spoons often used to measure ingredients like cornflour, arrowroot, and sugar?

Q 20
Collect different teaspoons. Check how much they vary in size. How would this affect the measurement of ingredients?

How accurate do kitchen scales need to be? See worksheet M14 for an experiment using eggs.

In this chapter you have investigated some of the reasons why there is such a variation in foods. You have learned how adaptable foods are, and practised some cookery skills.

You have also investigated different ways of measuring foods, and have had firsthand experience of the problem of having to convert units of measurement from one scale to another!

CHAPTER 7

Keeping food

Figure 7.1
'Sell by' dates help to make sure that food is fresh when it is sold.
Food labels often show how long the food can be kept after purchase, and how it should be stored.

FRESH CHICKEN
This food should be cooked on day of purchase or within 2 days if kept in a refrigerator.
Sell by 30 June

Figure 7.2
Mould growing on bread (× 1250).

7.1
WHY DOES FOOD GO OFF?

By law, shops must sell food of good quality that is safe to eat. Foods are processed in different ways to keep them. 'Sell by' and 'eat by' labels show recommended storage times. Many raw foods are not labelled and need special care to keep them fresh.

Food soon begins to loose its freshness. Even canned and packaged foods quickly go stale, once they are opened.

Nearly all food contains water in different amounts. Some foods quickly lose water and begin to wilt when they are stored. They must be packaged and stored to *control the rate* of water loss. Other foods attract water and become soggy. Biscuits and cereals need *moisture-proof* storage.

Fatty foods quickly go off if stored badly. Fat becomes rancid as it combines with air, or is affected by enzymes. Light and warmth speed up the staling process. Fatty foods need cool, dim, air-tight storage.

Enzymes are chemicals made inside the cells of all plants and animals. They are proteins which speed up chemical reactions. Even after a fruit has been picked or an animal slaughtered, enzymes continue to work. This is why green bananas or pears ripen after picking. Left unchecked, enzymes finally cause decay.

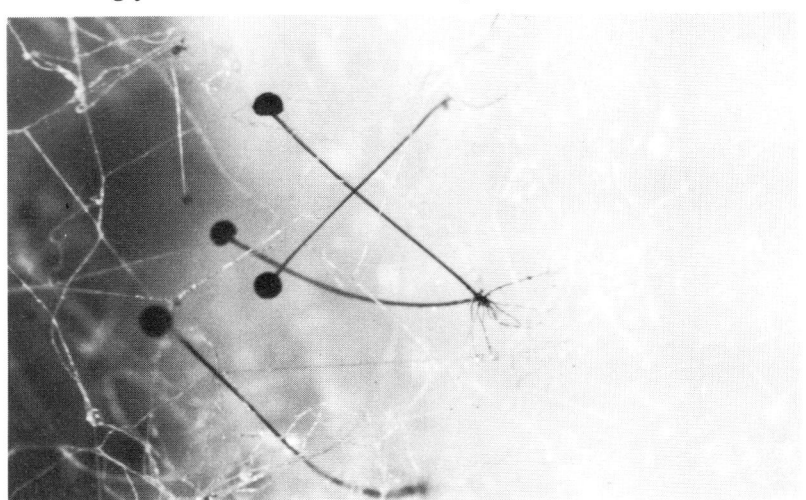

Enzymes are sensitive to different temperatures. As the temperature rises their activity speeds up, but at temperatures near the boiling point of water (100 °C, 212 °F) most enzymes stop working. As the temperature falls, enzyme activity is increasingly slowed down. This is why foods stored in cooler temperatures in the refrigerator keep fresh for longer. But even at temperatures as low as −18 °C (0 °F) some enzymes continue to work and can cause food to go off. This is why green vegetables such as runner beans are blanched (cooked for a short time in boiling water) before being frozen. Blanching inactivates the enzymes.

Other chemicals are used to halt or slow down the action of enzymes. These include acids, sugars, and salt.

Microbes (micro-organisms, such as yeasts, moulds, and bacteria) bring about both useful and harmful changes in food. Bread, cheese, vinegar, yoghurt, and wine are made by the action of useful microbes. But microbes which destroy food grow quickly at room temperatures. (So do those which cause disease.) They can be destroyed by heat and acid. Microbes don't grow quickly in cold temperatures. They slow down or may even stop working. (See figure 7.4.)

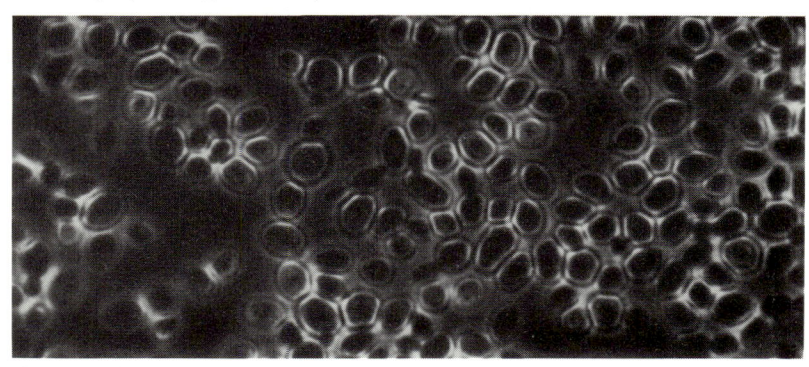

Figure 7.3 *Yeast (× 20).*

Figure 7.4

Despite the food manufacturers' or growers' careful preparation, processing and packaging, food can still be spoilt by the way you store it at home.

There are three storage areas — the refrigerator, the freezer, and shelf. They allow you to store foods at different temperatures. Different foods keep best at different temperatures. Usually, the cooler the temperature is the longer food can be kept. Some foods such as Brussels sprouts and butter can be kept in all three storage areas. It depends on the length of time you want to keep them for. Food storage containers must be hygienic and must control the effect of air and light on food.

7.2
KEEPING FOOD COOL

Just as there are different high temperatures in cooking, so there are different low temperatures in refrigeration. (Look at worksheet M15 to see how refrigerators and freezers keep foods cool.) Refrigerators and freezers have revolutionized shopping and cooking habits. Refrigerators will store food for short periods of time — about a week. Freezers store food at very low temperatures for longer periods of time — up to a year. This can save time and money. Foods can be stored prepared or partly prepared in advance.

There are different types and sizes of refrigerators and freezers. A family must decide what their needs are before they can know what suits them best.

Q 1
What would you have to consider in choosing fridges and freezers?

Figure 7.5
The uses of different temperatures in a refrigerator and a freezer.

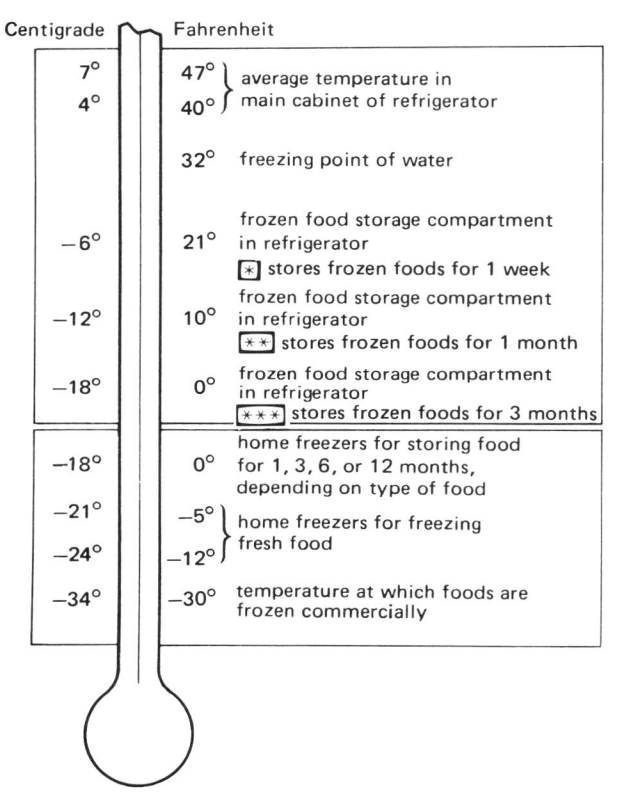

Centigrade	Fahrenheit	
7°	47°	average temperature in main cabinet of refrigerator
4°	40°	
	32°	freezing point of water
−6°	21°	frozen food storage compartment in refrigerator [*] stores frozen foods for 1 week
−12°	10°	frozen food storage compartment in refrigerator [**] stores frozen foods for 1 month
−18°	0°	frozen food storage compartment in refrigerator [***] stores frozen foods for 3 months
−18°	0°	home freezers for storing food for 1, 3, 6, or 12 months, depending on type of food
−21°	−5°	home freezers for freezing fresh food
−24°	−12°	
−34°	−30°	temperature at which foods are frozen commercially

Q 2
In figure 7.5, what is the range of temperature in
a a refrigerator
b a freezer?

Check the temperature of a refrigerator and freezer using an appropriate thermometer. Compare this with the temperature of kitchen shelves.

Q 3
Which part of the refrigerator is
a the coldest
b the least cold?

Q 4
a Why do you think the back part of the shelf of the refrigerator is likely to be colder than the front?
b Why do some upright freezers have solid fronts to the drawers?

Figure 7.6
a *A thermometer for measuring the temperature in a freezer and a refrigerator.*
b *An ordinary room thermometer.*
(Note the difference in the range of temperatures.)

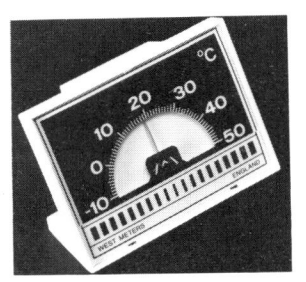

Table 7.1
The temperatures at which foods should be stored in a refrigerator.

Food	Temperature °C	°F
Fish	−5 to −1	23 to 30
Meat	0.5 to 3	33 to 38
Milk, butter, cream, *etc.*	3 to 8	38 to 46
Fruits and vegetables	7 to 10	44 to 50

Q 5
In which part of the refrigerator would you store
a fish
b fruits and vegetables?

7.3 ICE CRYSTALS IN FROZEN FOOD

What effect does freezing have on some foods?

YOU WILL NEED:
¼ cucumber
Vegetable knife and chopping board
Microscope and microscope slides
Freezer and freezer section of refrigerator

1 Slice the cucumber very thinly. Look at a slice under the microscope (low power, x 10).

2 Record your observations. Keep three slices for a control.

3   Freeze slices of cucumber in the ice-making compartment of the refrigerator with the setting
a   at coldest (for rapid freezing)
b   at warmest (for slower freezing).

4   Remove them and quickly examine them with a microscope (at low power, x 10, and at a higher magnification, x 40). Note the size and shape of crystals formed by
a   rapid freezing
b   slow freezing.

5   Compare the textures of the thawed slices with the cucumber slices which were not frozen.

Q 6
a   How do ice crystals in frozen foods vary with the rate of freezing?
b   Does this affect the texture of the thawed food?
c   List three foods unsuitable for freezing. (If you are not sure, check in a book on home freezing.)

Figure 7.7

7.4
WATER IN FOODS

Is there a link between the 'shelf-life' of foods (how long they keep) and their water content?

YOU WILL NEED:
Scraps of fresh, cooked, and preserved food (the contents of store cupboards and refrigerators)
Worksheet M19
Worksheet M21
Cobalt chloride paper

1   Wrap each scrap of food in the blue test papers (cobalt chloride papers).

2   Press firmly between two hard surfaces. Use a rolling-pin, microscope slides, or tiles.

3   Water squeezed out of food will give a pink patch on the blue test paper. Make a table of your results. List the foods in the correct column.

Figure 7.8

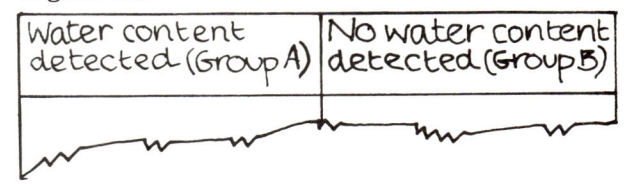

Water content detected (Group A)	No water content detected (Group B)

Q 7
a   Is there a link between which group the foods are in and how long they keep?
b   In which group do fats belong?
c   How is so much water held by fruits, vegetables, and meats?
d   Why did it run out when they were crushed?

4   Use a microscope to look at the cell structure of foods. (Ask your teacher about this.)

5   Look up food composition tables (worksheet M21) which show the amount of water in various foods.

Q 8
a   How dry are dried foods?
b   Compare the water content of 'perishable foods' such as meat and fish, and 'dry stores foods' such as flour and sugar. Is there a difference?

7.5
LOOKING AT WRAPPING MATERIALS

Moisture-proof storage is needed to protect foods stored on the shelf, in the fridge, and in the freezer. This helps to *control* the amount of water lost or gained by food. For example, to keep crisp foods crisp they must be kept dry. The effectiveness of different wrapping materials in doing this can be measured in a simple way using a 'Crispometer'.

YOU WILL NEED:
Potato crisps or cornflakes
Wrapping materials:
small polythene bags
cellophane
cling wrap
aluminium foil
grease-proof paper
kitchen paper
Large storage container

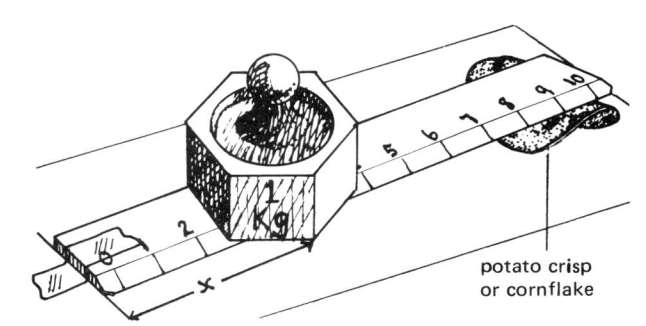

Figure 7.9
The 'Crispometer'.

1 Begin with the weight at the zero end of the ruler. Slowly slide it along until the crisp or cornflake breaks.

2 Read off the number at the point at which the food breaks as in figure 7.9. Test four more crisps or cornflakes from the same sample.

3 Find the average score. This is the 'crispness number'. The lower the number, the crisper the sample.

4 Put five crisps or cornflakes from the same packet in each different wrapping. Make the wrappings into bags or sealed packets.

5 Hang each bag in a damp atmosphere as in figure 7.10. Store overnight, or longer if possible.

Figure 7.10

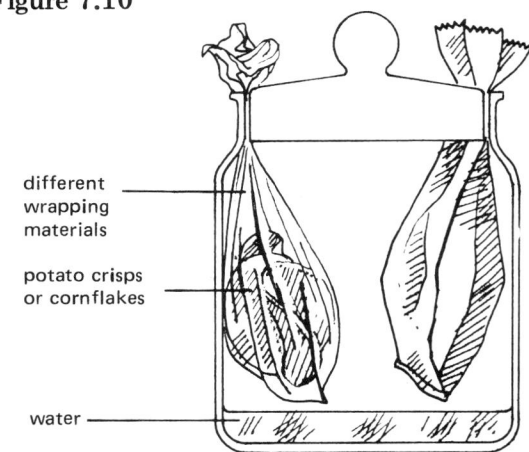

6 Remove the packets and test each sample of five crisps (or cornflakes) for crispness.

Q 9
a Which wrappings kept crispness well?
b Which were unsuitable for storing crisps (or cornflakes)?
c How could foods be made crisp again?
d What sort of container would be best for storing biscuits?

7.6
WATER AND DECAY

Does dampness encourage mould growth?

YOU WILL NEED:

2 slices of bread
Polythene bag
2 plates
Waterspray or sprinkler
Bread bin
Cheese dish
Biscuit tin
Sandwich box

1 Put a slice of bread on each plate. Leave them out in the kitchen area for 3 or 4 days, so that each slice is exposed to air-borne microbes.

2 Sprinkle each slice with an equal amount of water to make it damp.

3 Put one slice of bread in a polythene bag. Do it up loosely. Leave the other slice uncovered. Leave for 3 or 4 days.

4 Look for signs on each slice of bread of:
a mould growth
b dampness.

Q 10
a Which slice of bread developed most mould?
b Is there a connection between dampness and mould growth?

5 Look at the different food containers. Which have ventilation holes? Why?

Q 11
Which foods need to be stored so that air can circulate round them?

Understanding something about the science of cooking is only half the story. The main purpose of cooking is to make foods which are good to eat. Is a little of what you fancy all right? . . .

Nutrition is about people and their food. You will learn why you choose certain foods, and how foods are produced and cooked. You will also find out what different foods contain and how your body uses them.

Nutrition touches on lots of different subjects. It is important to everyone, because we all need food, and we all eat it. Learning about nutrition means learning about what other people eat as well as what you eat yourself.

Nutrition

Chapter 8   **Food in different countries** *page 46*

Chapter 9   **What is in our food?** *52*

Chapter 10   **Energy** *58*

Chapter 11   **Food choices** *64*

Chapter 12   **Digestion** *72*

Chapter 13   **Food and its effect on health** *78*

Chapter 14   **Choosing a nutritious diet** *84*

Chapter 15   **Solving nutrition problems** *90*

CHAPTER 8
Food in different countries

8.1
WHAT PEOPLE EAT

People in different countries eat very different kinds of food.

Figure 8.1
a A traditional British meal consists of meat, potatoes, and other vegetables.

b Hamburgers are part of nearly everyone's diet in the United States. Hamburgers are round cakes of minced meat, and are eaten in a bread roll and with pickles. It is a food you can eat very quickly.

c Italians eat a great deal of spaghetti and other pasta made from wheat. It is eaten with quite small amounts of meat or cheese and sauce.

d   Japanese dishes are often based on rice with fried prawns or thinly sliced meat, and finely chopped vegetables. Most foods are cooked in a very short time.

e   People in the eastern part of India eat rice, often with vegetables or meat flavoured with spices (curry). (In the western part of the country the main foods eaten are made from wheat.)

Q 1
Do all the children in figure 8.1 look happy and healthy?

Q 2
Are all the children eating the same food?

Q 3
Do all these children look as though they get enough to eat?

You can see from these pictures that all sorts of different foods can keep you healthy.

Knowing about food is important. To be as healthy as you can be you must eat the right mixture of foods. Even in countries where there are lots of different foods, you have to know how to choose foods to make you healthy. If you don't eat the right foods for many months you will become ill.

In all countries of the world, many people are well fed. But some people are malnourished. (This includes both too little food and too much.) For instance, in Uganda some children suffer badly from eating a diet that does not contain enough energy, proteins, or vitamins. This is because they cannot get enough food, or foods of the right kind.

Figure 8.1 (continued)
f   'Foofoo' is made from yams. It is rather like mashed potato, and is an important food for people in Ghana. It is eaten with vegetable, chicken, or meat stew.

Figure 8.2 (right)
This child cannot get enough food of any kind. He is very thin and miserable. He has 'protein/energy malnutrition'. He will probably get better if he has enough to eat.

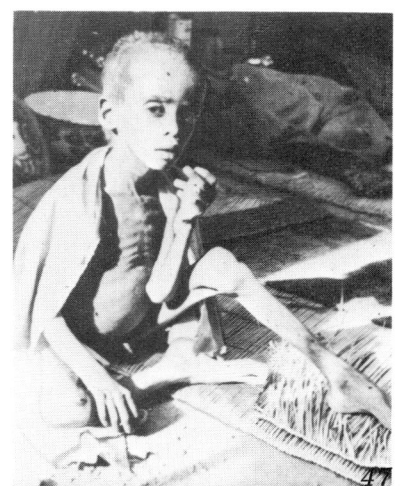

United Kingdom
dairy produce, barley, wheat, potato, meat

Italy
dairy produce, wheat, maize, potato

Japan
rice, fish, potato, dairy produce

United States
maize, meat, dairy produce, wheat

Ethiopia
barley, teff, sorghum

Uganda
plantain, cassava

India
rice in the East, wheat in the West

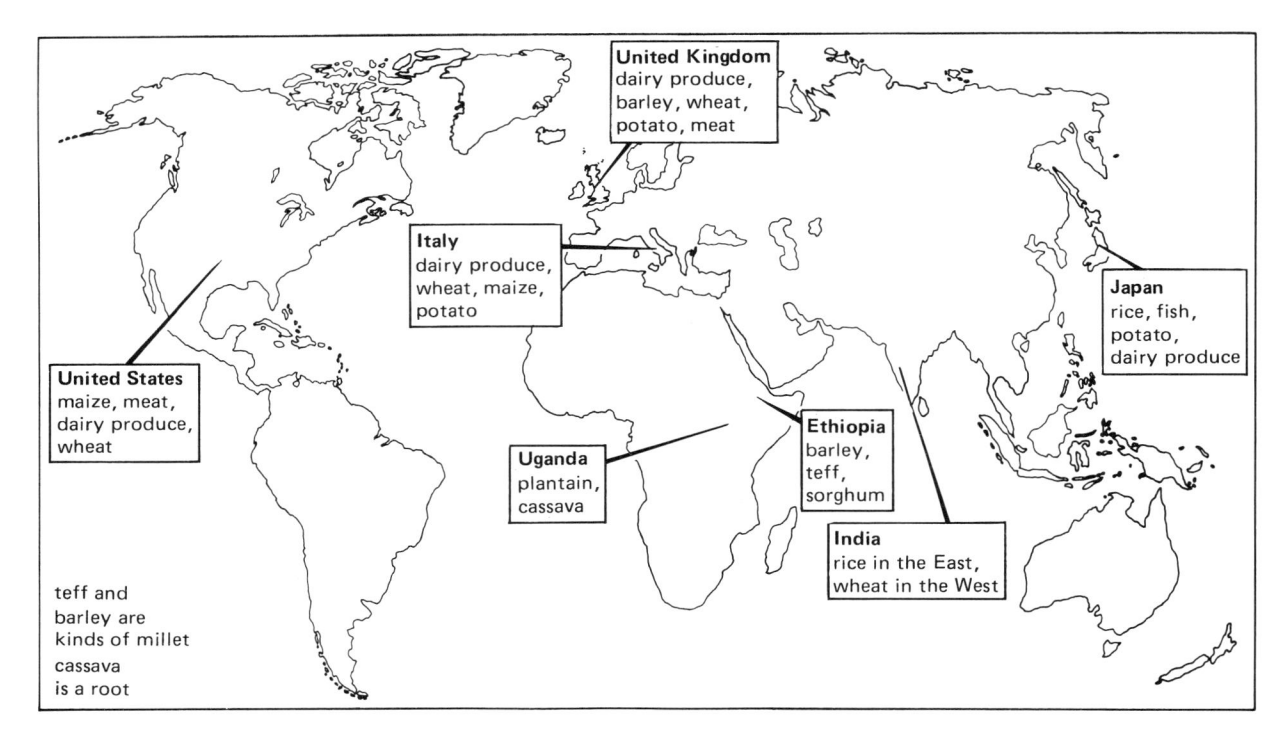

teff and barley are kinds of millet
cassava is a root

Figure 8.3
This map shows the main foods produced in some countries.

The United States, Britain, Italy, and Japan keep much better records of people and the foods they eat than Uganda, Ethiopia, and India. Even so, you can see in table 8.1 that there are big differences. For example, notice the large amounts of rice eaten in Japan.

Q 4
Who eats the most sugar?

Q 5
In which countries is meat an important part of the diet?

Q 6
Who eats the most food?

Your diet is everything you eat and drink. People can keep healthy on many different diets. But no matter what the local foods may be, people need certain substances in food called nutrients. Nutrients are some of the many chemicals in foods. Other chemicals include colours and flavours. You have probably heard of some nutrients already — they are carbohydrates, fats, proteins, vitamins, and minerals. These five groups together contain about fifty nutrients. You need them all to be healthy and grow well.

Table 8.1
The average weights of some foods eaten in different countries, in grams per person per day.

	Rice (g)	Potato (g)	Meat (g)	Wheat (g)	Fruit (g)	Sugars (g)
U.S.A.	9	116	200	143	191	137
U.K.	4	278	156	190	129	139
India	172	13	4	78	54	64
Japan	241	32	70	86	118	69
Italy	13	115	100	333	276	71
Ethiopia	0	13	53	58	10	8
Uganda	4	7	59	10	670*	55

*The main food eaten in Uganda is a fruit — the plantain, a type of banana.

Another essential part of food and drink is water. You lose a large amount of water from your body every day and have to replace it. If you did not get any water at all, even for just a few days, you would become very ill. You need energy from food to live and be active. But energy is not a substance like nutrients. Proteins, fats, starches, sugars, and alcohol all release their energy when broken down in the body.

Figure 8.4
Here are some comments from doctors working in countries where food is short.

> As a result of the tremendous population explosion that has occurred during the twentieth century, there have never before been so many children suffering from poverty and malnutrition. It is estimated that 500 million people in the world today, most of them children, are suffering from malnutrition and that a further 2000 million are suffering from undernourishment.
>
> The most recent studies show that lack of food is not the only problem; other factors, such as lack of affection and of mental and social stimulation, also have a negative effect on the child's intellectual and physical development. Families living in poverty are affected by all these factors.

Q 7
Read the magazine cutting. Why are there so many children who are short of food?

Q 8
Besides lack of food, what else affects your health and growth?

Figure 8.5

Name: Age: Average age of form:	Results
1 Weight.	
2 Height.	
3 Forehead (measure round it).	
4 Handspan (spread your fingers out and measure the distance between the tip of your thumb and your small finger).	
5 Chest measurement (breathing <u>in</u>) (breathe in as far as you can, then measure right around your chest).	
6 Chest measurement (breathing <u>out</u>) (breathe out as far as you can, then measure right around your chest).	
7 Shoe size.	
8 Length of each foot.	

8.2 HOW DO PEOPLE VARY?

What is the average size of people in your class?

YOU WILL NEED:
Bathroom scales
Tape measure
Ruler

1 Working in pairs, weigh and measure yourselves in the ways shown in the table in figure 8.5 below. Copy the table and record your results on it.

Figure 8.6

Figure 8.7

2 Now plot the class results of heights and weights as histograms (your teacher will show you how to do this if you are not sure).

Q 9
How accurately do you have to measure heights and weights in this work?

Figure 8.8
If you found that people in your class are different heights this is just what you should expect.

People in your class don't eat the same amount of food. Different people *need* different amounts of food. Even people of the same age do not all need the same amount.

8.3
A RANGE OF SIZES IS NORMAL

Figure 8.9

Throughout the world, different races of people have different physical characteristics. Some races are naturally taller than others. The Tutsi people of central Africa are very tall. They have an average male height of 1.72 m. But adult male pygmies living in Kinshasa, Africa (the Mbuti), average only 1.37 m. Both are normal within their own races, but a 1.72 m pygmy would be very unusual.

Figure 8.10
Compare the difference in height between these pygmies and the European.

8.4
WHAT IS HEALTH?

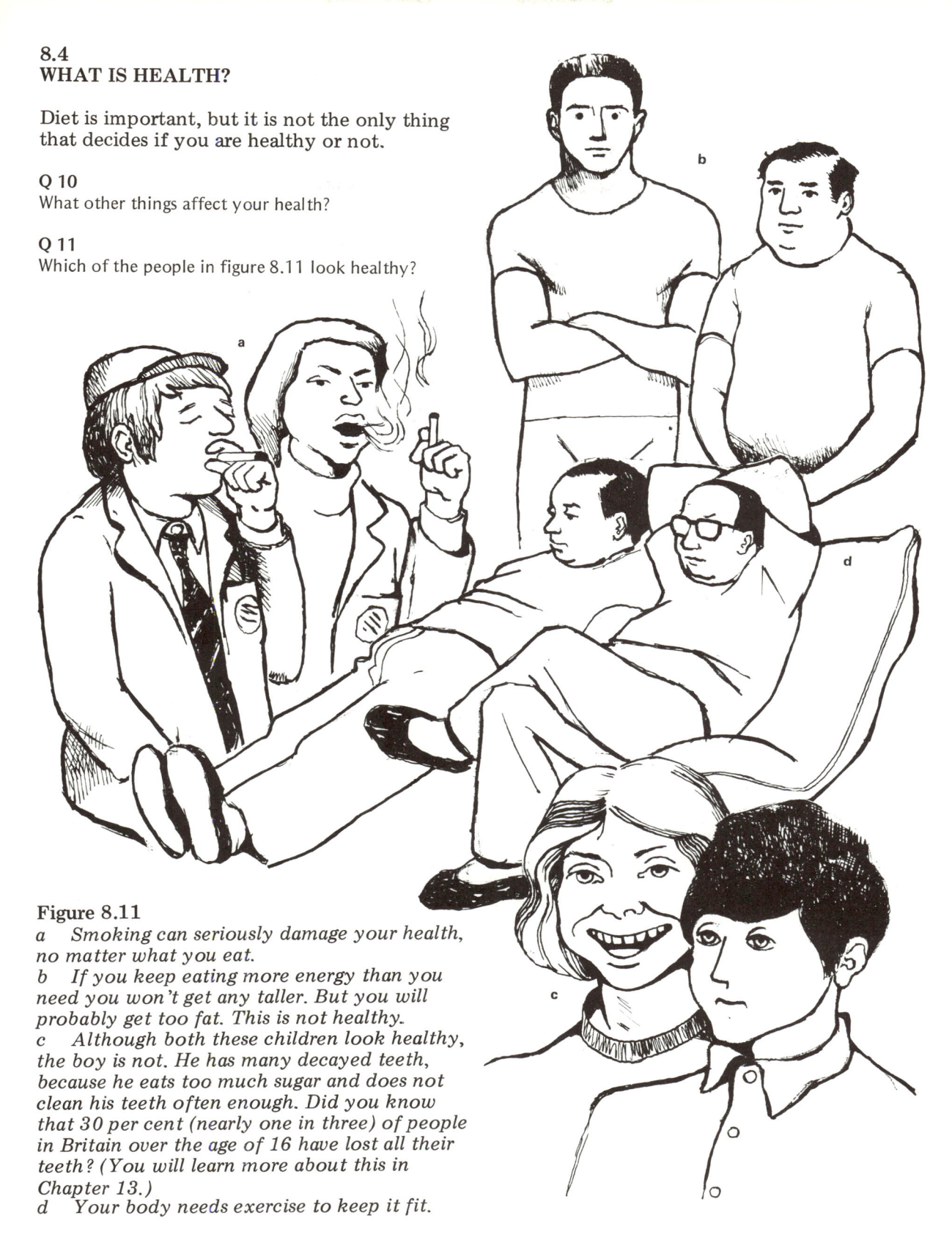

Diet is important, but it is not the only thing that decides if you are healthy or not.

Q 10
What other things affect your health?

Q 11
Which of the people in figure 8.11 look healthy?

Figure 8.11
a Smoking can seriously damage your health, no matter what you eat.
b If you keep eating more energy than you need you won't get any taller. But you will probably get too fat. This is not healthy.
c Although both these children look healthy, the boy is not. He has many decayed teeth, because he eats too much sugar and does not clean his teeth often enough. Did you know that 30 per cent (nearly one in three) of people in Britain over the age of 16 have lost all their teeth? (You will learn more about this in Chapter 13.)
d Your body needs exercise to keep it fit.

CHAPTER 9

What is in our food?

9.1
FOODS CONSIST OF MANY CHEMICALS

You saw in Chapter 8 that, given the choice, most people do not eat just one food at each meal; they eat several different kinds of food. Your diet is made up of a mixture of foods.

Figure 9.1a

Figure 9.1b

Q 1
If you could choose to eat one meal from each of the pairs shown here, which would you choose?

Q 2
Do you think small children would choose differently from adults? If so, say why.

Think about the colour and the taste of different foods. Many people hate tapioca pudding. Do you think it could have anything to do with the lumpy, slimy texture? Or is it because the pudding is not colourful?

Q 3
Why did you choose the meals you did?

Q 4
Did you stop to think about which meal would be better for your health?

Figure 9.2b

Figure 9.2a

The two plates of food in figure 9.1 have about the same amounts of nutrients and energy. So have the foods on the two plates in figure 9.3.

Q 5
Make a list of the ingredients used to make chocolate biscuits, orangeade, and sweets. (Use a recipe book to help you.)

Q 6
In figure 9.2, which meal do you think has more protein? (Look at worksheet M21 if you need help.)

Q 7
Can you find any links between how enjoyable food is to look at and how much fat, starch, sugar, or protein it contains? (Worksheet M21 will help you again.)

Figure 9.3a

Figure 9.3b

Q 8
Is the food which you think tastes best always more nutritious than food you dislike?

There are hundreds of chemicals which produce flavour and colour in foods. Some are naturally present in foods; others may be added by food manufacturers. They make the food pleasant to eat, but you could be healthy without them.

Figure 9.4
A simple diagram of some of the parts of the human body. The top lefthand corner shows some nerves. The top righthand corner shows the bone structure. The bottom lefthand corner shows muscles. In the bottom righthand corner are some large blood vessels.

Altogether foods contain a total of about fifty nutrients, which are all different chemicals. Most of them do not have much taste and most are white, but you cannot be healthy unless you eat every one of them. Many nutrients form part of the structure of your body *and* help it to function properly. Some of these nutrients and the work they do in your body are listed below.

Skin needs vitamin A to keep it healthy. Eyes need vitamin A to see in dim light.

Your teeth and bones need calcium and vitamin D to grow strong.

Muscles and nerves need sodium and potassium to work properly.

All your body cells need vitamin C (ascorbic acid) because it helps form the 'cement' that holds cells together.

Every cell in your body contains proteins as part of its structure.

A little fat is necessary to protect the body and to keep cell walls healthy.

You need vitamin K to help your blood clot over a skin wound.

Two-thirds of your body weight is water. Water is part of the structure of all body cells. Most chemical processes in your body take place in a watery solution.

All your body cells, especially your muscles, need iron and many vitamins in the B group to make use of food energy.

Your body uses *energy* to keep all the different parts working even while you are asleep. You use up more energy when you move, walk, or run about. Energy is provided by sugars and starches (carbohydrates), fats, proteins, and alcohol.

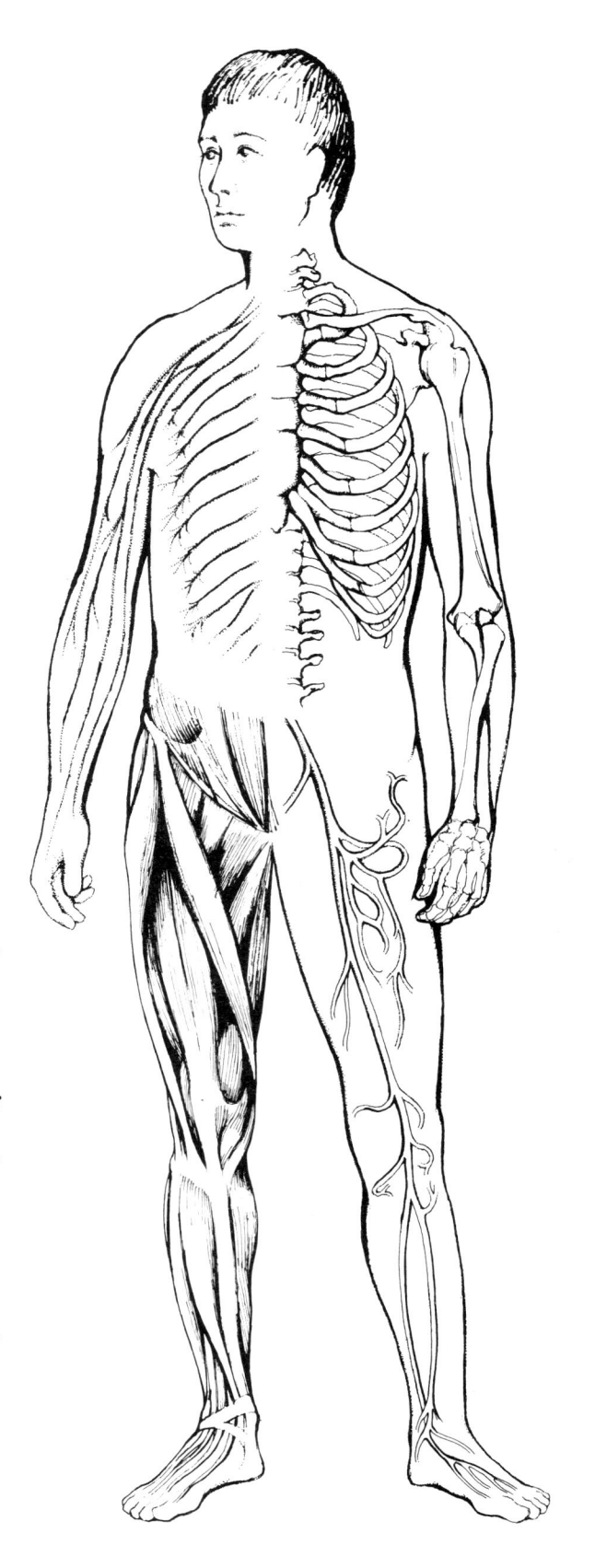

Nutrient	Foods
Vitamin A and carotene	margarine, carrots, liver
Calcium	bread, cheese, milk
Vitamin D	milk, fatty fish, margarine
Iron	liver, red meats, whole grain cereals, pulses
Sodium	salt, cured meats and fish, bread, butter, crisps
Potassium	nearly all foods
Vitamin K	leafy vegetables
Vitamin C	most fruits and vegetables
B group vitamins	meats, cereals, vegetables
Proteins	nuts, beans, meats, eggs, fish
Fats	butter, lard, meat fat, cheese
Sugars	sugar, sweets, jam
Starches	bread, potatoes, rice, pasta
Water	almost all foods

Table 9.1
Nutrients and some foods which contain them.

The problem is to know when you are getting these nutrients, since the colour, taste, and smell of food won't give you any help in choosing nutritionally balanced meals.

Even so, the appearance and taste of a meal are very important. If you don't like the look or smell of something, you won't want to eat it, so it won't matter how many nutrients it may contain! When you prepare food, you have to make sure it looks good and smells and tastes delicious, as well as choosing foods which will supply all the nutrients you need *and* enough energy (but not too much!)

How much do you need?

Different people need different amounts of each nutrient; even people of the same age, weight, and activity have different needs. The recommended daily intake (or recommended daily amount) of a nutrient is enough for a person with high needs. Most people will need less. (See worksheet M18.) The R.D.I.s or R.D.A.s for energy are averages, not maximum figures.

You will learn more about R.D.I.s and R.D.A.s in Chapter 14.

9.2 WATER IN FOODS

You may remember cooking baked beans in *Food science*, Chapter 1.

Q 9
What happened to the weight of the beans after they had been soaked?

Worksheet M21 will show you the amount of water in 50 grams of dried beans and 50 grams of soaked beans.

Q 10
How much water is there in the 200 grams of soaked beans that you used?

You can also see on worksheet M21 that 50 grams of dried beans contains far more of most nutrients than 50 grams of soaked or fresh beans. This is because of the extra water 'diluting' the nutrients. Most foods contain quite a lot of water. Water is vital to all life. If you lose only 10 per cent of the water in your body you will feel ill. Bacteria cannot grow in food if most of the water is removed. This means that drying preserves foods (see *Food science* Chapter 7).

9.3 FOOD TESTS

You cannot tell by looking what foods contain. But you can find out by doing tests. Use worksheet M19 to test foods for fats, starches, vitamin C, and glucose.

Glucose is one of the sugars in foods. It is different chemically from sucrose (table sugar) and is not quite as sweet. But equal weights of glucose and sucrose give you the same amount of energy.

The test for proteins uses dangerous chemicals. Your teacher may demonstrate this test to you.

Always be very careful when using chemicals like these. You must keep them well away from anything which might be eaten or used in food preparation. ⚠

1 Read the worksheet carefully.

2 Learn each test first by doing it on a pure nutrient to see the *positive* result; then on

water to see the *negative* result. Then test all the food samples.

3 Write down in the lefthand column of the table on the worksheet the list of foods to be tested. When you have carried out the tests, put a tick in the columns if you find a nutrient, and a cross if you do not.

4 Do the grease spot test first. Leave your filter papers to dry while you do the iodine test. This gives quick results. Wash the test-tubes.

5 Now record the grease spot results. Then do the Clinistix and DCPIP tests.

6 Interpreting results is very important. In the last column of the table, state which nutrients are present, and which nutrients have not been detected.

You cannot state that a nutrient is not present just because you did not find it. Discuss this with your teacher.

Q 11
Do your results agree with those of others in the class? If not, can you explain why?

The foods that were tested for fats, starches, glucose, proteins, and vitamin C were all brown.

Notice that although these foods have a similar colour, they contain different proportions of

Figure 9.5
Why might your results be different?

nutrients. In other words, *colour* does not tell you anything about the nutrients in food.

Q 12
a Does beef contain protein?
b Do all foods that contain protein also contain fat?
c Do all foods that come from animals contain protein?
d Are all foods without fat also lacking in starch?

Q 13
Can you find a link between the *taste* or the *texture* of foods and any of their nutrients?

9.4
SEPARATING A MIXTURE

Foods are mixtures of nutrients, colours, flavours, and other substances. Colours help to make food attractive. Often they are themselves mixtures of several different colours.

One method of separating mixtures is called chromatography. You will see how it works when you use it to separate out the colours in Smarties.

Table 9.2
Here is a guide to the amounts of fats, starches, sugars, vitamin C, and proteins in the foods you have tested. (You have not been able to measure the amounts — only whether the nutrients are present or not.)

Food portions	Nutrients					
	Fats	Starches	Sugars	Vitamin C	Proteins	
300 g brown rice (boiled)	*	**	*	—	*	KEY
200 g wholemeal bread	*	**	*	—	**	*** a lot
100 g stewed beef	*	—	—	—	***	** some
100 g chocolate	**	—	***	—	*	* a little
50 g demerara sugar	—	—	***	—	—	— none
500 ml tea (no milk or sugar)	—	—	—	—	—	
300 g baked potato	*	**	*	***	*	

YOU WILL NEED:
Smarties
Bowl of water
Filter paper
Teaspoon

1 Put one Smartie in the middle of a piece of filter paper. Label with the colour of the Smartie.

2 Slowly drop about 10 drops of water onto the Smartie from a teaspoon. Do this one drop at a time. Wait until each drop has spread across the filter paper before adding the next.

Q 14
How many different colours did you see from one Smartie?

3 Repeat the test with other, different-coloured Smarties.

Q 15
a Is there any one colour which all Smarties contain?
b Do they all have the same number of different colours?

Chromatography is also used for analysing very complicated mixtures like vitamins and drugs.

Figure 9.6

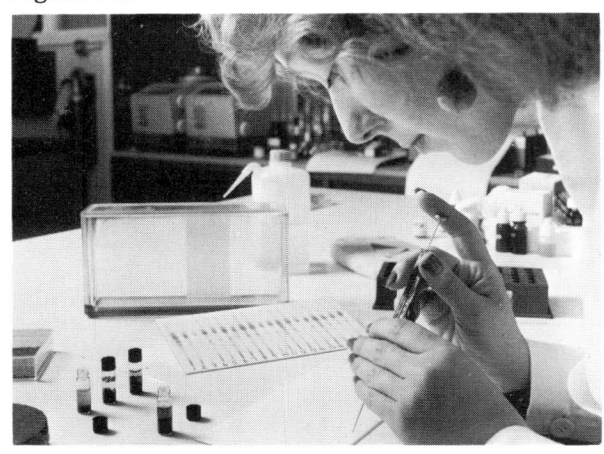

9.5
FOOD TABLES AND LABELS

You do not have to bother to test all your foods before you know what is in them. Many scientists have made thousands of tests on different foods, and you can make use of their results by using food tables and reading the labels on some packaged food.

Figure 9.7

Food tables are the average results of many food tests. You can get a pretty good idea of what a particular food may contain by looking up the figures in a table such as the one in worksheet M21.

Food labels on most 'recipe products' list the ingredients in descending order of the weights present, but they do not tell you *how much* of each ingredient there is. (See *Food science*, Chapter 1.)

Q 16
Can you tell how much of the different nutrients are in these two foods?

Figure 9.8

One portion of Cod in Parsley Sauce contains:-	
Protein	25g
Fat	5g
Carbohydrate	8g
Calories	175
	(27 per oz)

INGREDIENTS:
POTATO, WHEAT FLOUR, SHORTENING, MEAT, ONIONS, SALT, SPICE EXTRACT, CEREAL BINDER, MONOSODIUM GLUTAMATE, HYDROLYSED VEGETABLE PROTEIN.

Some food manufacturers put nutrition information on their packs. Others make this information available in booklets.

CHAPTER 10

Energy

Figure 10.1
The body shapes of these people changed as they lost fat.

Figure 10.2
Fat is stored in your body as fat pads. These areas are numbered in the figures drawn below, and in table 10.1.

Figure 10.3
These fat pads get thicker if you eat more energy than you use up, and so you slowly change shape.

10.1
ARE YOU THE RIGHT WEIGHT?

You put on weight or lose it depending on your diet and the amount of exercise you get. Growing children get heavier because they are growing taller. Bones and muscles get bigger. This is normal. It is not only your weight that changes as you build up or lose fat. The shape of your body changes too.

Adults put on weight if they eat more energy in food than they use up each day, because extra energy from food is usually stored as fat. Some body fat is essential to protect internal organs. A healthy man of twenty who is the right weight has about 12 per cent of fat in his body. But a very fat man may have so much fat that it accounts for half his weight.

Most women have a thicker layer of fat under their skin than men. The body of a girl of twenty is about 25 per cent fat. Unless she eats carefully, by the time she is fifty her body store of fat may rise to 45 per cent, about half her total body weight — or more! People should not go on getting heavier (fatter) all through life. Ideal weight at about twenty-five years of age is the ideal for the rest of a person's life.

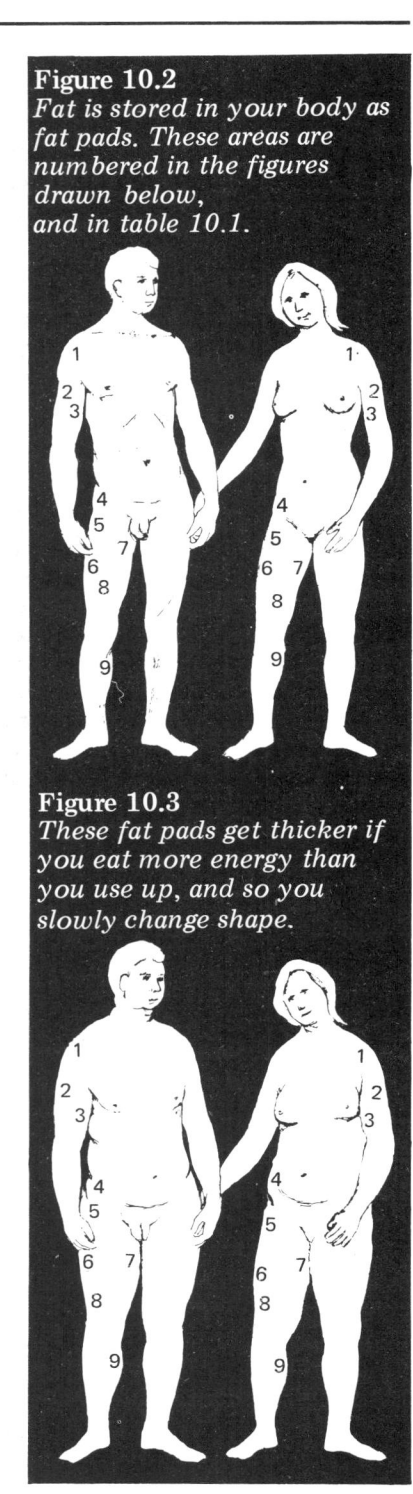

10.2
TEST YOURSELF FOR FATNESS

YOU WILL NEED:

Calipers
Honesty!
Pencil
Paper

Table 10.1
The average thickness of fat pads for men and women of normal weight. Notice the parts of the body where men and women have similar amounts of fat, and the parts of the body where women are fatter than men.

	Fat pads (in mm)	
	Men	Women
1 shoulder	18.0	17.8
2 outside arm	4.4	6.2
3 inside arm	3.5	6.6
4 hip	19.2	19.0
5 top of thigh	15.6	28.1
6 outside leg	4.8	7.4
7 inside leg	6.0	10.9
8 front of leg	2.6	4.1
9 back of leg	7.0	13.0

1 Measure the thickness of a fat pad. Try the outside of your upper arm. Use the calipers to measure a pinch of your skin at the back of your arm about halfway between your shoulder and elbow. (Don't include any muscle.)

Q 1
How thick is the fold of skin? (If it is less than 3 mm, you are slim! If it is about 18 mm or more for boys, or 23 mm or more for girls, that's fat!)

10.3
CHECK YOUR WEIGHT AND HEIGHT

YOU WILL NEED:

Bathroom scales
Tape measure
Pencil
Paper

Weight depends partly on your height. Your weight also varies with the size of your 'frame' (skeleton). For any given height, men should weigh more than women. The bones of people with wide shoulders or hips do not weigh much more than in small-framed people. But a large frame needs more muscle, skin, and so on to cover it. It does not mean that people with large frames should be fatter. Very athletic people may have large and heavy muscles. They will weigh more than people with under-developed muscles, but this does not mean they are fat. You can see whether someone is muscular or fat. Bones, muscles, fat, and blood account for most of the body weight.

1 Find your weight using the scales.

Q 2
How many kilograms should you allow for your clothes?

Q 3
Why should you use the same scales each time you weigh yourself?

2 Find your height (without shoes).

Q 4
Have your height and weight altered much since you did the class survey in Chapter 8? Why is this?

3 Check your weight using worksheet M17.
You won't get fat just by eating one or two very big meals a month It is a slow process. You would have to overeat almost every day for at least a week before you would notice that you were fatter. If you eat too much energy in food, no matter what sort of food it is, and do not use it all, you will gradually put on more weight than you should. Nearly everything you eat or drink gives you energy. If the proteins, fats, sugars, starches, and alcohol in your food give you more energy than you use, you will probably get fat. (There are some people who can overeat and won't get fat.)

10.4
USING UP ENERGY

Energy is measured in joules and calories (1 joule is about 0.25 calories). Because foods contain a lot of energy, food energy is measured in kilojoules and kilocalories.

('Kilo' means 1000, so 1 kilojoule = 1000 joules, and 1 kilocalorie = 1000 calories.)

You need energy just to stay alive:

to keep your vital organs such as heart, brain, and kidney working;
to keep breathing air in and out;
to keep burning up your food and to keep warm.

For all this you need about 4 kilojoules (1 kilocalorie) a minute.

Q 5
How many kilojoules do you need every minute just to stay alive?

Q 6
About how many kilojoules do you need in a day just to stay alive?

Q 7
About how many kilocalories is this?

Any activity, such as getting up, washing, dressing, going to school, or playing sport uses up extra energy. And everyone needs energy for growth.

Q 8
Adults are not growing taller. What parts of their bodies do grow all the time?

Use worksheet M23 to record all your activities for 24 hours. Work out how long you do each one for, and then how much energy you use.

How much energy do you use when climbing up stairs?

The amount of 'work' you do depends on two things: how *far* you move and how *hard* it is to move.

When you climb up stairs the height of the stairs is how *far* you move. Your weight is what makes it *hard* to move!

In other words:
Work done = height of stairs × your weight
(measured   (measured in   (measured in
in joules, J)   metres, m)   newtons, N).

(A newton is a unit of force used by scientists and engineers — it takes about 10 newtons to make 1 kilogram weight.)

So if you weigh 40 kilograms, you weigh about 400 newtons.

In the picture the person has moved 3 metres up the stairs. 400 newtons is how hard it was to move the weight being lifted.

So the work done is

3 m × 400 N = 1200 joules.

Figure 10.4

Figure 10.5a

Smartie
24 kilojoules
6 kilocalories

The energy in 1 Smartie is 24 000 joules.

Q 9
Work out how many times the person in figure 10.4 could climb up the stairs using the energy in 1 Smartie.

But in fact the human body only uses about a quarter of the energy eaten for doing work. The rest is used for making your body work faster, before eventually turning into heat. So:

Total energy used = energy to do work + energy to make your body function.

So to burn off the Smartie you would only need to run up about five flights of stairs.

Meringue
850 kilojoules
200 kilocalories

Figure 10.5b

Q 10
a How many flights of stairs would you have to run up to use the energy in one meringue?
b How long would it take to use up the energy in one meringue if you are just sitting down?

10.5 ENERGY IN FOODS

Almost everything you eat gives you energy. But some foods have a lot of energy in them while others only have a little.

Look at the 'Energy' column of the food tables on worksheet M21.

Figure 10.6

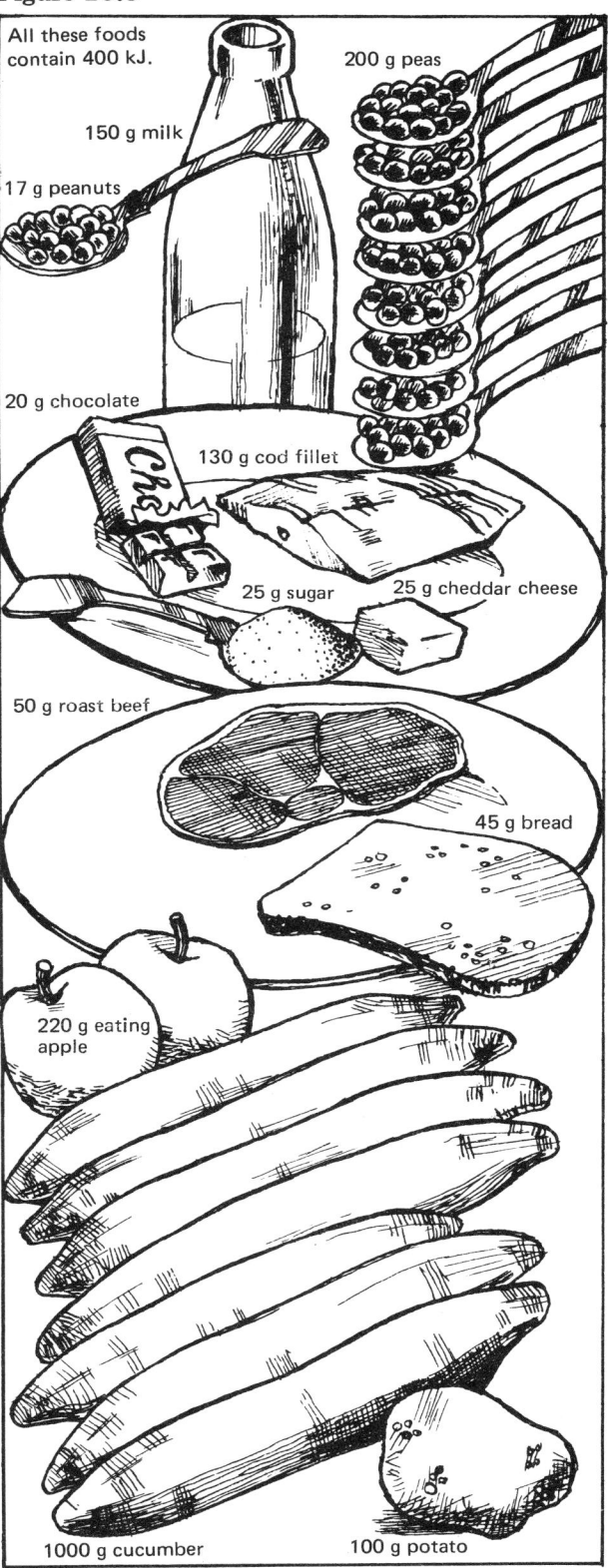

All these foods contain 400 kJ.
- 200 g peas
- 150 g milk
- 17 g peanuts
- 20 g chocolate
- 130 g cod fillet
- 25 g sugar
- 25 g cheddar cheese
- 50 g roast beef
- 45 g bread
- 220 g eating apple
- 1000 g cucumber
- 100 g potato

61

Q 11
Which food gives you the most energy? (Look for the biggest number.)

Q 12
Which food gives you the least energy? (Look for the smallest number.)

Notice the *amounts* of food the figures on worksheet M21 refer to.

Using worksheet M21, make a table like the one below to show the energy in kilojoules and kilocalories for these foods:

Food	Kilo-joules	Kilo-calories
50 g boiled egg		
50 g fried egg		
50 g beef burgers		
50 g chicken		
50 g sugar (about 10 teaspoons)		

Figure 10.7

Q 13
Which food would give you most energy?

Q 14
Do you think 10 teaspoons of sugar a day is a lot?

10.6
DO ALL SWEET FOODS GIVE ENERGY?

YOU WILL NEED:

2 different samples of orange drinks
2 teaspoons

1 Taste the orange drinks you have been given.

Q 15
Do they both taste sweet?

Q 16
Does one drink taste sweeter than the other?

Figure 10.8

2 Look at the list of ingredients on the labels.

Q 17
Which ingredient(s) would make the orange drink taste sweet?

Q 18
Which orange drink would give you more energy?

Q 19
Which orange drink would be better if you were slimming (trying to cut down on the amount of energy you get)?

Q 20
Why do people who are trying to lose weight still need some food energy every day?

10.7
PEANUT POWER

Energy in foods is measured by finding out how much heat they give out when they are burned.

Although food does not burn in your body, its energy still ends up as heat.

YOU WILL NEED:

Peanut
2 5-ml (tea) spoons cold water
Cork and long needle
Boiling-tube
Test-tube rack and holder
Matches or gas flame

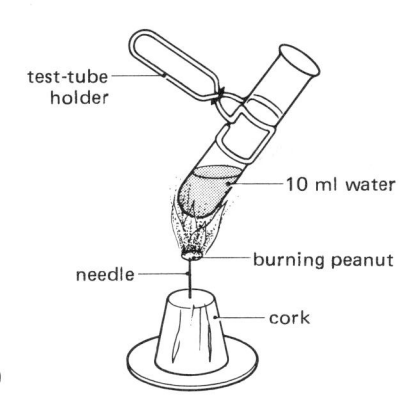

Figure 10.9

1 Set out the apparatus as in figure 10.9.

2 Pour 10 ml cold water into the boiling-tube.

3 Push the blunt end of the needle firmly into the cork.

4 Push the peanut carefully onto the point of the long needle.

5 Light a match and hold it under the peanut until the peanut starts to burn.

6 Use a test-tube holder to hold the boiling-tube in the flame from the burning peanut.

7 Hold the boiling-tube in the flame until the nut stops burning.

8 Watch the peanut carefully as it burns. Watch what happens to the water in the tube.

Q 21
What happened to the water?

Q 22
A lot of energy must have been put into the water to make this happen. Where did the energy come from?

Q 23
Do you think it was water or melted fat which bubbled out of the peanut and burned? How could you tell?

First, use your common sense to think of the answer. Which catches fire and burns — melted fat or water?

Q 24
a Look at worksheet M21 to check how much water and fat your 1-gram peanut contained.
b How much energy is there in a 1-gram peanut?

10.8
COOKING METHOD AND ENERGY

Copy the table below and use worksheet M21 to find out the energy value of each item.

Figure 10.10

1 large potato (about 200 grams)	Kilo-joules	Kilo-calories
Baked in its jacket		
Boiled		
Mashed		
Chipped and fried		
Made into crisps (thinly sliced and fried)		

Q 25
Which way of cooking potatoes would you choose if you wanted to:
a eat as much energy as possible?
b eat as little energy as possible?

Look at these three slices of cake. The large one has twice as many calories as the small one. So a good way to slim is just to eat less of your normal food!

Figure 10.11

lefthand slice	middle slice	righthand slice
1100 kJ	1500 kJ	2200 kJ
260 kcals	350 kcals	520 kcals

CHAPTER 11
Food choices

11.1
WHY DO PEOPLE CHOOSE THE FOODS THEY DO?

In Chapter 8 you saw that people in different countries often eat very different kinds of foods.

These differences in what people eat do not happen by chance. There are usually good reasons why there are differences between countries. There are at least eight things that affect what people eat. They are:

a   attractiveness of different foods
b   availability of foods
c   culture and religion
d   habit
e   customs
f   age
g   special body needs
h   ability to prepare food.

11.1a
Attractiveness of different foods

Q 1
Name three things about your favourite food which make you like it.

Q 2
a   List three foods you like very much, and three you dislike very much.

b   Use the lists to plot a class histogram to find out the most liked foods and the most disliked foods.

Figure 11.1
Sowing and harvesting rice in Japan.

11.1b
Availability of foods

Obviously, people cannot eat foods if they are not available. You will know from geography lessons about the climates in different countries. The weather is important in deciding what plants will grow in different parts of the world. For example, rice needs a warm climate with a lot of rain in the summer. This is a 'dry tropical climate' and is found in the far east in countries like Thailand, Vietnam, Burma, and Japan.

Figure 11.2
Wheat grows well in regions like central Canada and parts of Russia. The winters are cool and dry, and summers are warm with plenty of rain in the early summer. The climate is called 'prairie steppe'. Wealthy countries can afford to feed grain to animals as well as to people.

Figure 11.3
Countries such as the United States, Germany, France, and Sweden do not have to depend only on the foods they produce themselves. They are rich enough to have the money to buy all sorts of foods from other countries. Almost half of all the food eaten in the United Kingdom is imported.

11.1c
Culture and religion

Many of the world's religions control very strictly the kinds of foods their followers may eat.

It is also a part of some religions that people should fast (not eat) for a certain number of days in the year.

Q 3
a Name one food that Muslims must not eat.
b Name one food that Hindus must not eat.

11.1d
Habit

Q 4
a Write down what you eat and drink before you go to school.
b Do you eat the same foods each morning?

Q 5
Why is the first meal of the day called breakfast?

Q 6
Why do you think you eat the same thing for breakfast every day?

It is likely that you eat the same foods for breakfast every day of the week: most people do. There is much less variety in breakfasts than in mid-day or evening meals.

Everyone forms lots of habits as they grow older. Apart from food habits, you may visit a friend on the same day every week, and go shopping every Saturday morning. The members of your family may use the bathroom in just the same order every day.

65

When something is done in the same way often enough you don't have to think much about it — you form a habit. And some people have some very annoying habits! But forming habits makes life easier.

Some people have good habits in the way they choose foods; some have very bad habits. Food habits are very important because they affect the kind of food you eat almost every day. Once you get into the habit of doing something it is very hard to change. So don't get into the habit of buying sweets every day.

Figure 11.4
Here are shopping lists from different families.

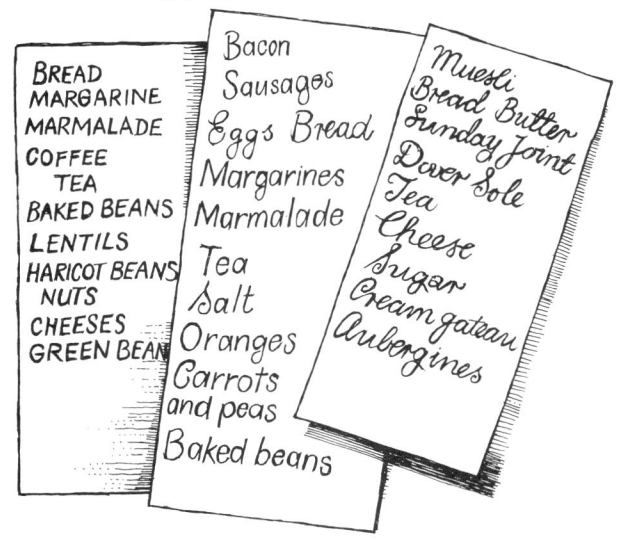

List 1: BREAD, MARGARINE, MARMALADE, COFFEE, TEA, BAKED BEANS, LENTILS, HARICOT BEANS, NUTS, CHEESES, GREEN BEANS

List 2: Bacon, Sausages, Eggs, Bread, Margarines, Marmalade, Tea, Salt, Oranges, Carrots and peas, Baked beans

List 3: Muesli, Bread, Butter, Sunday Joint, Dover Sole, Tea, Cheese, Sugar, Cream gateau, Aubergines

Q 7
a   Which foods are bought by all of them?
b   Which family does not eat meat?
c   Which is the most expensive diet?

11.1e
Customs

Nearly all countries, or parts of countries, have their own food customs. For example, seaweed is eaten by people in Japan and South Wales. Special foods are eaten on certain days. People in the United Kingdom eat pancakes on Shrove Tuesday.

Usually, customs like these have very little effect on the total diet. It does not really matter whether the foods are nutritious or not.

Figure 11.5

Q 8
List the special foods associated with these occasions:

a   Christmas in England
b   Birthdays in the United Kingdom
c   Chinese New Year
d   Easter
e   Thanksgiving in the United States
f   Hogmanay.

11.1f
Age

Q 9
a   What kind of food does a one-month-old baby eat?
b   What would a six-month-old baby have at mid-day?
c   What would a toddler eat for lunch?

Figure 11.6

Figure 11.7
Fathers can help with bottle-feeding!

Q 10
Why does a one-month-old baby eat such different food from you?

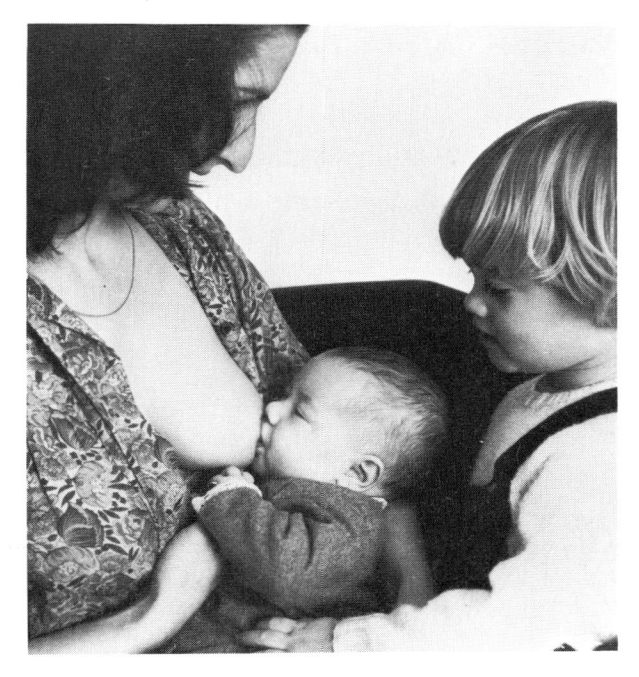

Figure 11.8
Breast feeding.

Sometimes, very old people have bad eating habits because they cannot go out shopping, or perhaps because chewing food may be difficult.

Q 11
Why else might some old people not eat well?

Some old people suffer from brittle bones, anaemia, or simply loss of weight.

Figure 11.9
Look at these foods one old lady ate on most days. She does not eat any meat, and not much milk or cheese.

Q 12
What two nutrients is the old lady likely to be short of? (Use worksheet M21 to find out the most important nutrients in meat, and in milk and cheese.)

Q 13
What effect will a shortage of these two nutrients have if this eating pattern goes on for a long time? (Look back to page 54 if you need help.)

11.1g
Special body needs

People who are very active need more energy from their food than people who spend most of their day sitting down. They do not usually need more proteins, vitamins, or minerals.

But there are times when some people do need to eat more proteins, vitamins, and minerals. For example, when a woman is pregnant her body needs more of all nutrients, and more energy so the baby can grow.

Q 14
When the mother is breast feeding she needs more of all the nutrients and energy. Why?

People with certain diseases need special foods. You will learn more about this in Chapter 15.

11.1h
Ability to prepare food

Look at the menus of the two Victorian families on worksheet M24.

Q 15
How many of the foods were:
a canned?
b frozen?
c dried?

Q 16
Do you think these families ate more or less sugary foods than you do?

If no one in the Victorian household was good at preparing food, or no one liked that job, meals would have been very boring. But today things are different. Even if you are not very good at cooking, you can buy tasty and nutritious foods. The food manufacturer prepares the food for you.

Figure 11.10

Eating many different foods, whether they are prepared at home or in a food factory, helps to ensure you eat enough of all nutrients. You will learn more about choosing foods in Chapter 14. But the food industry has also given you a huge range of sugary foods. Eating some of these is all right. But it is important not to eat too many.

Q 17
Why should you not eat too many sweets and chocolates?

Figure 11.11

Q 18
Can you think of any more things which affect the kinds of foods you choose to eat?

Q 19
Look at the different meals at the top of the next page.
a Which one of these would you *not* like to eat?
b Do you think it is nutritious?

Q 20
One of these menus provides a lot of sugar and fat. Which one is it? (Use worksheet M21 to help you work this out.)

Q 21
Use worksheet M21 to change some of the foods in this menu so that there is less fat and less sugar.

Q 22
Which menu is short of vitamin C?

Q 23
Menus B and C are equally good for you. Which would you like to eat? Can you say why?

	Menu A	Menu B	Menu C
Breakfast	toast, butter, and jam Coke	porridge tea	orange juice cornflakes and milk tea
Mid-morning	bar of chocolate		apple
Lunch	fried egg and chips jam sponge	cod, butter beans, and lumpy potato cornflour mould	grilled hamburger, peas, and chips ice-cream
Snack	peanuts	sponge cake	
Evening meal	cold pork pie and crisps Coke	liver and Brussels sprouts natural yoghurt	baked beans on toast fruit yoghurt
Snack	cold milk cheese and biscuits	glass of hot milk	

Table 11.1

11.2
HOW MUCH CAN YOU EAT?

To help you choose a balanced diet it helps to know which foods are good sources of the different nutrients. Food tables often tell you the amount of nutrients in 100 grams of food. But you have to know *how much* of each food you eat too. Two of the most important things which affect how much you eat of a food are its taste and texture. The nicer the taste and texture the more you feel like eating.

Figure 11.12
Choosing foods.

How much of each of these foods do you think you could eat at one go? Take a guess now. Then check your estimate by trying to eat the foods.

a   white flour
b   white bread
c   skimmed milk powder
d   skimmed milk.

YOU WILL NEED:

About 1 5-ml (tea) spoon white flour
About 1 5-ml (tea) spoon skimmed milk
2 slices white bread
Glass of skimmed milk
2 teaspoons

1   Work in pairs.

2   Get one person to eat about half a teaspoon of white flour; then eat two slices of bread.

3   The second person eats about a teaspoon of skimmed milk powder; then drinks the glass of skimmed milk.

Q 24
Is it easier to eat a lot of flour or the two slices of bread?

Q 25
a   Is it easier to eat a lot of skimmed milk powder or to drink the milk?
b   Why do you think this is?

Q 26
a What is the main ingredient by weight in bread? Look up a recipe to check.
b What is the second main ingredient in bread?

Q 27
How is skimmed milk powder made into liquid milk?

Q 28
a Why is it easier to eat bread than flour?
b What happens in your mouth when you eat very dry foods?

Q 29
Think of other reasons why you may like eating bread better than flour.

Q 30
Do you think you could eat even more bread if you put some butter on it? Why?

11.3 FOODS AS GOOD SOURCES OF NUTRIENTS

Table 11.2
The amount of protein in bread flour and bread.

Food	Protein (g)
50 g white bread flour	5.6 g
50 g white bread	3.9 g

Q 31
Which food seems to have more proteins?

Now check which food you are likely to get more protein from.

YOU WILL NEED:
Small sliced white loaf
Bag of flour
Kitchen scales
Tablespoon

1 Weigh 50 g white flour.

2 Weigh 2 slices of white bread — they should be about 50 g.

3 Look at the two 50-g portions.

Q 32
Would you find it easy and enjoyable to eat:
a 50 grams of flour?
b 50 grams of bread?

Figure 11.13
Food can be very enjoyable!

Most people could just manage to eat about 5 grams of flour if they really had to, but they would not enjoy it.

Q 33
How much protein would 5 grams of flour give you?

Copy figure 11.14 into your notebook and fill in the amount of protein each food would provide.

Figure 11.14

Food	Protein (g)
5 g white bread flour	
50 g white bread	

Q 34
Which food gives more proteins?

Q 35
Compare the answers to question 34 and question 31. What two things do you have to know before you can say how much protein a food gives you?

Q 36
50 grams of bread flour has more protein than 50 grams of bread. So bread flour has a higher:
a density; *b* concentration;
c combination; *d* distribution
of protein than bread. Which is the right word?

11.4 COOKING VEGETABLES

Does cooking affect the amount of food and nutrients you can eat?

Usually you cook foods to make them nicer to eat, but cooking can also make you eat more. Some nutrients are also affected by cooking.

YOU WILL NEED:

About 175 g cabbage or green beans or cauliflower
Saucepan of boiling water
Vegetable knife
Chopping board
Kitchen paper
Strainer
Plate
2 tablespoons and 2 forks
Clock or watch
Balance

1 Wash and then slice the cabbage or beans, or divide the cauliflower into florets.

2 Weigh three lots of vegetable — one of 25 grams and two of 75 grams each.

3 Measure the time it takes to eat the 25-gram sample.

Q 37
How easy is it to chew and swallow?

4 Boil one of the 75-gram samples for five minutes, or until just tender.

5 Strain the cooked vegetable and put it onto kitchen paper. Reweigh it. Note the weight in your notebook.

6 Compare the size (volume) of the 75-gram raw and cooked samples.

Q 38
a Has cooking caused any change in the weight of the food?
b Can you suggest why?

7 Eat the 75-gram cooked sample and time yourself.

8 Compare the time it takes to chew and swallow it with the time the 25-gram sample took you.

Figure 11.15

Q 39
Which was nicer to eat, the raw or cooked vegetable?

Usually it is much easier to eat more of a cooked food than a raw one. Cooking vegetables means that some of the vitamin C is lost. But this may not be as bad as it sounds.

Table 11.3 shows how much vitamin C there is in raw and cooked vegetables. Look back at page 54 to remind yourself why you need vitamin C.

Food	Vitamin C (mg)
100 g raw cabbage	55
100 g raw cauliflower	60
100 g raw green beans	20
100 g cooked cabbage	20
100 g cooked cauliflower	20
100 g cooked green beans	5

Table 11.3

9 Work out the amount of vitamin C in the 25-gram raw sample you ate.

10 Work out the amount of vitamin C in the 75-gram cooked sample you ate.

Cooking can mean some vitamin C is lost from foods. But you can eat more cooked than raw food, so you may be getting as much, or more, vitamin C from the cooked food.

This chapter has shown why some people choose certain foods. You have also found that cooking makes many foods nicer to eat.

CHAPTER 12

Digestion

12.1
MAKING FOOD USEFUL

Every part of your body needs feeding. Food cannot get to your muscles until it has been changed and carried in your blood. Imagine sausage and peas chugging down your arm!

Before nutrients can be absorbed into your body, they have to be soluble in water and a suitable size. Some nutrients, such as proteins, have molecules which are too big to get through the walls of blood vessels. They have to be *digested* into smaller molecules.

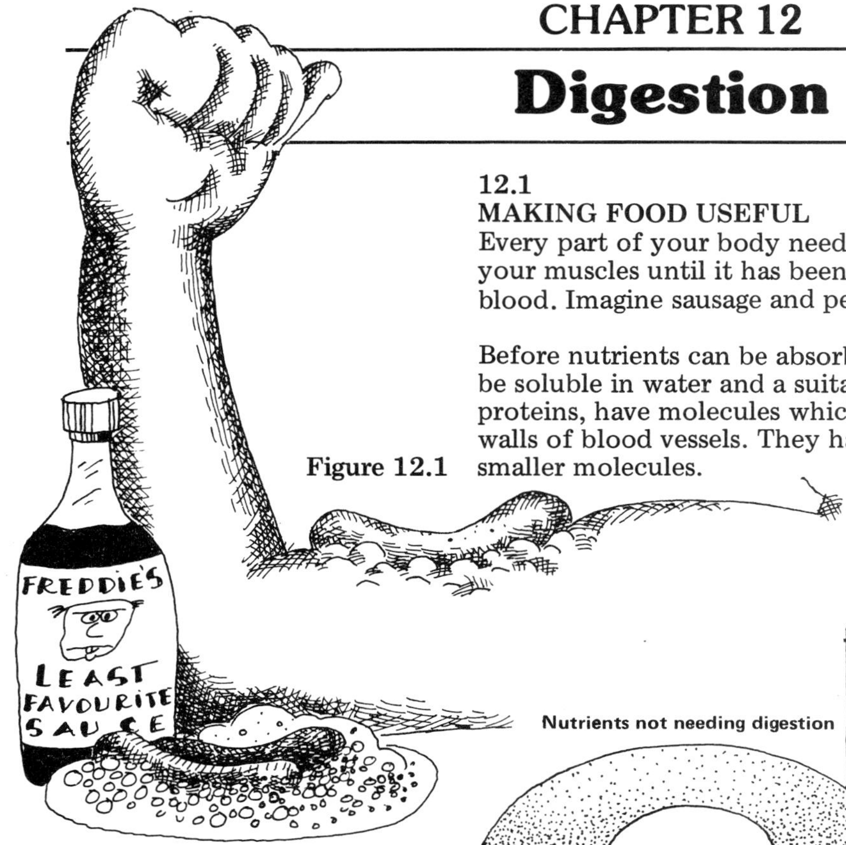

Figure 12.1

Carbohydrates are all made up of sugar molecules (units). For instance:

Glucose is a one-unit sugar

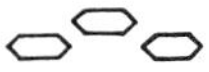

Maltose is a two-unit sugar

Starch is made of chains of units

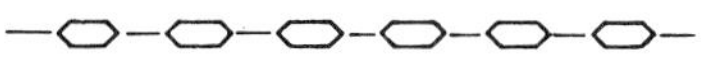

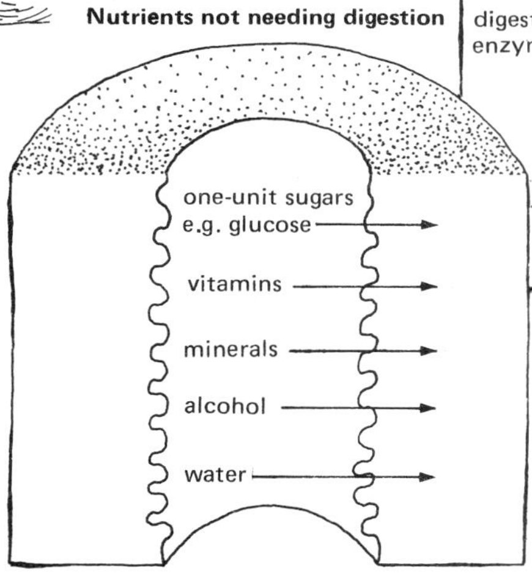

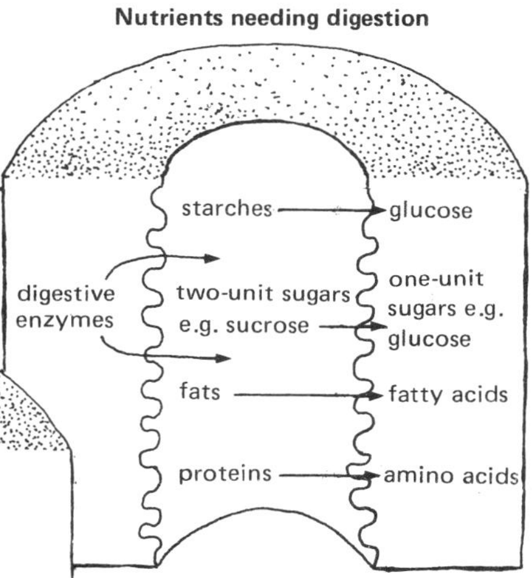

Figure 12.2
Which nutrients need to be digested and which do not.

12.2
ENZYMES

Enzymes are proteins. They make all the chemical processes in your body happen at the right speed. Enzymes are *catalysts*. (They take part in chemical reactions but are not changed themselves.) Some enzymes work in your *alimentary canal* (gut) to digest your food. You can see some of the work the digestive enzymes do in table 12.1 and figure 12.3.

About four hours after you have eaten, your food reaches your small intestine. At this stage you couldn't tell by looking at it whether it started out as fish and chips or beef and vegetables! All your food gets mixed up with digestive enzymes and finishes up as a thick liquid.

Table 12.1
Some of the digestive enzymes and secretions.

Enzyme or other secretion	What it does
Salivary amylase	begins to digest starch
Pepsin	begins to digest proteins
Pancreatic amylase	digests starches to dextrins and then to maltose
Bile (not an enzyme)	emulsifies fats
Lipase	digests fats to fatty acids
Trypsin	digests proteins to amino acids
Maltase	digests maltose to glucose

After food has been digested (broken down) the nutrients are absorbed (taken up) through the wall of your small intestine. Most absorption takes place in the small intestine. But water can be absorbed in your stomach and your large intestine too.

12.3 DIGESTING FOOD

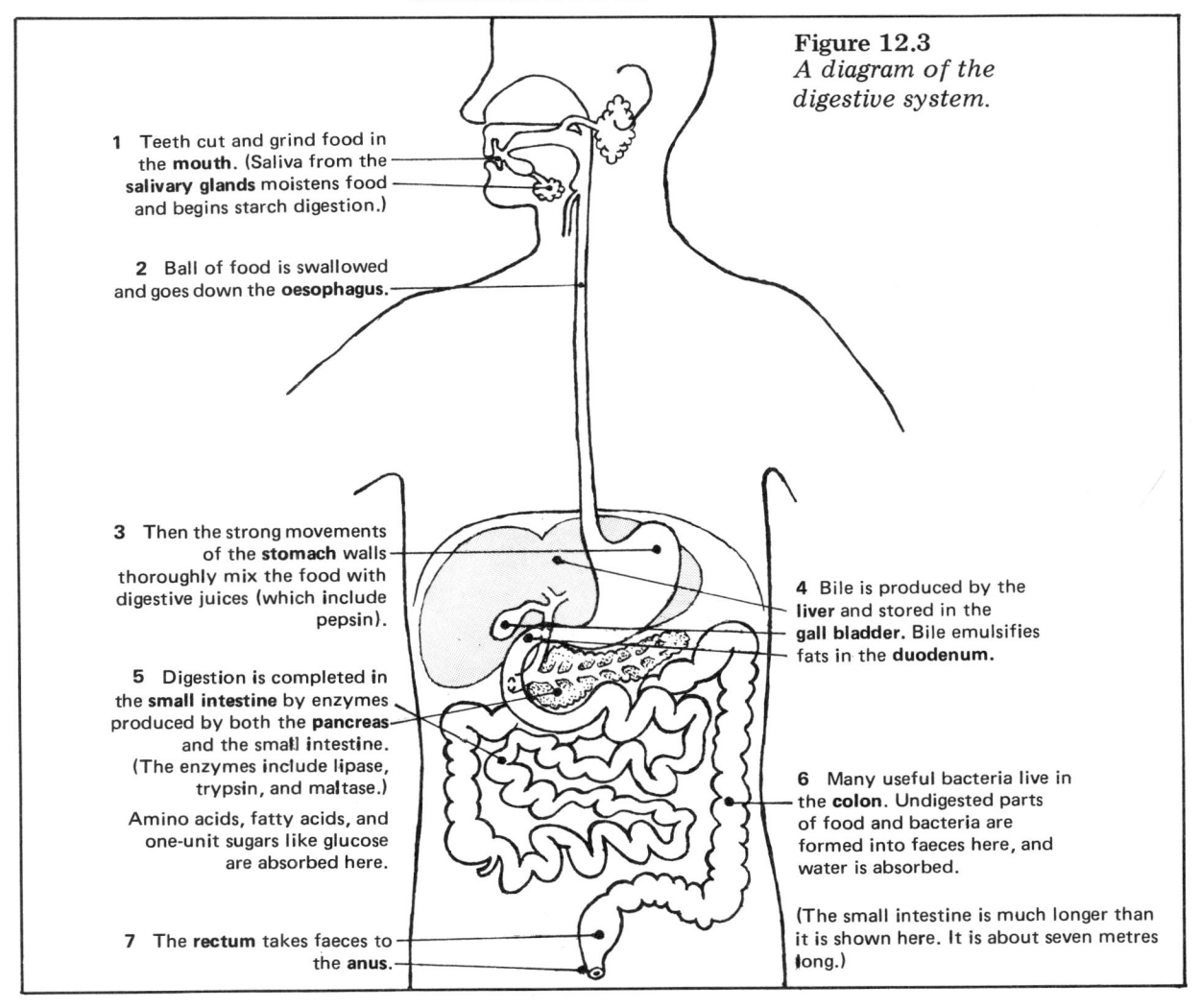

Figure 12.3
A diagram of the digestive system.

1 Teeth cut and grind food in the **mouth**. (Saliva from the **salivary glands** moistens food and begins starch digestion.)

2 Ball of food is swallowed and goes down the **oesophagus**.

3 Then the strong movements of the **stomach** walls thoroughly mix the food with digestive juices (which include pepsin).

4 Bile is produced by the **liver** and stored in the **gall bladder**. Bile emulsifies fats in the **duodenum**.

5 Digestion is completed in the **small intestine** by enzymes produced by both the **pancreas** and the small intestine. (The enzymes include lipase, trypsin, and maltase.)
Amino acids, fatty acids, and one-unit sugars like glucose are absorbed here.

6 Many useful bacteria live in the **colon**. Undigested parts of food and bacteria are formed into faeces here, and water is absorbed.

(The small intestine is much longer than it is shown here. It is about seven metres long.)

7 The **rectum** takes faeces to the **anus**.

12.4
SPECIAL FEEDING

Some people need special feeding. For example, if someone has a badly injured mouth and cannot swallow, they will need 'digested' nutrients put directly into their blood through a vein. This is called *intravenous feeding*.

Figure 12.4
The bottle contains a solution of glucose, amino acids, vitamins, and minerals. Sometimes a second bottle containing fat may also be used to provide extra energy.

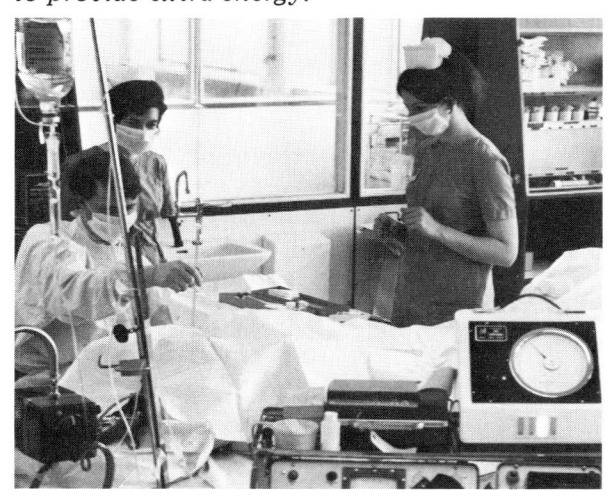

12.5
DIGESTING STARCH

Starch is an important part of many foods (see *Food science* Chapter 5). In some parts of Africa and India, starch makes up 70 to 80 per cent of people's total energy intake. In the United Kingdom it is about 25 per cent.

Q 1
List three foods you eat often which contain a lot of starch. Use worksheet M21 to check your ideas.

Starch cannot be absorbed by your body. It must first be digested by enzymes called amylase and maltase. Your body makes amylase in your mouth and pancreas. Maltase is made in your small intestine.

How do amylase and maltase change starch?

YOU WILL NEED:

Good pinch of starch
10 ml water
Pinch of amylase
Pinch of maltase
Iodine solution
Clinistix
Worksheet M19
2 test-tubes
Test-tube holder
Watch or clock
Access to gas burner

1 Work in pairs. Read the starch and glucose tests on worksheet M19.

2 Put the starch and water in a test-tube. Shake to disperse the starch.

3 Pour a few drops of the liquid into the other test-tube. Test for starch. Note the result. Wash out the test-tube.

4 Gently heat the test-tube containing the starch mixture. (It does not have to boil.)

Q 2
What happens to the viscosity (runniness) of the liquid?

5 Test the liquid for glucose. Note the result.

6 Let the test-tube cool until it feels just warm.

7 Add a pinch of amylase to the test-tube. Shake it.

8 After 5 minutes, test for glucose. Note the result.

9 Pour a few drops of liquid into the spare test-tube and test it for starch. Note the result.

Q 3
Does amylase change starch to glucose?

Q 4
What has happened to the viscosity of the liquid?

10 Add a pinch of maltase. Shake the test-tube.

11 After 5 minutes, test the liquid for glucose. Note the result.

This test has shown you that starch is digested in stages. Starch is first changed to dextrins and then to maltose by amylase. Then maltase changes maltose to glucose. See figure 12.5.

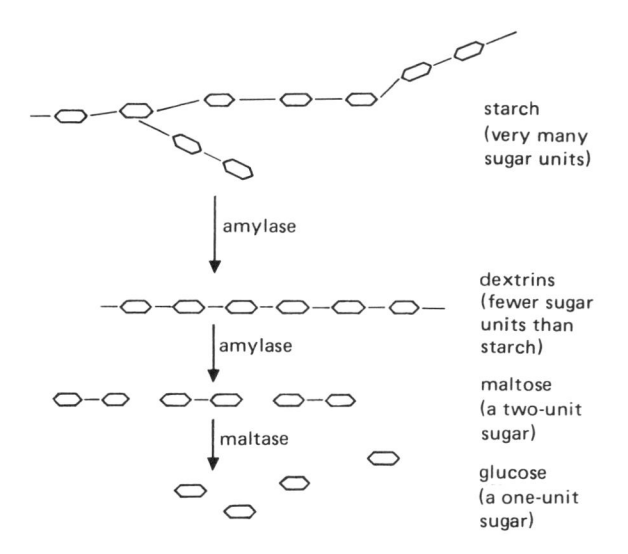

Figure 12.5
The digestion of starch to glucose.

Q 5
Why is it necessary for starch to be changed to glucose? (If you are not certain, look back at figure 12.2.)

12.6
MOVING AND USING NUTRIENTS

After digestion and absorption, nutrients are moved in blood from the gut to where they are needed.

Many nutrients, such as proteins and some minerals, are needed to build body cells. Other nutrients are needed to give you energy to grow and be active. To remind yourself, look back at page 54 of Chapter 9 and page 60 of Chapter 10.

Q 6
Name the nutrients which give you energy.

When nutrients have been used they are changed to other molecules like carbon dioxide, water, and urea. These have to be removed or they would poison your body.

12.7
WHAT NEEDS FEEDING?

Every part of your body, from the top of your head to the tip of your toes, needs to be fed. For example, your bones, blood, muscles, and nerves contain different chemicals and need different nutrients to make them.

Bone is made of proteins, with minerals such as calcium to make it hard. Figure 12.6 shows a cross-section of a small part of a bone. A whole bone would contain many of these side by side.

Figure 12.6

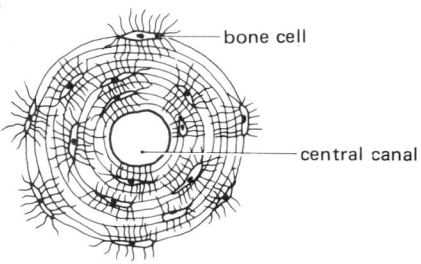

Blood consists of different kinds of cells floating in a watery liquid. Some of the cells contain iron. They all contain proteins. There are many important proteins in the liquid part of blood too.

Figure 12.7

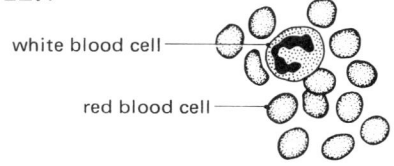

Muscles are solid but soft, and can contract (get shorter). Iron, proteins, sodium, potassium, and calcium are important for their structure and proper working. Figure 12.8 shows the kind of muscle there is in your arms and legs.

Figure 12.8

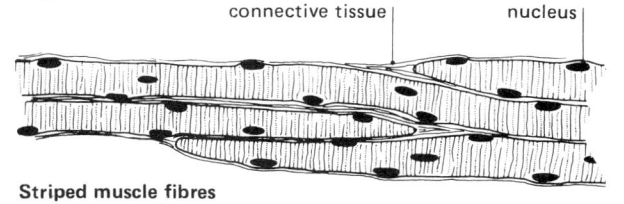

Striped muscle fibres

Nerves are made of long thin cells. They carry messages to and from your brain. They are made mainly of proteins with a fatty casing.

Figure 12.9

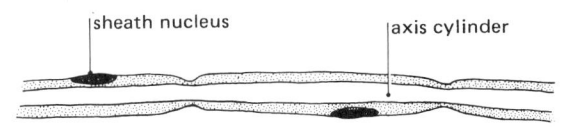

Portion of a nerve fibre

Nutrient	Where needed	What for
Amino acids	all tissues	building body cells, making enzymes, providing energy
Glucose	all tissues especially brain	providing energy
Fatty acids	all tissues especially muscle	providing energy
Calcium	bones and teeth	structure (giving rigidity)
Iron	blood and other tissues	forming part of red cells which transport oxygen, controlling activity *e.g.* muscle contraction
Iodine	thyroid gland and other tissues	making thyroxine — a chemical which controls the rate of chemical reactions in the body, forming part of enzymes which release energy from food

Table 12.2
Where some of the nutrients you eat in food are needed in your body and what they are for.

Even when a cell is formed it does not stay in your body for ever. A blood cell may last for four months, and a bone cell for several years. But because all cells eventually wear out, they have to be rebuilt. So you need to go on eating to get the nutrients to rebuild your cells. And when you are growing you need to make even more cells.

12.8
ALL NUTRIENTS CAN BE STORED

Your body can store all the nutrients you need. So if you don't get enough of one particular nutrient on one day there is no need to panic.

If you are getting a good diet, your body can store large amounts of some nutrients. But it can store only small amounts of others.

If a well-fed person suddenly stopped eating vitamin C or vitamin A he would not be ill immediately. Table 12.3 shows how long full body stores of some nutrients would last.

Vitamin	Time it would last
Thiamin (vitamin B_1)	2—3 weeks
Vitamin C	about 2 months
Vitamin B_{12}	many years
Vitamin A	1—2 years

Table 12.3

If you eat more than you need, extra nutrients are stored in your body. You saw in Chapter 10 that fat is stored mostly under your skin. But lots of nutrients are stored in your liver. (This is why animal livers give you such a rich supply of nutrients.)

When you have filled your body stores, extra nutrients are mostly got rid of (excreted) and are lost from the body.

But some nutrients such as iron, vitamin A, and vitamin D are not lost from your body in this way. The more you eat of these nutrients the more your body stores. So if you take vitamin tablets and mineral tonics in stupidly large amounts you will get very ill, and could even die.

Figure 12.10
A lesson to us all!

Health fan who died a carrot juice addict

A health food addict drank himself to death on carrot juice. And an inquest at Croydon heard today the dead man drank up to a gallon a day.

Before his death, 48-year-old scientific adviser Mr Brian X of Kenley, Surrey, was warned of the dangers by his doctor.

Dr John Fabricius told the hearing that he had warned Mr X about his addiction to Vitamin A after he was told that in a ten-day period Mr X had taken 70 million units.

Later he heard he was drinking as much as eight pints of carrot juice a day.

The doctor added that Mr X, of Heathview Lane, was an intelligent man, but had a low opinion of doctors.

Pathologist Dr David Haler said that vitamin A poisoning produced a condition indistinguishable from alcoholic poisoning. 'Anything taken in sufficiently large amounts will be poisonous', he said.

Coroner Dr Mary McHugh recorded a verdict of death from carrot juice addiction.

Q 7
What happens if you eat too much energy?

So the right amount of all nutrients does you good. Eat much too much or much too little for a long time, and you are in trouble.

12.9 DIETARY FIBRE

Some parts of food are not digested by body enzymes. Doctors and scientists used to think that roughage was not very important because it was not absorbed. But now a great deal more is known about it and it is realized that it is important for good health. Roughage is now called dietary fibre, because the fibre in most foods is not rough at all.

Dietary fibre is not one chemical, but a mixture of many. Three of them are cellulose, pectin, and lignin.

These are all parts of plant cell walls, as you can see in figure 12.11.

Figure 12.11
Simplified diagrams of a plant cell and an animal cell.

cell wall, made mainly of cellulose; also contains other dietary fibre chemicals

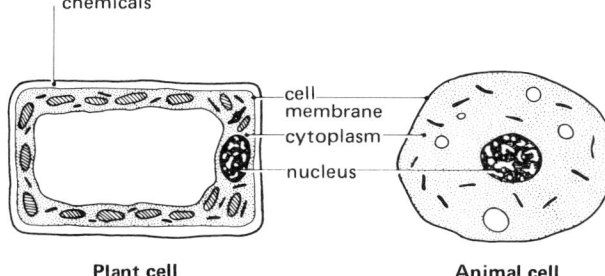

cell membrane
cytoplasm
nucleus

Plant cell   **Animal cell**

Q 8
Do any animal foods contain dietary fibre? (Use worksheet M21 and figure 12.11 to help you decide.)

Q 9
Does a slice of wholemeal bread contain more or less dietary fibre than a slice of white bread?

Q 10
Which three vegetables on the worksheet (M21) have the most dietary fibre?

Q 11
Using worksheet M21, plan two meals: one with a lot of fibre (about 15 grams), and one with very little fibre (less than 5 grams).

Q 12
Think about the high fibre meal you have planned.
a   Would it look attractive?
b   Does it contain foods with different textures?
c   Would you *really* like to eat it?

In 1978 the average dietary fibre intake in the United Kingdom was 20 grams per person per day. Many nutritionists think that this is not enough. Some say that an average intake of 30 grams would be healthier.

Find several high fibre recipes. Choose one and make it.

12.10 DIETARY FIBRE HOLDS CHEMICALS

Dietary fibre absorbs water and forms a large bulk which is easily expelled or removed from the body. This helps to prevent constipation.

Some parts of dietary fibre can hold molecules other than water. Because dietary fibre does not stay in the body very long, it can take harmful chemicals out with it before they do any damage. So many doctors believe that dietary fibre may help to prevent cancer of the large intestine. But they haven't definitely proved this yet.

If your food doesn't contain enough fibre, the muscles in your colon have to contract more than they should to make the contents move along. This causes high pressure inside the colon, and sometimes the inner lining of the colon is forced through weak spots in the muscle wall (see figure 12.12b). Pouches are formed which can be painful.

Figure 12.12

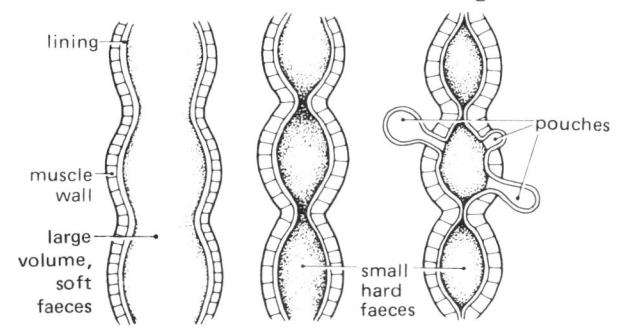

lining
muscle wall
large volume, soft faeces
pouches
small hard faeces

a   high-fibre diet   b   low-fibre diet

Dietary fibre is not digested by the enzymes produced by the gut wall. But it is broken down a bit before it leaves your body, by the bacteria which live in your large intestine. Because dietary fibre is bulky it makes you feel full. So a diet with a lot of fibre may help you stay the right weight and not get too fat.

CHAPTER 13

Food and its effect on health

Figure 13.1
Hospital food must be particularly nutritious.

13.1
FINDING OUT WHAT PEOPLE EAT

You need to eat about fifty nutrients if you are to be healthy and strong, and able to get over illnesses quickly. Eating well when you are healthy is important, but it is even more important when you are ill.

You learned in Chapter 9 that the amount of nutrients and energy groups of people ought to eat are called *recommended daily amounts*. To find out if people are eating enough of all the nutrients and energy, nutritionists carry out dietary surveys.

There are three types of survey. You can do one for yourself.

24-hour recall survey

1   Try to remember all the food and drink you had yesterday. Include meals and snacks.

2   Write down the kind of food and estimate the amount of each food. Use a table like the one below. (Don't bother to work out any nutrients or energy.)

Figure 13.2

Food	Description	Amount
Potato	boiled	1 medium

Q 1
a   Was it easy to remember everything you ate and drank yesterday?
b   Would it be easier or more difficult to remember what you had the day before that?

Q 2
a   Was your diet yesterday like your diet for every other day of the week?
b   Do you eat different foods on Saturdays and Sundays compared with weekdays?

Because it is difficult to remember what foods you ate, and because you eat differently on different days, one 24-hour survey may not tell you much about your total diet.

Weighed survey
It is much more accurate to weigh food just before you eat it and to fill in the diet record at each meal and snack.

Q 3
Why might this kind of survey be difficult to do? (Think about the people in the world who cannot read or write. What equipment would you need to do the survey? How many people would be needed to carry out the work?)

Figure 13.3
Importing apples.

Figure 13.4
A health worker making an epidemiology study at an urban centre in India. If there is anything wrong, the worker can find out what it is. She may also be able to help the mother to put things right.

Food balance survey
A third kind of survey finds out how much food is produced in a country or area and how much is imported and exported. This kind of information was used to compile the data in table 8.1 in Chapter 8.

The total weight of each food available is divided by the number of people in the country or area. This tells you the average amounts of food available per person.

Q 4
Does this survey tell you anything about what each individual person eats? (Might some people eat more than others?)

Q 5
Is this kind of survey more or less accurate than the weighed survey?

Accurate dietary surveys take a long time to do, and many workers are needed to make sure that people being surveyed fill in the records properly. But these surveys are important because they help to find the links between food and its nutrients and health.

13.2
LINKING FOOD AND HEALTH
Lots of things affect health. It is not only the food you eat. When nutritionists try to find out what affects health, they often find out what people eat and drink, and whether they are active or use cars a lot. They check whether people smoke or drink lots of alcohol.

The diseases people suffer from can sometimes be linked to what they eat or do. This kind of study is called *epidemiology*. On the next page is an example of the kind of evidence this gives you, and the questions that still have to be asked.

Children in some countries like India and Uganda do not eat nearly as much protein or food energy as children in the United States and United Kingdom.

Q 6
Many children in Uganda are not healthy. What is often wrong with them? (Look back to Chapter 8 if you can't remember.)

This suggests that not getting enough protein and food energy *may* be the cause. But it is not *proof*. The disease could be caused by a virus. To prove for certain that it is a lack of protein and energy, the children would need to be given more protein and energy. Doctors would then be able to see if it made any difference.

Q 7
Look at figure 13.5. What do you think is the matter with this girl? What is she drinking?

Figure 13.5

Everyone who becomes ill has drunk water at some time.

Q 8
a Does this mean that drinking water causes illness?
b How could you prove whether it does?

There are some questions about diet and health that scientists cannot answer yet. They don't know what causes heart attacks.

By doing different kinds of surveys, scientists have found out that in countries where people eat a lot of fat many of them get heart attacks. This means that fat *may* be the cause of heart attacks. Or it may be *one* cause. But people who eat a lot of fat also eat a lot of protein. They also smoke more cigarettes, and they watch more television than people who do not get much heart disease. A lot more work is needed to find out exactly what causes heart attacks, and how to prevent them.

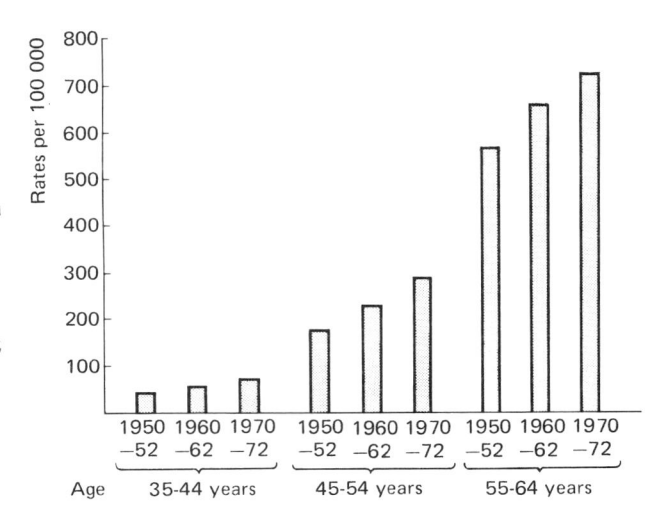

Figure 13.6
a *The annual death rate from coronary heart disease for men aged 35 to 64 years in England and Wales.*
b *The percentage of energy derived from fat in the diet of the average household in the United Kingdom.*

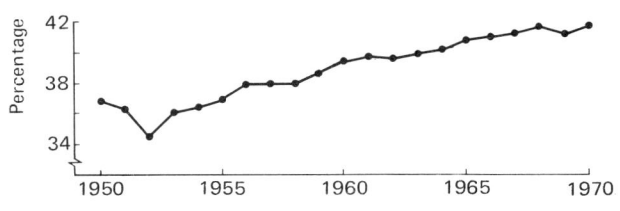

Figure 13.7
People who are too fat are more likely to have a heart attack than thin people. Research is going on to find out how some people can eat a lot of energy-giving foods but still stay thin.

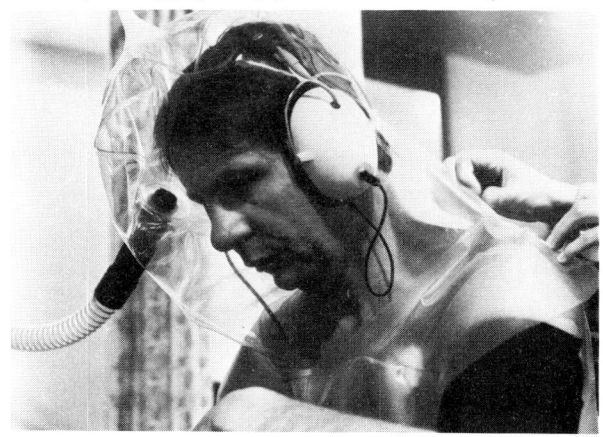

13.3 SUGAR AND TOOTH DECAY

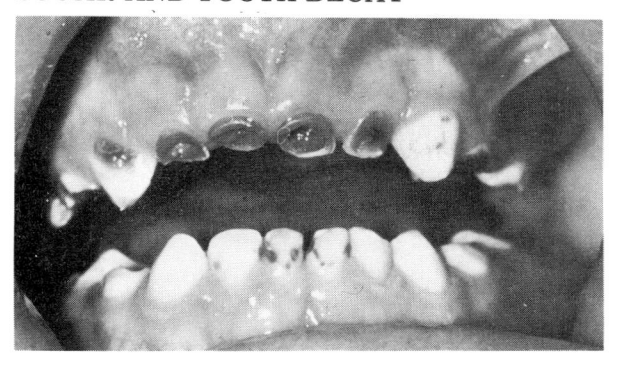

Figure 13.8
The ugly remains of the teeth of a child who was given sugary foods every day.

Q 9
a Look at worksheet M21. What foods contain large amounts of sugar?
b Can you tell which foods have a lot of sugar just by tasting them?
c How many times a day, on average, do you eat sugary foods?

1 Work in pairs and find out how many fillings you have.

2 Plot a histogram to show how many fillings people in your class have. Your teacher will help you do this.

Q 10
a What is the least number of fillings any one person has?
b What is the average number of fillings?

In countries where a lot of sugar is eaten, many people have badly decayed teeth. Lots of children have bad teeth.

Q 11
How could you prove that sugar causes tooth decay?

Table 13.1
Tooth decay in the United Kingdom.

Age (years)	Average number of decayed, missing, or filled teeth	% of children with some bad teeth
5	3.4	71
8	5.0	91
15	8.4	97

About 30 per cent of adults (people over sixteen years of age) in the United Kingdom have none of their own teeth left.

Q 12
a In table 13.1, what percentage of five-year-olds have some decayed teeth? (That is, how many out of every hundred?)
b What percentage of fifteen-year-olds have *no* decayed teeth?
c On average, how many decayed teeth do eight-year-olds have?

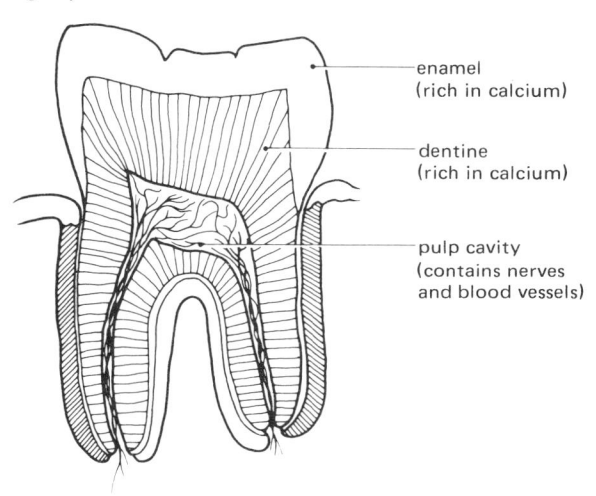

Figure 13.9
The structure of a tooth.

Bacteria are always in your mouth. They live on your teeth in a substance called *plaque*, and their main food is sucrose (table sugar). As they eat the sugar, they make acid as a waste product. If sugary foods are eaten many times a day, the bacteria will be producing acid almost all the time.

13.4 ACID AND TOOTH DECAY

What does acid in vinegar and orange juice do to your teeth?

YOU WILL NEED:

2 teeth — either animal teeth from the butcher or from a younger sister or brother who is losing milk teeth (without your help!). If this is not possible, use 2 chips of marble (calcium carbonate)
10 ml vinegar
10 ml orange juice
2 test-tubes
Test-tube rack
2 labels

1   Work in pairs.

2   Put a tooth or small chip of marble into each test-tube.

3   Pour 10 ml vinegar into one tube. Label it.

4   Pour 10 ml orange juice into the other tube. Label it.

Q 13
What do you see?

5   Leave the test-tubes for a day or two and look at them again.

Q 14
What has happened now?

Q 15
What is the chemical name of the group of substances which neutralizes acids?

Nuts and cheese are much better than apples for preventing tooth decay because they help neutralize the acid in your mouth. These foods are neutral or slightly alkaline. They also make you produce more saliva which is alkaline.

Figure 13.10

The *total amount* of sugar you eat is not the most important thing in deciding the amount of tooth decay you have. The *number of times* you eat sugary foods in a day is more important. You should eat sugar only at meal times, not between meals. If you can't brush your teeth after every meal, you should eat nuts or a small piece of cheese to help prevent tooth decay.

Look back at your 24-hour recall survey. How many times did you eat sugary foods yesterday? (Use worksheet M21 to check if you are not sure which foods contain sugar.)

13.5 VITAMIN D, CALCIUM, AND RICKETS

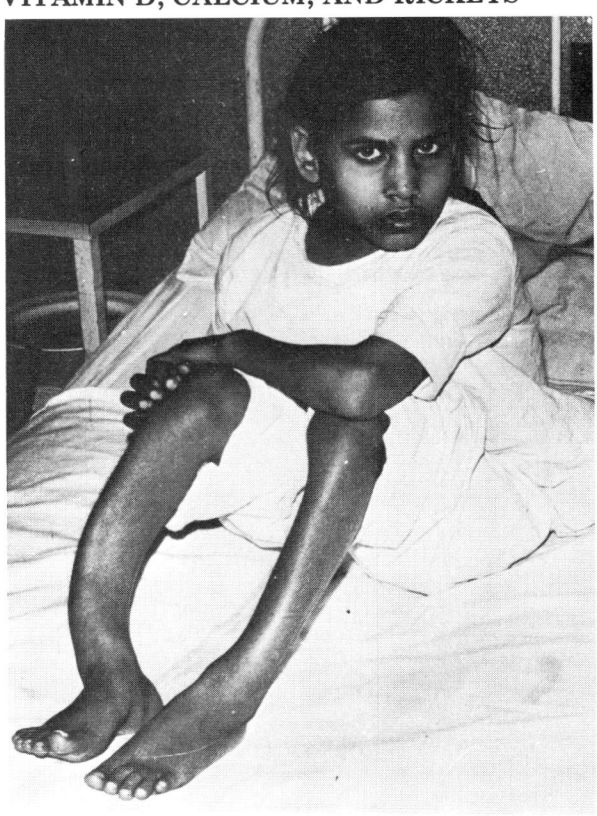

Figure 13.11

Q 16
Look at figure 13.11. What is unusual about this child?

This photograph shows what happens when a child has rickets. This child never ate much butter or margarine, cheese, or fatty fish. She drank very little milk.

Q 17
Look at table 13.2. Which nutrient do butter, margarine, cheese, and fatty fish have, which is *not* in fruits, vegetables, and meat?

Q 18
What nutrient do bones and teeth contain a lot of? (Look back at Chapter 12 if you can't remember.)

Your bones and teeth do not contain much vitamin D, but this nutrient is important for bones and teeth. This is because it helps you to absorb calcium from food into your blood. Vitamin D also helps you use calcium to build strong bones and teeth.

Food (100 g)	Protein (g)	Calcium (mg)	Iron (mg)	Vit C (mg)	Vit D (µg)
Meat	20	7	2.0	0	0
Fatty fish	20	30	1.0	0	22
Fruit	0	15	0.5	5—30	0
Green vegetables	1	30	0.5	15—30	0
Butter/margarine	0	10	0.2	0	1—8
Cheese	26	800	0.4	0	0.3
White fish	20	30	1.0	0	0
Cooked rice	2	0	0.2	0	0

Table 13.2

Even if you eat lots of calcium, your body cannot use it to make strong bones and teeth unless you get enough vitamin D. Your bones will be soft and your legs will bend easily under the weight of your body. Look at figure 13.11 opposite. In this case, one leg in particular has gradually become bent. This is permanent.

These are the foods the man in figure 13.12 ate when he was a child: rice, vegetables, white fish. He did not eat much else.

Figure 13.12

Q 19
Do these foods give him any vitamin D?
(See table 13.2 opposite.)

Q 20
Do his legs look strong and healthy?

The reason why this man has good straight legs is that when he was a child he made his own vitamin D.

Everyone can do this if they spend long enough in the sun. *Ultra violet rays* from the sun fall on your skin and change a chemical in it to make vitamin D. If children are out in the sun enough they don't need to eat much vitamin D. But if they move to colder countries they will need to wear more clothes to keep warm and they will not play in the sun so much. Also, the culture of some groups means that many young girls spend most of their time inside the home. Then they need to eat more vitamin D.

Figure 13.13

You have seen what happens if you eat sugar a lot and don't clean your teeth. You also know what happens if you don't get enough vitamin D. If you don't get enough of any nutrient for a long time you will become ill in some way.

In nutrition there are lots of things to find out about, and there are lots of discoveries still going on. Chapter 14 shows you the short cuts to eating well. Chapter 15 is about solving nutrition problems and eating healthy food that tastes good.

CHAPTER 14
Choosing a nutritious diet

14.1 PEOPLE EAT MANY DIFFERENT FOODS

Figure 14.1
Both humans and cows live on milk when they are very young.

Figure 14.2
Older cows eat grass. Older humans eat many different foods.

Q 1
Why do you have more foods to choose from than cows or sheep?

Cows and other animals don't know much about nutrition, but they generally get enough of all nutrients. There are three reasons for this. Firstly, most animals can make their own vitamin C, and the bacteria which live in many animals' guts make enough of many vitamins for the animals' needs. Secondly, most wild animals have only a small number of foods to choose from. These foods (such as other animals and grass) are nearly all very nutritious. Thirdly, domesticated animals often eat foods prepared specially for them. They are made so that they contain enough of all nutrients.

Humans have hundreds of foods to choose from. Many are prepared by the food industry. Some are very nutritious, some are not. You cannot eat them all, so you have to eat some and leave the rest. To be able to choose the right mixture of foods it helps if you know about the nutrients in different foods.

Q 2
Why don't you eat just one food all the time? (Would you like eating only one food?)

Q 3
Look at worksheet M21. Does any one food in this list give you all nutrients?

bread	meat	milk
potatoes	fish	cheese
rice	oranges	butter.

Q 4
If you ate just one of these foods for your whole life, would you be healthy?

Q 5
a About how many different foods do you eat in a week?
b Make a list under two headings:

foods you eat every day
foods you eat less often.

14.2
A HEALTHY DIET IS A VARIED ONE
No single food can keep you healthy for ever. Most foods are completely lacking in at least one nutrient.

Q 6
Look at worksheet M21. What nutrients are missing from the following foods?

| beef | rice | bread |
| apple | butter | cod. |

If you eat a mixture of all these foods — and others — you will probably get every nutrient. Nutritionists say you should eat a varied diet to be healthy.

Q 7
Discuss what nutritionists mean by varied. Is it eating ten different flavours of crisps? Or six different colours of sweets? Or a mixture of soft, crisp, and chewy foods?

Q 8
Does the flavour, colour, or texture of food tell you what nutrients it contains? (Look back to Chapter 9 if you can't remember).

14.3
MEALS OR SNACKS
These days many families don't eat meals together. They eat meals at different times of the day and often in different places.

More food is now eaten as snacks. A snack is a food or meal which is quick to prepare (or needs no preparation). It is usually eaten without a knife and fork. And you probably don't think of it as a main meal.

Usually the kind of meals you eat with a knife and fork contain meat, fish, or cheese, with cereals or vegetables. These meals are usually nutritious. Some snacks such as pizzas, hamburgers, and milk shakes are nutritious too. Snacks like chocolate, biscuits, crisps, and sweets, which contain a lot of sugar or fat or both, are more likely to give you lots of energy, but not many vitamins or minerals.

Figure 14.3

85

14.4 AMOUNTS OF NUTRIENTS IN FOODS

Figure 14.4 (Weights of foods are edible weights.)

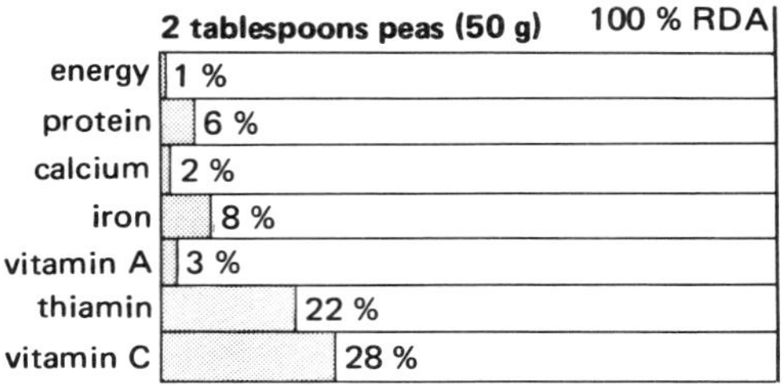

Even if a food seems to contain a lot of different nutrients, some of them may be there in only tiny amounts.

Look at figure 14.4. See which foods give you a lot of *one* nutrient. See which give you a lot of *more than one* nutrient. To understand what these bar charts mean, look first at the vitamin C line of cabbage.

The length of this shaded line shows you that 2 tablespoons of cabbage gives you about a third of the vitamin C you should eat on average each day.

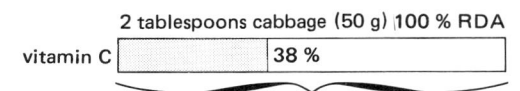

2 tablespoons cabbage (50 g) | 100 % RDA
vitamin C — 38 %

This is 100 per cent (the total amount) of the vitamin C that teenagers need each day. R.D.A. stands for recommended daily amount.

2 tablespoons peas (50 g) — 100 % RDA
energy	1 %
protein	6 %
calcium	2 %
iron	8 %
vitamin A	3 %
thiamin	22 %
vitamin C	28 %

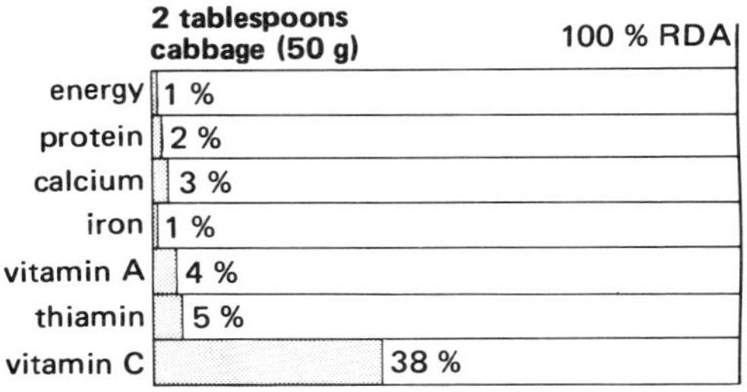

2 tablespoons cabbage (50 g) — 100 % RDA
energy	1 %
protein	2 %
calcium	3 %
iron	1 %
vitamin A	4 %
thiamin	5 %
vitamin C	38 %

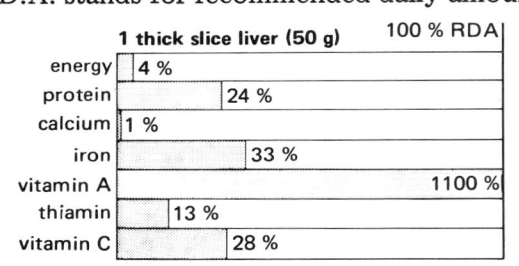

1 thick slice liver (50 g) — 100 % RDA
energy	4 %
protein	24 %
calcium	1 %
iron	33 %
vitamin A	1100 %
thiamin	13 %
vitamin C	28 %

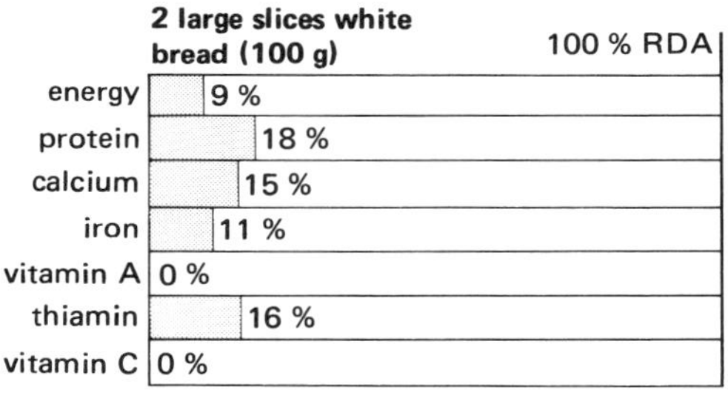

2 large slices white bread (100 g) — 100 % RDA
energy	9 %
protein	18 %
calcium	15 %
iron	11 %
vitamin A	0 %
thiamin	16 %
vitamin C	0 %

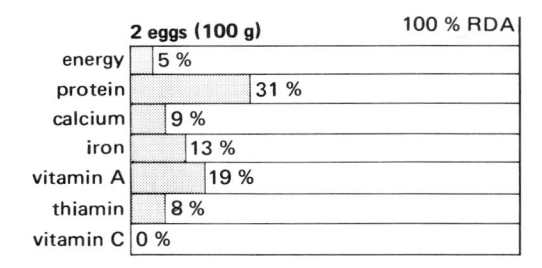

2 eggs (100 g) — 100 % RDA
energy	5 %
protein	31 %
calcium	9 %
iron	13 %
vitamin A	19 %
thiamin	8 %
vitamin C	0 %

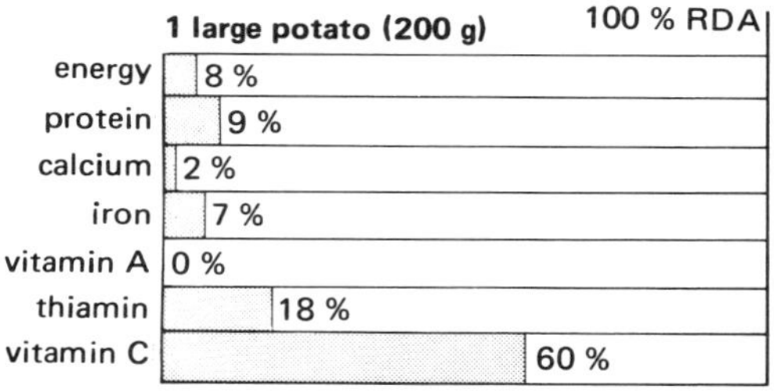

1 large potato (200 g) — 100 % RDA
energy	8 %
protein	9 %
calcium	2 %
iron	7 %
vitamin A	0 %
thiamin	18 %
vitamin C	60 %

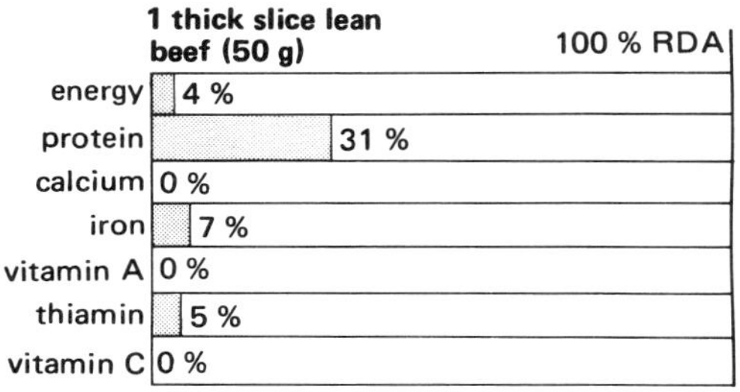

1 thick slice lean beef (50 g) — 100 % RDA
energy	4 %
protein	31 %
calcium	0 %
iron	7 %
vitamin A	0 %
thiamin	5 %
vitamin C	0 %

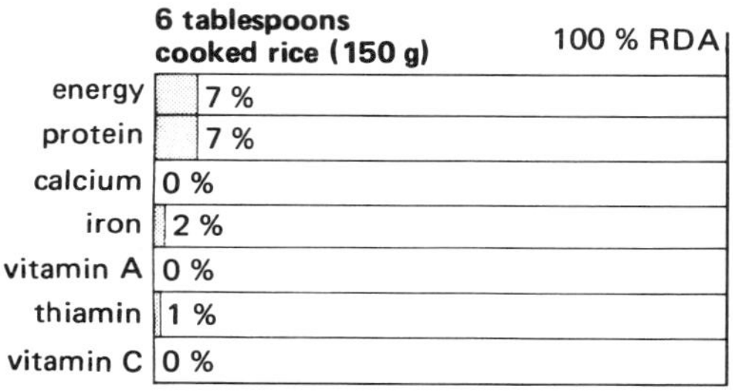

6 tablespoons cooked rice (150 g) — 100 % RDA
energy	7 %
protein	7 %
calcium	0 %
iron	2 %
vitamin A	0 %
thiamin	1 %
vitamin C	0 %

1 glass milk (200 ml) — 100 % RDA

energy	5 %
protein	15 %
calcium	37 %
iron	1 %
vitamin A	10 %
thiamin	7 %
vitamin C	8 %

Can sugary drink (250 ml) — 100 % RDA

energy	2 %
protein	0 %
calcium	2 %
iron	0 %
vitamin A	0 %
thiamin	0 %
vitamin C	0 %

1 orange (125 g) — 100 % RDA

energy	2 %
protein	2 %
calcium	8 %
iron	3 %
vitamin A	1 %
thiamin	9 %
vitamin C	240 %

2 small packets crisps (50 g) — 100 % RDA

energy	10 %
protein	7 %
calcium	3 %
iron	7 %
vitamin A	0 %
thiamin	9 %
vitamin C	30 %

1 small bar milk chocolate (50 g) — 100 % RDA

energy	10 %
protein	9 %
calcium	17 %
iron	5 %
vitamin A	0 %
thiamin	4 %
vitamin C	0 %

Q 9
Look at the bar chart for two slices of bread. What percentage of the amount of protein you should eat each day does this bread give you?

Q 10
a Which is a better source of vitamin C: six tablespoons of rice or one large potato?
b Do all foods contain vitamin C?
c Do all or almost all foods contain thiamin?

Q 11
a Add up the percentage figures for protein, vitamin C, iron, and energy in two slices of lean beef, two slices of bread, and a glass of milk.
(This shows you how much of your daily nutrient and energy needs a beef sandwich and a glass of milk gives you.)
b Add up the same percentage figures for nutrients and energy in beef, potato, and cabbage.

Foods and meals which give you a high proportion of many nutrients are called *nutritious*.

Q 12
Is the hot meal in question 11 much more nutritious than the sandwich?

Q 13
Are sugary drinks nutritious? (Remember that energy is not a nutrient.)

Q 14
If you eat twelve potatoes to give you all the energy you need, would you also get enough of all the nutrients listed?

14.5
A LITTLE OF WHAT YOU FANCY ...

When nutritionists talk about a varied diet they mean you should eat a little of many foods. That can include some sugary drinks, but not too many. Sugary drinks give you energy but almost no nutrients other than sugars.

Copy figure 14.5 into your notebook.

Use figure 14.4. Look at each food. For each one write down the names of all the nutrients which have bars longer than the energy bar. This means that the food is a good source of these nutrients. For example, in the case of bread write down protein, calcium, iron, and thiamin. (Thiamin is vitamin B_1.)

Food	Main nutrients
Cabbage	
Oranges	
Milk chocolate	
Sugary drink	
White bread	
Beef	
Potato	
Peas	
Milk	
Eggs	
Rice	
Crisps	
Liver	

Figure 14.5
(See previous page.)

Q 15
Which are the most nutritious foods? (In other words, which foods have two or three or more nutrients written by them?)

Q 16
a What is the most important nutrient in milk?
b If you don't like milk, which other foods could you eat to give you calcium?
c What does calcium do in your body? (Look back to Chapter 13 if you can't remember.)

14.6
EATING ENOUGH IRON

You need iron to make healthy blood cells. These cells carry oxygen from your lungs to every part of your body. In muscles oxygen allows your body to use the energy from digested foods.

Q 17
Which are the most important sources of iron in figure 14.4?

In fact, the richest source of all is liver. Iron is also deliberately added to some foods like flour and breakfast cereals.

Q 18
Which nutrients help provide energy? (Look at Chapter 10 if you can't remember.)

Look at the red blood cells in figure 14.6. Iron deficiency anaemia is a common disease in many countries including the United Kingdom.

Figure 14.6
a *Normal red blood cells from a healthy person.*
b *Red blood cells from a person with iron-deficiency anaemia. (There are fewer cells.)*

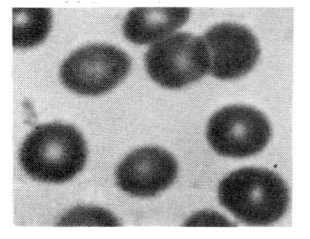

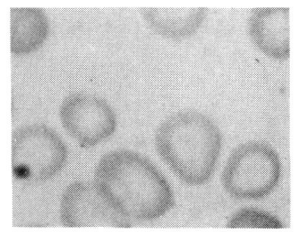

Figure 14.7
Hard exercise makes your breathing change, even if you are healthy.

If you don't have enough iron in your blood, even slight exercise, like walking up stairs, can make your breathing change. You feel a bit out of breath.

Q 19
Why? Look back to the beginning of this section for a clue.

Q 20
Look at worksheet M18. Women need more iron than men. Why?

Q 21
Use worksheet M21 to find out how much of the following foods you would need to eat to get half your recommended daily amount of iron:
a bread; *b* liver; *c* beef; *d* potato.

Liver and kidney are the best sources of iron, but many people don't like the taste or texture. A very important part of nutrition is making nutritious food nice to eat. Try some liver recipes which are good to eat, such as liver paté or stroganoff, and some iron-rich dessert recipes.

14.7
VEGETARIANISM

Some people don't eat any meat or fish. This may be because they don't like the idea of killing animals. But for millions of people in the world, meat is not available. Animals are too expensive to raise, and it makes better economic sense for people to eat grain instead of feeding it to cattle, sheep, or pigs.

Figure 14.8
Fruits and vegetables for sale in the streets of Jaipur (India).

Most vegetarians eat cheese, milk, and eggs, as well as fruits, vegetables, and cereals.

The main nutrients in meat are proteins, fats, iron, and some B group vitamins like thiamin.

Q 22
Use figure 14.4. If you didn't eat any meat, would you be able to get these nutrients from other foods?

Some people cut out more foods than just meat. They don't eat any food which has any connections with animals. These people are called *vegans*.

Q 23
a What foods do vegans refuse to eat?
b What foods do they eat?
c Do you think they can still be healthy?

Q 24
If you decided to eat only one food, like rice, for your whole life, what nutrients would you be short of? (Use figure 14.4 to help you.)

Whether the single food is rice, bread, eggs, meat, or milk, eating only one food is bound to lead to deficiency of one or many nutrients. This would make you ill. The more foods you eat, the better your chance of eating all nutrients.

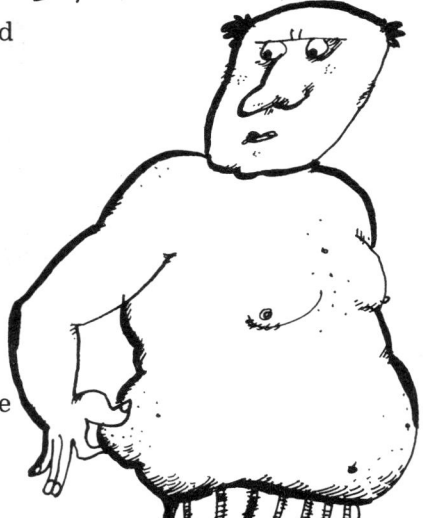

CHAPTER 15
Solving nutrition problems

15.1
BUT I DON'T LIKE CABBAGE
The easiest way of getting all nutrients is to eat many different foods. This does not mean you have to eat *every* food to be healthy. Every nutrient is in more than one food.

Not eating one or two foods won't matter. But if there are lots of foods you refuse to eat you may well be short of one or more nutrients. And you won't be very popular in other people's homes either if you are fussy.

Figure 15.1

15.2
EATING TO SLIM

Q 2
When you are trying to lose weight what nutrients should you eat less of?

Q 3
Why do you still need the same amount of vitamins and minerals and proteins?

Q 4
Write down four foods with a high fat content, and four foods with a high sugar content.

Q 1
a Jane doesn't like cabbage or liver. What are the main nutrients in these two foods? (Use figure 14.4 to help you.)
b What other foods do you know contain these nutrients in good amounts?

These foods, and others like them, are the ones you must cut down on if you need to lose weight.

Every kilogram of body fat contains 32 000 kilojoules (7700 kilocalories). It is a store of the energy you ate, but did not use up, in activity and staying alive. To lose 1 kilogram of body fat you have to eat 32 000 kilojoules less than you need. You could do this in about a week by eating 4500 kilojoules a day less than you use.

Most good slimming eating plans allow you 4000–6000 kilojoules (1000–1500 kilocalories) a day, depending on age, sex, and activity. If you ate even less than this you would certainly lose more weight. But it would be muscle you were losing, not more fat. This won't make you look any better and it could be dangerous to your health.

Figure 15.2
EVERY KILOGRAM OF BODY FAT CONTAINS 32,000 KILOJOULES

15.3
HEALTHY EATING FOR COELIACS
Even though some people may like all foods, there may be some they must not eat because their bodies cannot cope with them.

For example, coeliacs (see'lee'acs) cannot digest and absorb a part of wheat called gluten. This is a protein. Small amounts are also in rye, oats, and barley. So children and adults with coeliac disease cannot eat foods which contain any gluten. Even the tiny trace in powdered mustard might make them ill. If they do eat gluten they get diarrhoea and feel very sick. Children don't grow well and they have pot bellies.

Q 5
Do meat, fish, eggs, rice, fruits, vegetables, or milk contain wheat?

Q 6
Will a coeliac be able to get enough of all the nutrients even though he can't eat wheat, rye, oats, or barley? (Look at figure 14.5 which you filled in in your notebook if you need help.)

Q 7
Which single food, made mainly of wheat flour, would you miss most if you were a coeliac?

Q 8
Write down the foods you ate yesterday. Which of the foods contained gluten? Could you follow the same recipe but use something else instead of wheat flour?

It is possible to make bread, biscuits, and cake without wheat flour. The textures are different from normal. Your teacher may give you some recipes to try.

15.4
EATING WELL WHEN YOU ARE OLD
Most old people in the United Kingdom eat varied diets. Most of them get enough of all nutrients and energy. But sometimes the elderly don't eat enough. They don't have different nutrient needs from younger adults, but their diets change as they get older.

Q 9
Why might an old person not eat well?

Figure 15.4

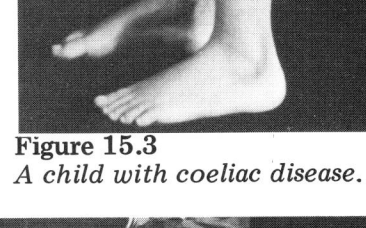

Figure 15.3
A child with coeliac disease.

91

15.5
STARTING GOOD EATING HABITS EARLY

The best food for the young baby is his mother's milk. Most mothers can breast feed if they want to. The amounts of proteins, fats, carbohydrates, vitamins, and minerals in mother's milk are in the right proportions for the baby's growth and health.

A few mothers cannot breast feed. Their babies can have one of the modified milks on the market. Straight cow's milk is not suitable. It is designed for the growing calf who grows much more quickly than the human baby. It has to be modified before it can be given to human babies.

Figure 15.5
Many changes have to be made to cow's milk before it is like human milk.

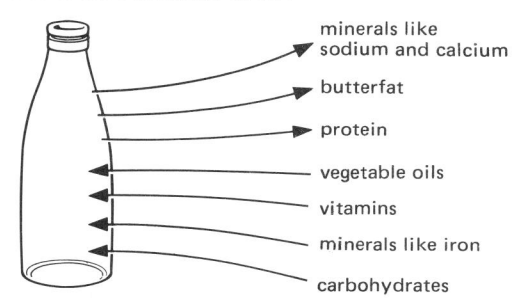

minerals like sodium and calcium
butterfat
protein
vegetable oils
vitamins
minerals like iron
carbohydrates

Many baby milks are bought in powder form. When the feed is made up with water it is very important to use the exact amounts of powder and water recommended by the manufacturer or doctor. The balance of powder and water is very important. If this balance is upset it could be dangerous. Not enough powder means the baby won't grow well. Not enough water can mean that losses from the body are not made up. This leads to dehydration which could give the baby convulsions (twitching of all the muscles in the body).

Most children can grow well on milk for about four or six months. After that they need to eat solid foods. They are weaned.

If a mother is well fed in pregnancy her baby will have enough vitamin C and iron in its body to last for several months, even though milk does not contain much of these two nutrients. But when the stores are used up, other foods must be eaten to get enough vitamin C and iron.

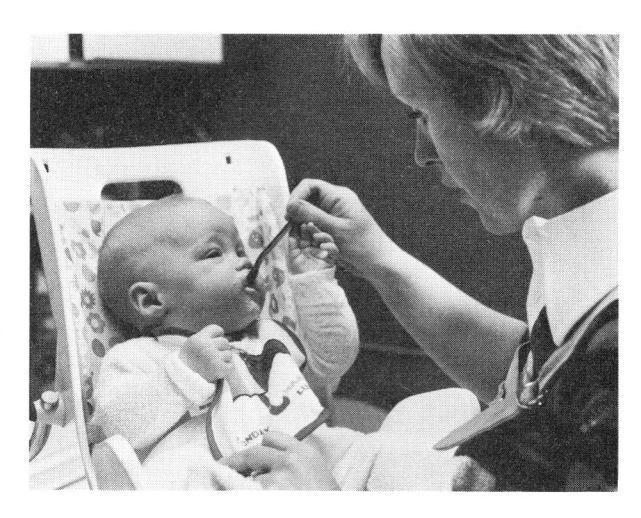

Figure 15.6

Q 10
Use worksheet M21. Which two foods contain a lot of
a iron
b vitamin C?

There are two other reasons for eating a mixed diet. Living on milk alone is boring and you would have to drink a lot of it to get enough energy.

Q 11
Work out how many pints of milk you would need a day to get your recommended daily intake of energy. Use worksheet M21 to help you.

Quite a lot of people do not eat some foods. Maybe they don't like them, or their religion forbids them, or they have an illness which makes it impossible for them to eat certain foods. But as long as lots of foods are available to choose from, it is possible to get all nutrients in the right amounts so that everyone can be as healthy as possible.

Now that you know something about nutrition you will know that a little of what you fancy is all right. But . . . .

This area of study looks at fabrics and the fibres they are made from. With modern technology we can make a great range of different fibres for different purposes. You will learn about this, and investigate the structure of fabrics too. You will look at the properties of fabrics and how these affect their use in everyday life.

In *Fibres and fabrics* you will look at the reasons why particular fabrics are used for particular purposes. This will help you to choose the right fabric for the job you want it to do.

Fibres and fabrics

Chapter 16 The importance of fabrics *page 94*

Chapter 17 Fabric structure and properties *100*

Chapter 18 Yarns *106*

Chapter 19 Textile fibres *112*

Chapter 20 Fabrics and colour *118*

Chapter 21 Fabrics for clothing *124*

Chapter 22 Soiling and cleaning *130*

CHAPTER 16

The importance of fabrics

16.1
WHAT WOULD THE WORLD BE LIKE WITHOUT FABRICS?

Suppose one morning you got up and found that everything made out of fabrics had disappeared. You would certainly notice a difference. For a start, there would be no clothes for you to put on, and it would be no good trying to go back to bed. All the bedding would have gone too. There would be no curtains at the windows, and no carpets on the floor. You and the world would seem very bare. But fabrics and fibres are also used for many more things than you would think of at first.

Look carefully through the pictures shown in figures 16.1 to 16.9 — they have been chosen to teach you something. Read the captions and answer the questions.

Figure 16.1
Fire hoses and motor tyres are both reinforced (made stronger) with fabrics. Fabrics used for jobs like this have to be strong and hard-wearing. Lives depend on them.

Figure 16.2
These fabrics have to be very open. The net lets water through but catches the fish. The net curtains let through light and air.

Q 1
a What other qualities do you think would be important for a fisherman's net?
b What for curtains?

Figure 16.3
Fabrics used for the sails of the boat and the wings of the glider have a lot in common.

Figure 16.4
Sport uses fabrics in many ways. Tennis balls have a fabric covering. The footballer's shirt shows his team colours. A tracksuit keeps an athlete warm before and after an event.

Q 2
What must the fabrics in figure 16.3 be able to do? List what you think would be right for them and what would be wrong:
a light; *b* strong; *c* flexible (able to bend easily); *d* stretchy; *e* non-stretchy; *f* not easily damaged by sunlight; *g* porous (lets air through easily); *h* non-porous; *i* absorbent (soaks up water); *j* non-absorbent.

Figure 16.5

Q 3
a Why does the tracksuit cover the whole of the athlete's body while the footballer's clothes leave legs and arms bare?
b In what ways might fabrics used for the tracksuit and the footballer's shirt be different?

Q 4
a What do the fabrics in figure 16.5 help to keep out?
b Why would each fabric be different from curtain netting?

Traditional styles of dress suit the local climate. Cold-climate clothes must slow down the loss of your body heat by keeping out chill winds. In hot climates clothing must let air blow over your skin to cool you and let body perspiration dry.

Q 5
Is traditional Arab dress loose or close fitting? Why?

Figure 16.6 (right)
Traditional Eskimo and Arab clothing.

Different jobs need different clothes. The paint sprayers wear clothes which can easily be washed. The spacesuit is airtight, pressurized, and air-conditioned to give the astronaut his own private surroundings so that he can live on the air-less moon. The spacesuit must also be tough, lightweight, and flexible.

Q 6
What qualities are needed for the motorcyclist's outfit?

Figure 16.7

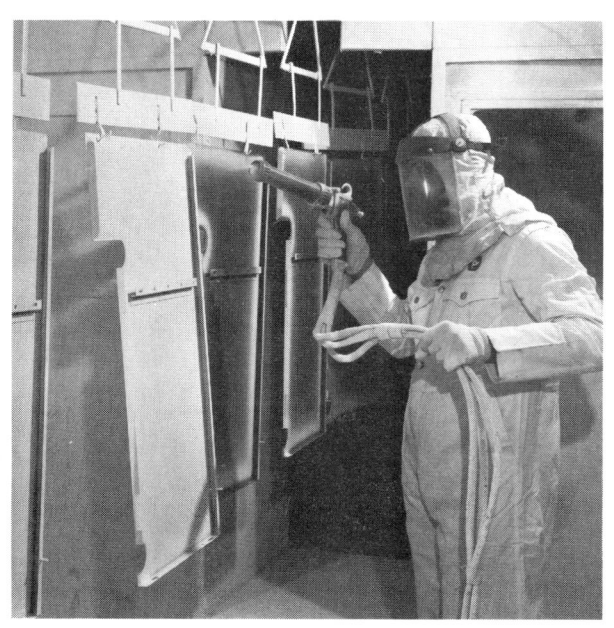

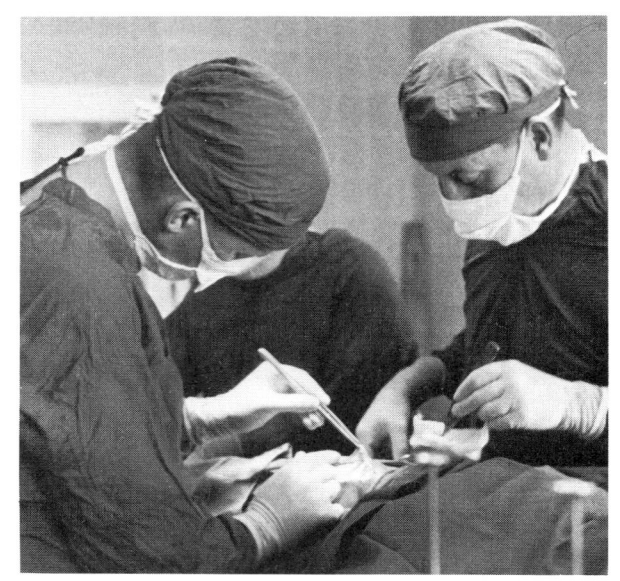

Figure 16.8a and b
Fabrics are used by doctors and nurses.

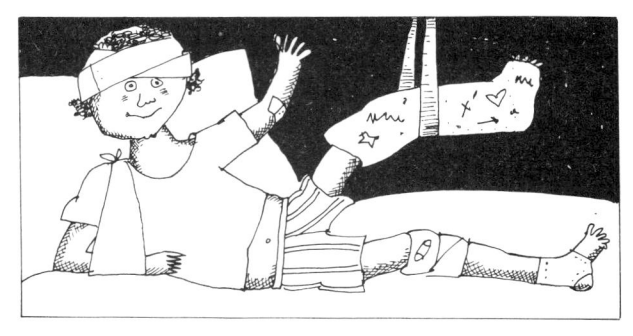

Q 7
How many medical uses of fabrics can you list?

Figure 16.9
Fabrics are used a great deal in the home to give colour, texture, and design. They also keep us warm.

Q 8
How many uses can you spot in figure 16.9?

The photographs and drawings show you some of the ways we all rely on fabrics in our everyday lives. You will probably have noticed that clothing cropped up more often than anything else. This is right, because about half of all the fabrics made is used for clothes of one sort or another. The other half is used for home furnishings and in industry. Fabrics are important at home, at work, and at play.

16.2
THE RIGHT FABRICS FOR THE JOB

Some of the questions above asked you to think about the fabric qualities needed for certain uses. Now you have a chance to try your skill on real fabrics.

YOU WILL NEED:

Labelled fabric samples

1 Look at and handle the fabric samples provided by your teacher. Each is labelled with its use.

2 Make a table in your book like the one below.

3 For each fabric, read the list of properties and put a tick against those you think are important. Put a cross if the property seems wrong for that particular use.

4 Check with your teacher that you have ticked the right properties.

Would it be sensible to swap any of the uses around? Would you go up a mountain in an anorak made from curtain netting? Would upholstery fabric make good underwear? You will see that each use requires fabric with its own special set of properties.

Properties	Use								
	Upholstery	Net curtains	Winter overcoat	Men's underwear	Towel	Anorak	PVC coat	Summer dress
Lightweight								
Heavyweight								
Open texture								
Close texture								
Very flexible (bendy)								
Stretchy								
Windproof								
Waterproof								
Absorbent (soaks up water)								
Hard-wearing								
Insulating (slows down heat loss)								

Figure 16.10

Q 9
Say why you think each sample fabric suits its particular job. Use your completed property table to help you.

Fabric manufacturers have to be able to make cloth with the right properties for each purpose. Some of the things that cause fabrics to be different from one another are discussed in the next chapters.

CHAPTER 17

Fabric structure and properties

17.1 WHAT ARE FABRICS?

Some fabrics can be very different from others; think of your own clothes. But all fabrics have something in common — and you can find out what this is.

YOU WILL NEED:

Fabric samples
Pin
Hand lens

1 Use your pin to tease out a little material from the edge of each of your fabric samples, as shown in figure 17.2.

Figure 17.1

You will find that you are pulling out strands of one kind or another from each fabric sample. These strands may be single, hair-like fibres or bigger yarns (threads) which are made up of lots of fibres.

Figure 17.2

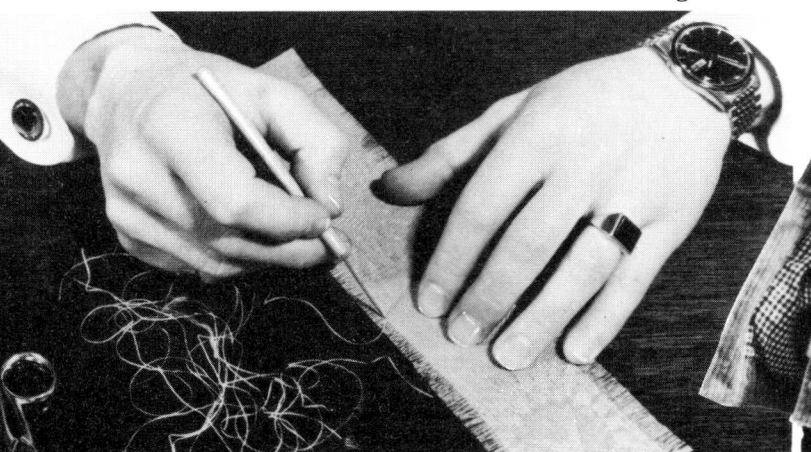

2 See if you can find examples of these two kinds among your samples. Use the hand lens.

Now you can see one thing fabrics have in common. Every fabric is made from pliable fibres or yarns which are linked together to give a flat, flexible, and fairly thin material.

Figure 17.3
Lawnmowers contain felt! It is used to carry oil for the bearings.

17.2 WHAT AFFECTS HOW A FABRIC BEHAVES?

Here are two questions to set you thinking.

Q 1
If two fabrics were made in the same way, but one was made just of wool fibres and the other just of cotton, would they feel, look, and behave the same?

Q 2
If wool fibres were used for two materials, but one was made thick and heavy and the other thin, open, and light, would each fabric be just as good for making an overcoat?

To help you answer these questions try looking at some actual fabrics.

YOU WILL NEED:

10 cm × 10 cm samples of
fine worsted fabric
hairy tweed
flannelette
scrim
Hand lens

Q 3
The worsted and the tweed are both made from all wool. What differences do you notice?

Figure 17.4
Felt can be cut and shaped under moist heat and pressure, so it is ideal for making hats. These hats are all made of felt except the policeman's helmet.

1 Compare the worsted fabric and the tweed. Feel their texture; look at them carefully. Use a hand lens for a closer look.

2 Do the same with the flannelette and the scrim.

A fabric's properties, or behaviour, depend both on what it is made from and how it is made.

Q 4
Flannelette and scrim are both made from cotton. What do you notice?

Q 5
Do fabric properties depend just on the type of fibre used?

Q 6
Does the thickness of the yarns and the way they are linked together make any difference to the fabric?

Q 7
Are there any differences between the wool fabrics and the cotton fabrics? (Clue: try creasing them.)

17.3 NONWOVEN FABRICS

All fabrics contain fibres. Usually the fibres are twisted together to make yarns, and then the yarns are woven or knitted into cloth. But this is not always the case. Sometimes the fibres are made straight into fabrics. Wool felt, probably the oldest of all cloths, is made like this. So are some of the most recently invented fabrics.

Have a close look at some felt and some modern nonwoven fabrics. How are the fibres arranged?

YOU WILL NEED:

Felt and other nonwoven fabrics
Powerful hand lens or microscope
Needle or pin

1 Handle each of your fabrics. Try stretching them gently. Test them for flexibility.

Q 8
a Are the fabrics flexible or stiff?
b Do they go back into shape after stretching?

2 Look at the fabrics under a powerful lens or, better still, a microscope. (Worksheet M27 shows you how to use one.) Answer these questions for each of the fabrics examined.

Q 9
a How are the fibres arranged?
b Can you see any pattern, or are they all higgledy-piggledy?
c Are there any yarns?
d Do any of the fabrics seem to be made in layers?

3 Try unravelling an edge of each fabric with your pin.

Q 10
Was it easy to separate the fibres?

In all nonwoven fabrics, the trick is to make the fibres cling together in a flat sheet. But how is this done? With wool felt it is comparatively easy. If you have ever washed a woollen sweater and found that it had gone matted, you are half way to the answer. Wool is covered with tiny scales which open in hot, soapy water to give each fibre a spiky, clinging surface. Pressure and rubbing is then all that is needed to make the wool fibres lock together or 'felt'.

Most fibres do not have spikes, so something different is needed to stop them separating. Sometimes several very thin webs of loose fibres are laid over one another and glued together to give what is called an 'adhesive-bonded fabric'. Another method of turning a sheet of loose fibres into a cloth is to pass it through a needle-punching machine. In this, thousands of barbed needles move quickly up and down, punching through the sheet and pulling out little tufts of fibres. Each tuft is like a tiny rivet, holding the sheet of fibres together.

Because their structure is similar, many nonwoven fabrics have similar properties. A good point is that they do not fray, so edges need no finishing. But the firm fixing of the fibres, which stops fraying, has a bad side as well. Since the fibres cannot slide easily over one another, most nonwoven fabrics are stiff. They do not drape in soft folds. More serious still is their lack of elasticity. Once stretched out of shape, the nonwovens stay stretched.

But there are plenty of uses where stretchiness is not important. Modern adhesive-bonded fabrics are widely used for interlinings and cleaning cloths, while needle-punched fabrics are made into filters, waddings, and underfelts. Wool felt is even used for clothes, though these must not be too tight-fitting or they would stretch out of shape or go baggy. The pictures on the previous page show some other uses.

Q 11
What clothes do you think could successfully be made from felt?

17.4
WOVEN FABRICS

Most fabrics are not made directly from fibres. Instead the fibres are first twisted into yarns or threads. Then the yarns are woven or knitted to make fabrics. A woven cloth has two sets of yarns crossing each other at right angles. Knitted fabrics have interlacing loops of yarn.

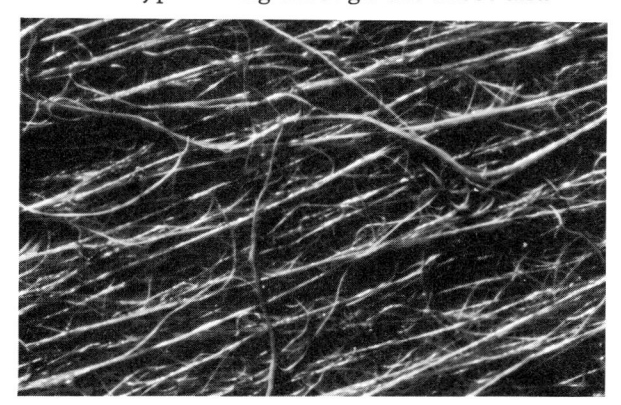

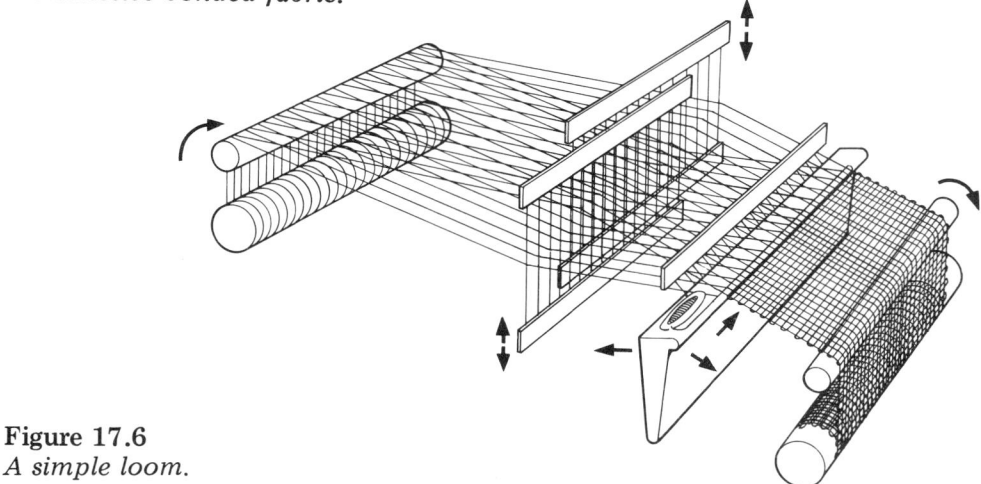

Figure 17.5
An adhesive-bonded fabric.

Figure 17.6
A simple loom.

Figure 17.7
Mending a broken warp thread on a modern loom.

In weaving, the warp threads are usually stronger than the weft threads. Warp threads run down the length of the cloth, parallel to its selvedge. Weft threads go over and under the warp, to form the cloth. The order in which the yarns cross over each other makes a pattern called a 'weave'. When yarns are woven together to produce cloth, the threads can still slip over one another. They can bend and stretch in different directions as the fabric is moved about. This is why woven fabrics are flexible and can take up different shapes.

By using different yarns and weaves, and by altering the spacing between threads, fabrics can be woven to show all sorts of repeating designs. Different weaves also give different properties of stiffness, roughness, lustre, elasticity, smoothness, and stretch.

Investigating weaves
Here is how you can discover the interlacing pattern of some simple weaves.

YOU WILL NEED:
Fabric samples labelled A, B, and C
Pieces of squared paper with 10 squares per side
Magnifying glass or hand lens
Fine needle

1 Take sample A and pull out a few warp and weft threads, to leave a small fringe all round.

2 Use a magnifying glass as in figure 17.8 to look at how the weave pattern is made.

Figure 17.8

3 Use the needle as a pointer to help follow the threads as they pass over and under one another. Record the weave patterns on squared paper. Warp threads run up and down the fabric parallel to the selvedge. Weft threads run across the fabric, as figure 17.9 shows.

Figure 17.9

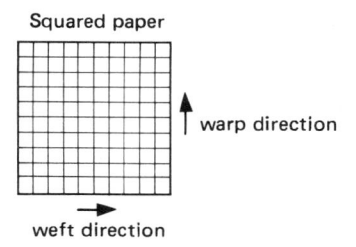

4 Plot the way the warp threads weave. If the warp yarn goes *over* the weft, shade in the corresponding square for each thread. If the warp yarn goes *under* the weft, leave that square blank.

5 Fill in each column of squares for a different warp yarn, until 10 columns have been filled in. Label the paper with an A and put it to one side.

Q 12
Does the pattern repeat itself?

6 Record the weave of fabric samples B and C on squared paper in the same way.

7 When you have finished, compare the squared papers from the three samples. Your

records should show repeating patterns similar to those in figure 17.10.

Figure 17.10

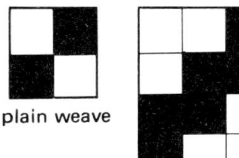

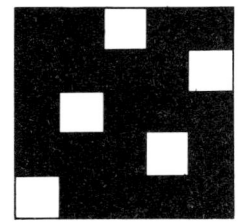

plain weave

twill weave

satin weave

Q 13
a Can you identify the weave used in each of your samples?
b Which weave was the most shiny?
c Which stretched most easily?
d Which tended to be the most flexible?
e Which was the smoothest?

Figure 17.11
If you were to look at a piece of woven fabric along the edge you might see something like this.

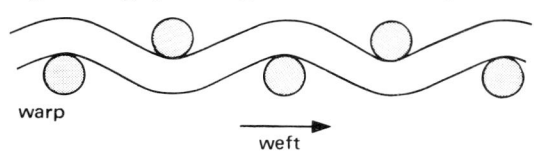

warp

weft

Try stretching the three fabrics. As you pull, yarns straighten, allowing the cloth to stretch. The more the yarns interlace, the more will be their 'crimp' and the greater will be the stretchiness of the fabric.

Q 14
Did your answer to question 13c agree with this?

Plain weave fabrics will tend to have more 'give' to them than satins because they have more interlacings. Twills come about half way between the more stretchy plain weaves and the firmer satins.

17.5
KNITTED FABRICS

In knitted fabrics there are no rows of yarns crossing at right angles. Instead there are rows of loops which interlock to form a fabric.

The simplest kind of knitted fabric, called weft-knitted fabric, is made with one single length of thread. The rows of loops run across the fabric. You can do weft-knitting yourself, using two needles. Weft-knitting is also swiftly made by large machines in the clothing industry as figure 17.12 shows.

Figure 17.12
A circular weft-knitting machine.

Warp-knitting is more complicated. It can only be made by machine, and uses many threads, each with its own needle. The row of needles runs the whole width of the fabric. The rows of loops are made down the length of the cloth instead of across it.

Figure 17.13
a The structure of weft-knitted fabric.
b Warp-knitted fabric.

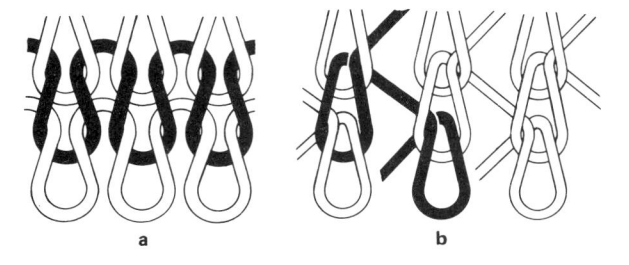

104

Investigating the stretchiness of knitted fabrics
Stretchiness is an important property of fabrics, and determines their use. (If your overcoat stretched as much as a pair of socks it would cause you problems!) How much do knitted fabrics stretch?

YOU WILL NEED:

Knitted garments — a selection of fine and coarse, plain and fancy knits
Ruler
Tailor's chalk or pins

1 Draw a 10-cm square on each of the garments with tailors' chalk. Or mark it out with pins. The sides of the square should run exactly up and across the rows of loops.

2 Draw the diagonals of the square (lines from corner to corner). Measure 10 cm along both diagonals with a ruler and mark it with chalk. A diagonal line across a fabric is called 'on the bias'.

3 Now see how far the garments will stretch (don't tear them) in a lengthwise, crosswise, or bias direction. Pull the garments along the chalk lines, and measure how much longer each line has become with the ruler.

4 Record your results in a table like figure 17.14 below.

Q 15
In which direction did most of the garments stretch:
a most?
b least?

Q 16
Do ribbed garments stretch more along or across the ribs?

Q 17
a Have any of the garments not fully recovered from the stretching?
b What are they made of? (Look at the garment label.)

Figure 17.14

Very stretchy knitted fabrics which recover well from stretching are used in clothing where a close fit is important, such as socks, gloves, hats, and skinny rib sweaters.

Less stretchy knitted fabrics are used in clothes which don't have to fit so closely to the body, such as skirts and jackets. Knitted fabrics are often used in place of woven fabrics because the slight 'give' or stretch of knitted fabrics is more comfortable to wear.

The softness and close fit of knitted fabrics are useful in medicine. Knitted fabrics are also used to cover seats in cars, trains, and the home.

Figure 17.15
A knitted head bandage.

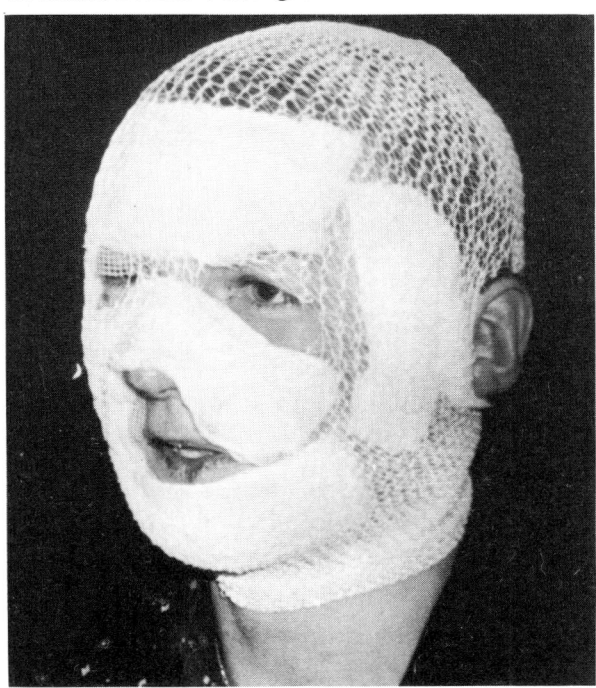

Q 18
a Make a list of the clothes you are wearing.
b Which garments are knitted?
c Which garments are woven?

Garment	Stretched from 10 cm to ... lengthwise	crosswise	Stretched from ... to ... bias
Pullover			to
Tights			to

CHAPTER 18

Yarns

18.1
THE IMPORTANCE OF YARNS

In Chapter 17 you saw that changing the way the yarns interlace changes the fabric. Each weave pattern has its own properties, and knitted and woven fabrics look and feel completely different. But what about differences between the yarns themselves? Shouldn't they affect how a fabric behaves?

How do yarn properties affect how a fabric behaves?

1 Make a table like the one below.

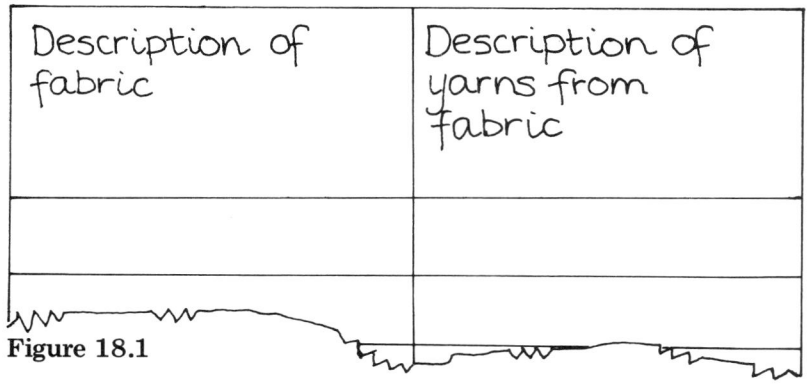

Description of fabric	Description of yarns from fabric

Figure 18.1

YOU WILL NEED:

Samples of woven fabrics
Needle or pin for unpicking
Hand lens

Q 1
Is there a connection between the yarns and the way the fabrics look and feel?

2 Look at each fabric and decide how to describe it. Is it thick, thin, soft, hairy, or smooth? Write a description of each fabric in the first column of the table.

3 Using the needle or pin, pull out warp and weft yarns from each fabric in turn. Look at the yarns carefully with your hand lens. Are they thick, thin, wirelike, soft, hairy, or smooth? Are warp and weft yarns always the same? Write down what you find in the second column of the table.

You have seen that yarns are not all the same. They can be made thicker or thinner by twisting more or less fibres together. They can be made to feel hard or soft by altering the amount of twist. Tight twisting gives a hard wirelike thread. Loose twisting produces a much softer yarn. Other characteristics such as warmth, weight, or texture can be altered by changing the type of fibres used to make the yarn.

Now look at figure 18.2. It shows how thickness can be built up by twisting or plying several single yarns together.

A textile manufacturer can make a huge range of cloths by using different types of yarn, and by altering knit or weave patterns. For any use the right combination of the yarn and construction must be found. The fabric must be suited to the job.

Figure 18.2
Differences in yarns.

a single strand (ply)
b two-ply
c four-ply
d multi-ply
e cable yarn
(3 strands of multi-ply)

So, to be able to make fabrics for different purposes, the manufacturer needs to know a lot about yarns. He must know what fibres they should be made from. He must also know how much twist yarns should be given and what thickness they should be. He will have found out how much stress and strain the yarns can stand, and how long they are likely to last in normal and extra hard wear. (See figure 18.4!)

18.2 LOOKING AT FIBRE LENGTHS IN YARNS

YOU WILL NEED:
Fabric samples A and B
Ruler
Needle or pin for unpicking

1 Unpick a yarn from the edge of sample A and measure its length.

2 Untwist the yarn so that it starts to come to pieces. Pull gently as you untwist. Try to get as many separate fibres as you can. Be sure not to snap any fibres by pulling too hard.

3 Measure the length of the fibres you have separated.

4 The first yarn you looked at might not be typical, so untwist another yarn from Fabric A and measure its fibres.

Q 2
Are all the fibres the same length as the original yarn, or are most of them shorter?

Q 3
Are the results from the first yarn the same as the second one?

5 Measure two yarns taken from Fabric B. Then untwist them and measure their fibres.

Q 4
Are the fibres from Fabric B the same length as the yarns, or are they shorter?

Q 5
Have you noticed any special difference between the yarns from Fabrics A and B? What is this difference?

Figure 18.3
Fine yarns generally make fine fabrics; heavy yarns make heavy fabrics.

Figure 18.4

107

Textile fibres come in two basic sorts — the long and the short. The long fibres can be thousands of metres in length without a break, and so are called 'continuous filaments'. Silk from the spinnerets of the silk worm is a natural continuous filament. All other continuous filaments used in textiles are man-made. Short fibres, such as wool and cotton, are only a few centimetres long. They are called *staple fibres*. Some yarns are made from the long continuous filaments; some from the shorter staple fibres.

If the same filaments run right through a yarn, very little twist is required to keep them together. But shorter staple fibres have to be twisted (or spun) more tightly to hold them together. Otherwise the yarn will fall to pieces. So continuous-filament yarns need less twist than staple-fibre (or spun) yarns.

But let's get back to Fabrics A and B. One is made from continuous-filament yarns and one from spun yarns.

Q 6
Can you decide which fabric had the continuous-filament yarns? Which had the spun ones?

Figure 18.5
a A spun yarn is made from short fibres. Twisting is needed to stop the yarn coming to pieces.
b A continuous-filament yarn has fibres which run its entire length without a break. Very little twist is needed to keep the filaments together.

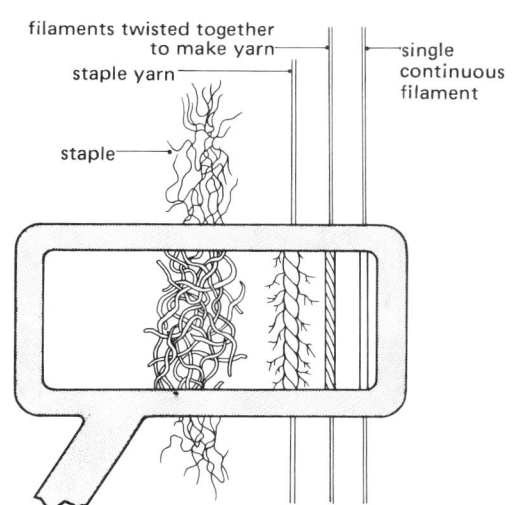

18.3
COMPARING DIFFERENT YARNS

YOU WILL NEED:

Fabric samples A and B, as used in section 18.2
Several different spun yarns
Several different continuous-filament yarns
Hand lens

1 Pull out one yarn from Fabric A and one from Fabric B. Look at them side by side, using the hand lens.

2 Move the hand lens slowly along the length of each yarn. Look for slight changes in thickness.

3 Compare the other spun and continuous-filament yarns in the same way.

Q 7
Which is the more even in thickness — a spun yarn or a continuous-filament yarn?

Q 8
Which type looks the more shiny?

Q 9
Which type has the greater number of loose ends of fibre sticking out?

Figure 18.6

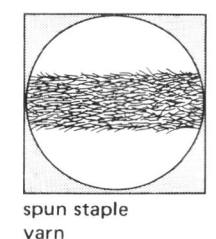

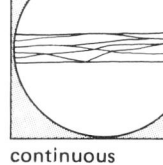

Because of their differences, spun and continuous-filament yarns are often put to different uses. The loose fibre ends in spun yarns give a fabric a soft, fluffy feel, warm to the touch. This is useful for things like coats, sweaters, and some kinds of furnishings. Continuous-filament yarns are particularly good where a smooth, shiny cloth is required.

Sometimes man-made continuous filaments are chopped into short lengths before being spun into yarn. This makes a softer-feeling fabric. (See figure 18.7.)

Figure 18.7
This skirt and top are both made of man-made fibre.

Continuous-filament yarns can be altered to look and feel more like staple-fibre yarns. One of the ways of doing this is to force the straight yarn against itself in a heated 'stuffer box', so that the filaments buckle and form crimps or coils. This makes the filaments take up more space. Yarns made like this are said to be 'bulked'. (Pull a thread out of a pair of old tights to see the bulked yarn.) (See OHP M29.)

Figure 18.8
A 'stuffer box'.

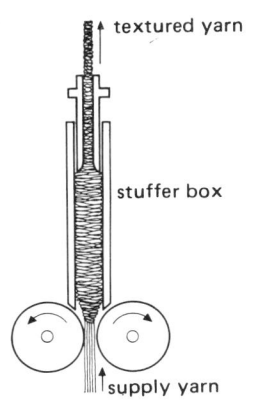

Bulked yarns can be very stretchy, and so make stretchy fabrics. These are used for socks, tights, underwear, and stretch covers on furniture.

Figure 18.9
Gymnasts need stretchy clothing. (Emilia Eberle of Rumania at the 1980 Olympic Games.)

Figure 18.10
Some fabrics can stretch a surprising amount! (The photograph was taken at a rugby match between Llanelli and the All Blacks in 1980.)

Figure 18.11
These coats are made of man-made fibres and cotton.

18.4
BLENDS AND MIXTURES

Yarns are not always made entirely of just one type of fibre. Sometimes they have two or more types. You may have a yarn containing both cotton and polyester fibres. Other yarns may be made of wool and nylon. Many socks and jerseys are made of yarns which are a mixture of wool and nylon. Shirts, sheets, and pillowcases are often made of cotton and polyester.

Different fibres can be combined to make yarns in two ways — by blending or by mixing.

In a blended yarn, the different types of fibre are combined before spinning. The blend is fed into the spinning machine, which twists two or more types of fibre together into a single yarn. The fibres can be in any proportion the manufacturer wants.

Figure 18.12
In blended-fibre yarns all types of fibre present in the complete yarn are found in each ply.

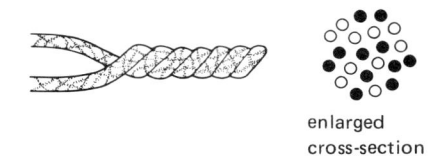

enlarged cross-section

In a mixed yarn, two or more plies are twisted together. Each ply contains only its own particular type of fibre. A mixed cotton and rayon two-ply would contain one ply made entirely of (100 per cent) cotton and one made entirely of (100 per cent) rayon.

Figure 18.13
In a mixed yarn the different fibres are in separate plies.

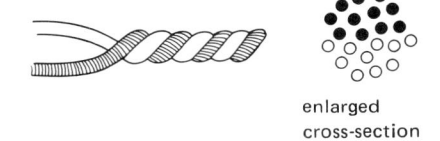

enlarged cross-section

Figure 18.14
School clothes need to be practical and hard-wearing. They often contain blended or mixed-fibre yarns to combine desirable properties. Look at the labels in your clothes and check for yourself.

By careful blending and mixing, yarns can be made which combine the better properties of each of the fibres used. For instance, in a wool and nylon blend, the nylon is there because it is hard-wearing. The wool makes the blend softer to the touch.

18.5 YARNS FOR SPECIAL EFFECTS

The appearance and feel of a fabric can be completely altered by the use of 'special-effect' yarns. These are ply yarns into which loops, curls, twists, or slubs (thickened areas) have been purposely introduced. Usually a 'special-effect' yarn has three parts: the core ply, the binder ply, and the effect ply.

Figure 18.15

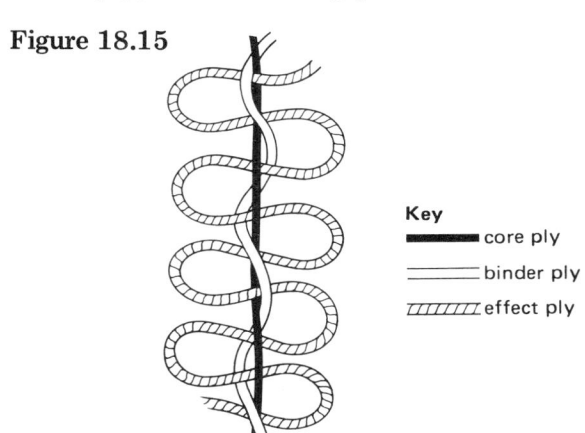

Key
— core ply
= binder ply
▨ effect ply

Figure 18.16
Terylene net curtains made of a simple 'special-effect' yarn.

But let's look at some actual yarns.

YOU WILL NEED:

A selection of 'special-effect' yarns
Fabric samples
Pin
Hand lens

1 Look at each yarn and decide how to describe it. Does it have loops, twists, or knots? Can you see any slubs (thick, lightly-twisted parts)? Does it spiral? Or does it corkscrew?

Figure 18.17
A 'spiral' yarn.

Figure 18.18
A 'corkscrew' yarn.

2 Use the pin to separate the core, binder, and effect plies. Look through the lens and try to decide how the special effect was created.

3 Read the yarn labels.

Q 10
Is there any connection between fibre content and the way a particular yarn looks and feels?

Q 11
Compare the prices of your selection of yarns. Can you decide why some yarns are cheaper than others?

4 Compare the two fabrics given to you by your teacher. Look closely at the yarns used.

Q 12
How have the texture and appearance been created in each case?

Your teacher may give you a worksheet (M30) for this section.

CHAPTER 19
Textile fibres

19.1
FIBRES IN TEXTILES

To be of any use in the textile industry, fibres must be reasonably strong, flexible, and resistant to common household chemicals such as soap and other detergents. But above all, fibres must be thin in comparison with their length, so that they can easily twist around each other and cling together in the stable yarns needed for the manufacture of woven and knitted cloth. To make acceptable yarns, fibres must be at least a thousand times as long as they are thick (length-to-thickness ratio of at least 1000:1).

There are many fibres in nature. But very few have all the properties needed to make good quality fabric.

Figure 19.1
Charts of some of the main types of natural and man-made fibres.

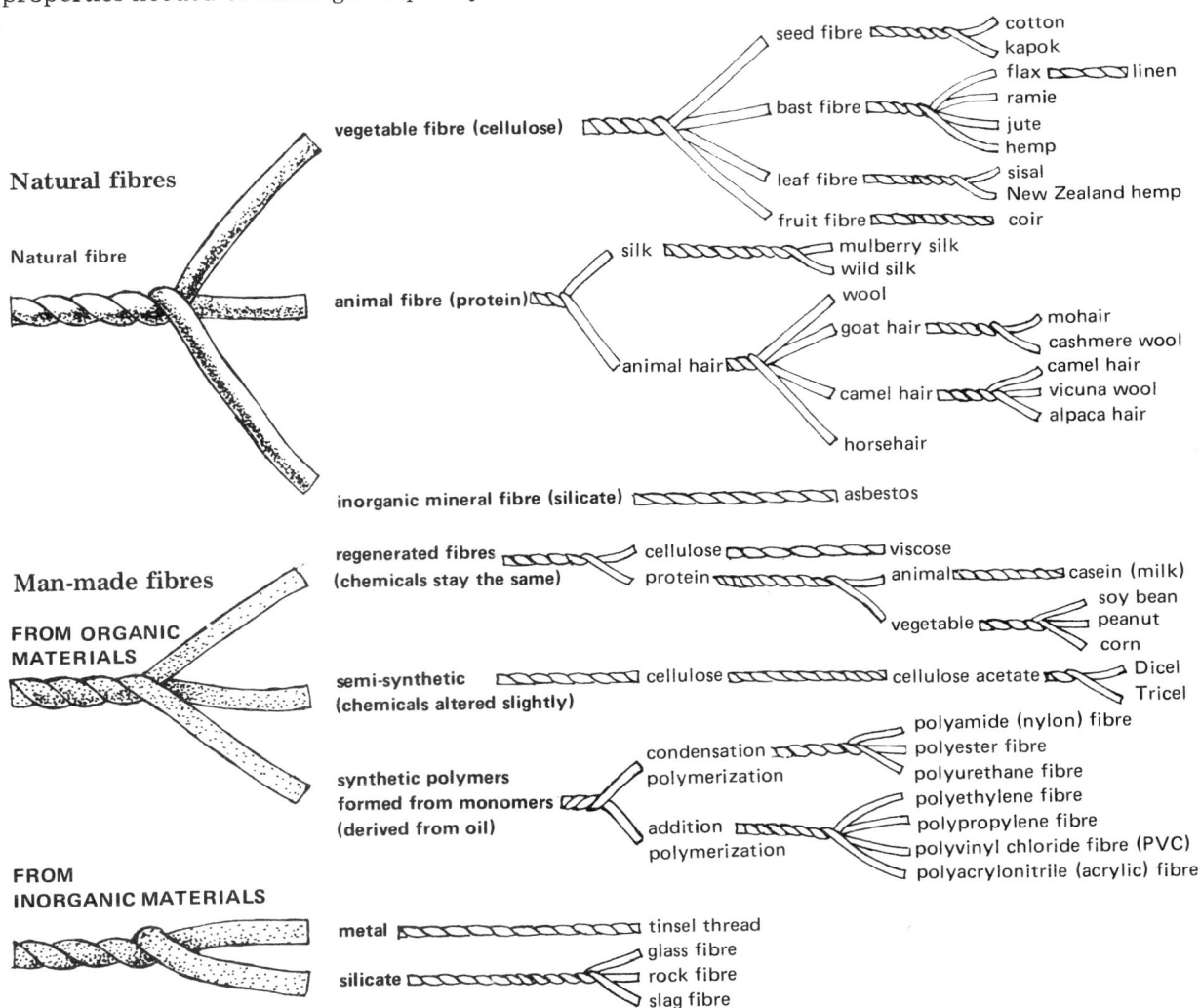

Natural fibres

- Natural fibre
  - vegetable fibre (cellulose)
    - seed fibre — cotton, kapok
    - bast fibre — flax → linen, ramie, jute, hemp
    - leaf fibre — sisal, New Zealand hemp
    - fruit fibre — coir
  - animal fibre (protein)
    - silk — mulberry silk, wild silk
    - animal hair — wool; goat hair → mohair, cashmere wool; camel hair → camel hair, vicuna wool, alpaca hair; horsehair
  - inorganic mineral fibre (silicate) — asbestos

Man-made fibres

FROM ORGANIC MATERIALS

- regenerated fibres (chemicals stay the same)
  - cellulose — viscose
  - protein — animal → casein (milk); vegetable → soy bean, peanut, corn
- semi-synthetic (chemicals altered slightly)
  - cellulose — cellulose acetate — Dicel, Tricel
- synthetic polymers formed from monomers (derived from oil)
  - condensation polymerization — polyamide (nylon) fibre, polyester fibre, polyurethane fibre
  - addition polymerization — polyethylene fibre, polypropylene fibre, polyvinyl chloride fibre (PVC), polyacrylonitrile (acrylic) fibre

FROM INORGANIC MATERIALS

- metal — tinsel thread
- silicate — glass fibre, rock fibre, slag fibre

112

Fibres seen under magnification

Cotton ×360

Silk ×900

Wool ×200

×900

Fibre	Typical fibre length	Typical fibre thickness	Approximate ratio of length to thickness
Cotton	2.5 cm	0.018 mm	1400 to 1
Silk	often over 1000 m	0.010 mm	very large
Wool	7.5 cm	0.025 mm	3000 to 1

Table 19.1 *Sizes of natural fibres.*

These traditional natural fibres are still used for clothing and household textiles. But increasing use is made of the man-made fibres produced by twentieth-century technology.

Man-made materials could be made in almost any shape or size, but they are usually formed into filaments of about the same range of thickness as the natural fibres. Experience has shown that these thicknesses are just about right to make yarns.

Tricel

Terylene

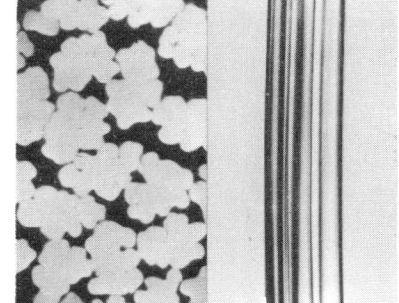

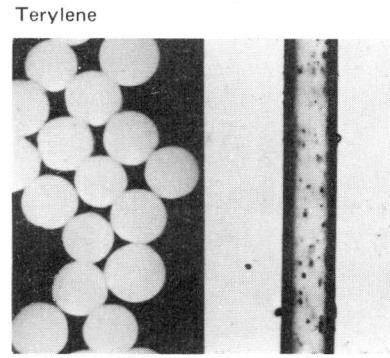

Figure 19.2 (above)
The most important natural textile fibres are cotton, wool, and silk. Here are pictures of what they come from and what they look like under a microscope.

Figure 19.3 (right)
Man-made fibres can be made in a variety of shapes.

19.2
DON'T FORGET FABRIC STRUCTURE

Because individual fibres are so delicate, you will find it easier to study their properties after they have been made into fabrics. But it would not be scientific to experiment on a haphazard collection of fabrics. If you used all sorts of weaves and thicknesses, it would be difficult to decide which properties were due to fibre content and which to fabric structure. To make a fair comparison of fibre properties, all the fabric samples should have the same weave and, as nearly as possible, the same yarn thickness and spacing.

Figure 19.4
In these three fabrics differences in structure would make it difficult to recognize differences in fibre properties.

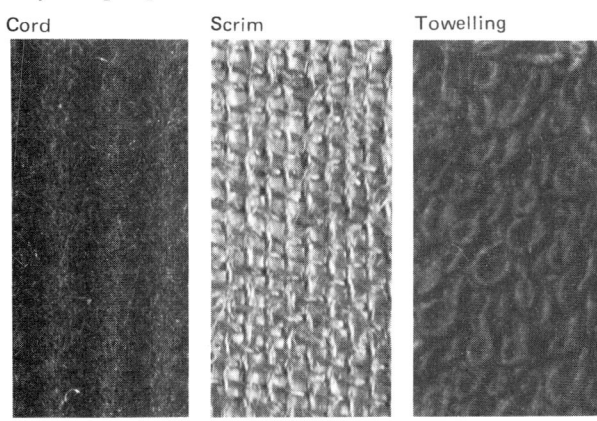

Cord   Scrim   Towelling

Figure 19.5
A wear-testing machine in Marks and Spencer's laboratories.

19.3
WEAR-TESTING

Fabrics often have to stand up to a lot of hard wear. So it is a good idea to know which fibres and fabrics wear best.

Clothes manufacturers and retailers need to know how well their fabrics will wear. For instance, Marks and Spencer do extensive tests on the clothes they sell. In their laboratory, special equipment submits textiles to all sorts of different treatments, including rubbing, stretching, pulling, snagging, tearing, and washing. People are sometimes asked to wear clothes, and to report on fit, comfort, and how well they behave in use. Marks and Spencer also test all their other products. Tests like these are part of 'quality control' to maintain standards and keep their customers satisfied.

Here is how you can find out about wear for yourself.

YOU WILL NEED:

Fabrics of different fibre content but similar thickness and construction
Wear machine
Low voltage power supply
Ruler
Scissors

1 Mark out and cut the fabric samples to fit the wear machine. Fix them around the rim of the wheel.

2 Connect the wear machine to the low voltage supply and switch on. After 5 minutes, stop the machine and examine the samples. If no wear shows up, switch on again. Continue doing this until several of the fabrics have clear signs of wear.

3 Take the samples off the wheel and lay them out side by side. Try to arrange the fabrics in ascending order of wear, with the least worn to the left, and the most worn to the right. Number the fabrics from left to right, so that fabric 1 is the least worn (the hardest-wearing), fabric 2 is the next least worn, and so on.

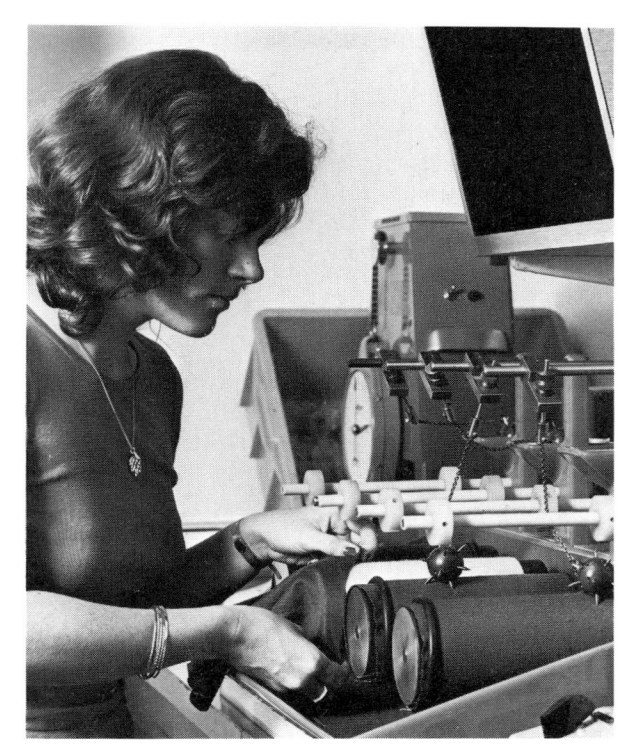

Figure 19.6
Testing for snagging at Marks and Spencer's.

4   Enter your findings in a table like the one below. (Remember that these results can only be taken as a rough guide, because you are working with fabrics and not directly with fibres.)

Figure 19.7

Fibre content of fabric	Order of resistance to wear

Hard-wearing fabrics are needed for a lot of different uses in daily life. As you learned in Chapter 18, blended fabrics are made from more than one type of fibre. This means that the good qualities from both fibres can be combined. Each fibre is chosen to make up for shortcomings in the other. Hard-wearing fibres are frequently combined with more fragile fibres to give a longer-lasting cloth.

Q 1
Which man-made fibres are often combined with wool to give better wear performance in socks, trousers, and sweaters?

19.4
THE EFFECT OF HEAT ON FABRICS

It is very important to know how fibres behave at high temperatures to avoid unnecessary damage while tumble-drying or ironing them. Try the following experiment to find out which fibres are sensitive to the temperatures reached during ironing.

YOU WILL NEED:

Selection of fabrics, each of known fibre content, cut into 5 cm × 5 cm squares (2 squares of each fabric)
Cooking foil
Scissors
Electric iron
Ironing board with heat-resistant stand
Watch or clock with seconds hand
Tweezers

1   Switch on the iron, and set it to the highest setting. Put the iron on its stand to heat up.

2   Fold the first fabric sample in two.

3   Cut out a square of cooking foil, 10 cm × 10 cm, fold it in two, and tuck the fabric sample inside.

4   Put the foil with the sample tucked inside it on the heat-resistant stand. Hold the iron down on it for exactly one minute.

5   Lift up the iron (take care — it will be very hot), and remove the hot foil with tweezers.

6   Open the foil and look for changes to the fabric. Compare it with a fresh piece of the same fabric.

7   Test all the other fabrics in the same way, recording your results like this.

Figure 19.8

Fibre content of fabric	Change, if any, caused by contact with hot iron

Q 2
Which fibres need to be ironed at a low setting?

Clothes usually have a care label sewn into them which gives washing information. It also tells you the recommended iron setting for different fabrics.

19.5 FLAMMABILITY OF FIBRES

Many deaths and injuries are still caused by clothes catching fire. Some fabrics catch fire so easily that they will burst into flames at the least contact with fire. Even fabrics which do not burn readily will often burn while actually in a flame, though they may go out when removed. Clothes must always be kept well away from any open fire or other source of heat.

A thick, heavy cloth will burn more slowly than a thin, lightweight one of the same material. But the flammability of a fabric depends mainly on the type of fibre it is made from.

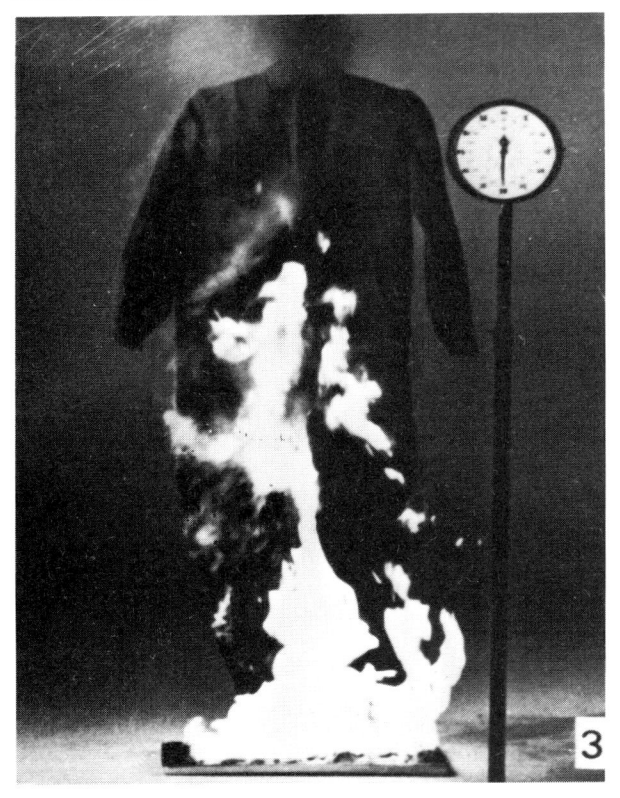

Figure 19.9
A cotton overall with a flame-retardant finish was burning like this after 30 seconds in one test.

You can do tests yourself by burning fabrics made of different fibres to test their flammabilities. (The older word 'inflammable' is not used here because some people think it means non-flammable.)

YOU WILL NEED:
Fabric samples
Scrap paper
Ruler
Ballpoint pen
Scissors
Wire cooling stand
Two clean, empty tins of the same size
Bulldog clip
Old baking tray
Small stapling machine
Matches
Stopwatch
Ovencloth

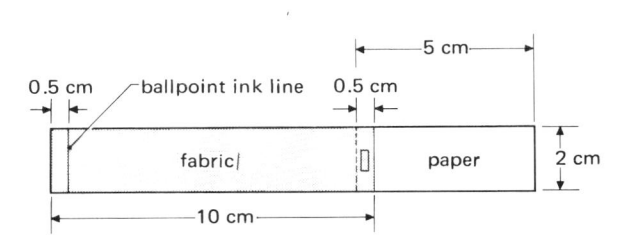

Figure 19.10
Sample testing strip.

1 Cut a 10 cm × 2 cm strip from the first fabric to be tested. Mark ballpoint ink lines as shown, measuring the distances carefully with a ruler. Use a staple to attach a paper 'fuse' made to the size shown. The experiment will not be a fair test unless you make all the fabric samples in exactly the same way. They must also all be the same size.

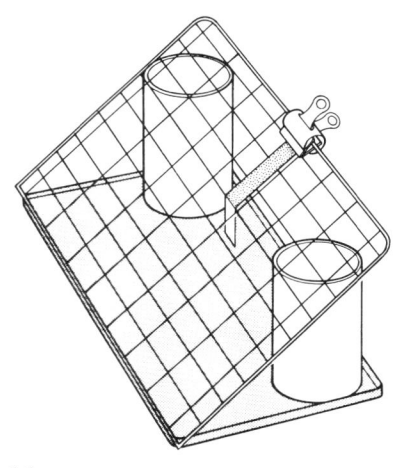

Figure 19.11
Burning frame.

116

2 Set up the cooling stand as shown in figure 19.11 so that it makes a sloping burning grid. The old baking sheet goes underneath to prevent any damage to the working surface.

3 Fasten the fabric to the top of the grid with a bulldog clip. Check that the edges of the jaws are level with the top ink line. Smooth the fabric sample down the grid, and at a convenient point tuck the paper fuse through the mesh, so that it hangs down as in figure 19.11.

4 Light the bottom of the fuse, taking care to keep your clothing and hair well out of harm's way. Have the stopwatch ready, and start it immediately the black of the burning fuse reaches the bottom of the fabric.

5 Stop the watch when the black of the 'flame front' reaches the jaws of the bulldog clip. Record the time taken for the sample to burn. If the flames go out before reaching the top of the sample, do not bother with the time, but instead measure the length of fabric left unburnt. Write the results in a table drawn up in the way shown below.

Figure 19.12

Fibre content of fabric	Time taken if burning complete (seconds)	Length left unburned if burning incomplete (cm)

6 Open the clip, using an ovencloth if the fabric burned right up to the top, and clean away any ash with a spent match.

7 Test the rest of the fabric samples in the same way.

8 Draw up a table as shown and list each of the fibres tested in the correct column.

Figure 19.13

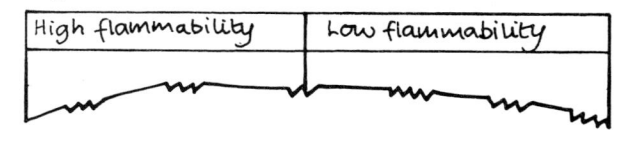

High flammability	Low flammability

Q 3
What fabrics would you avoid if you were buying material to make a child's nightie?

19.6 CREASE RECOVERY

Clothes must not crease too easily if they are to look good when they are worn. The fabrics from which they are made must be able to recover quickly from the folds and creases which happen in wear. Crease recovery largely depends on the type of fibre, but cloth structure is also important. To make a fair comparison, crease recovery tests must be carried out on fabrics which are as nearly as possible the same. Try the following activity to see how different fabrics compare for crease recovery.

YOU WILL NEED:

10 cm × 10 cm samples of fabrics with different fibre content but similar construction

1 In turn squeeze each of the samples into the tightest ball you can manage.

Figure 19.14

2 Lay out the samples side by side on a flat surface. Arrange them in order, starting at the left with those showing the greatest crease recovery. Fabrics at the lefthand end of the line have good crease recovery. Those in the middle, fair, and those at the right, poor.

3 Make a table of your results like the one below. Put a tick in the correct column.

Figure 19.15

Fibre content of fabric	Good crease recovery	Fair crease recovery	Poor crease recovery

117

CHAPTER 20

Fabrics and colour

Figure 20.1
A nineteenth-century batik sarong from Indonesia.

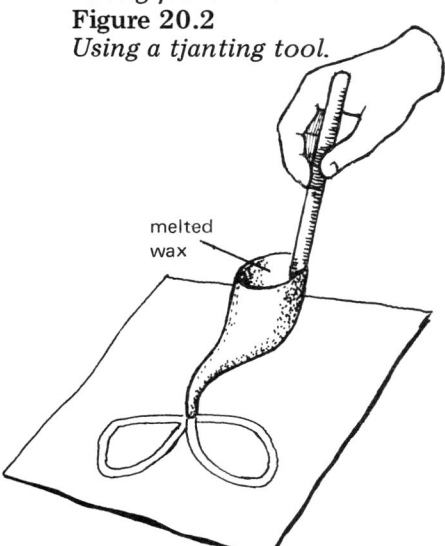

Figure 20.2
Using a tjanting tool.

20.1
DYES

One of the most important uses for dyes is to colour fabrics. Usually, the colour is just for decoration. This is the case with the beautiful Indonesian fabric shown in figure 20.1 below.

You can see from the picture how colour and pattern are used in batik design.

Batik is a method of dyeing invented centuries ago in Java. A pattern is drawn or brushed on the fabric with melted wax. Usually this is done with a *tjanting* tool. The brass nib is filled with melted wax, and used to 'paint' a pattern on the fabric.

The waxed parts of the cloth do not pick up any dye, leaving a white pattern on the dyed material.

But sometimes fabrics are coloured for more practical reasons. Motorway policemen wear clothes dyed in bright colours, so that they are easily seen (see figure 20.4).

The browns and greens of a soldier's combat uniform are selected for the opposite reason. His clothes must match his surroundings to make it hard for the enemy to spot him (see figure 20.3).

No one knows exactly when dyeing started, but the earliest pieces of dyed fabric found come from ancient Egypt and date back 5500 years.

Figure 20.3
Colour and pattern for safety.

Figure 20.4

Figure 20.5a
The woad plant makes a blue dye.
Figure 20.5b
The madder plant produces a red dye.

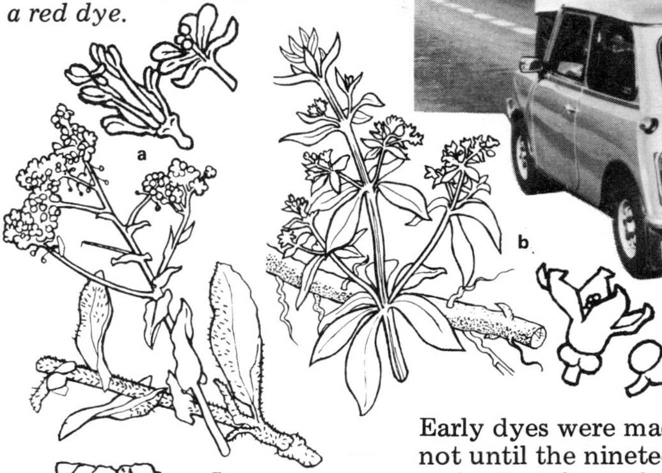

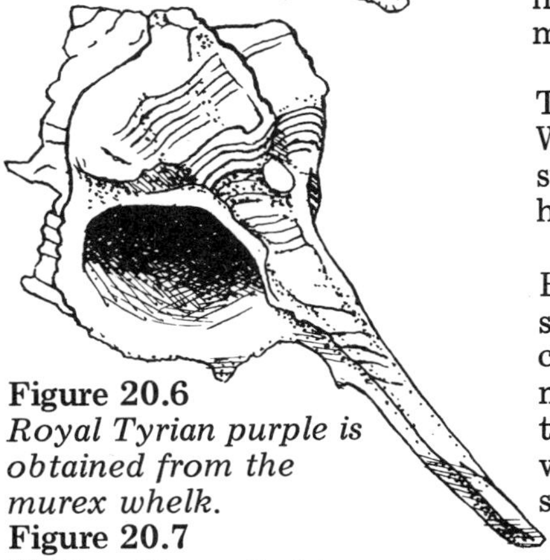

Figure 20.6
Royal Tyrian purple is obtained from the murex whelk.
Figure 20.7
William Henry Perkin (1838–1907).

Early dyes were made from plants, animals, and minerals. It was not until the nineteenth century that scientists learned how to make dyes from chemicals.

The first synthetic dye was discovered accidentally in 1856 by William Henry Perkin, an eighteen-year-old chemistry student, experimenting in a rough-and-ready laboratory he had set up at home.

He was working on substances obtained from coal-tar, when he saw a bright lilac colour form. This was the dye which was later called mauveine. With his father, Perkin built a factory to manufacture the new dye. Before he was twenty he was well on the way to making his fortune. By the time he was thirty-six he was able to retire from business and concentrate on scientific research.

Perkin's chance discovery led to the giant synthetic dye industry of today. Chemical dyes are cheaper and often more effective than those made from plants and animals, so most dyeing is now done with synthetic dyes. (See OHP M33 for more information.)

20.2
DYEING WITH NATURAL DYES

Although most dyes are now synthetic, it is still fun to try colouring fabrics with natural substances. All sorts of things (leaves, berries, flowers) will give a colour, so there is plenty of scope for experimenting on your own. Most natural dyes need the help of a special chemical compound (mordant) to work really well. Mordants are chemicals that fix the dye firmly to a cloth. Try out one of the dyes described below.

Caution: wear an overall for all dyeing activities.
Accidental splashes of dye can stain your clothes badly.

YOU WILL NEED:

Tin(II) chloride and cream of tartar for the mordant
Blackcurrants or elder leaves for the dye
Undyed woollen fabric
Synthetic detergent powder

Measuring jug
Balance
Blender
Strainer
2 enamelled saucepans
Wooden spoon
5-ml (tea) spoon
Scissors
Spin drier
Iron
Overall

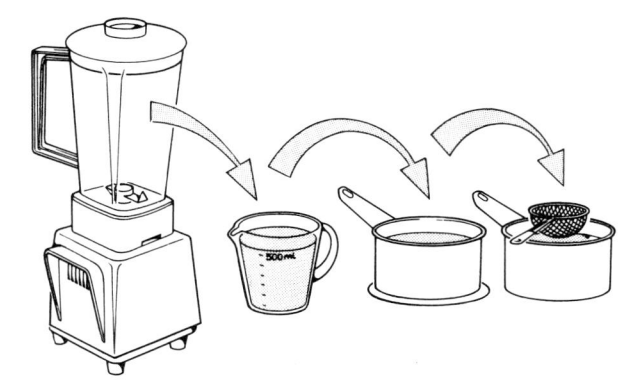

Figure 20.8

To make the dye

1 Put 30 g of the berries or leaves in a blender with a little water and liquidize them.

2 Empty into a measuring jug. Rinse out the blender with water, and pour it into the measuring jug.

3 Add extra water to make the dye up to 500 ml. Tip it into a saucepan and boil for at least 5 minutes.

4 Cool and strain into another saucepan. Your dye is now ready to use.

To make the mordant

1 Measure 500 ml of water in a jug and dissolve 0.5 g of tin(II) chloride and 2 g of cream of tartar in it.

Dyeing

1 Cut five small samples (5 cm × 5 cm) from the woollen cloth. (Five samples are needed because one is to be left undyed to show what the original cloth looked like, two are to be put in the mordant before dyeing, and two are to be dyed without mordant treatment.)

2 Pour the mordant into a clean saucepan and put in two of the fabric samples. Simmer for 10 minutes.

Figure 20.9

3 Lift out the pieces of cloth with a wooden spoon. Let the samples cool and then squeeze them gently to wring out surplus mordant.

4 Mark these samples by snipping off a corner from each.

5 Put the two mordanted samples and two untreated pieces into the dye bath. Simmer for 10 minutes. Lift out the samples with your wooden spoon. Save the dye for the next experiment.

Figure 20.10

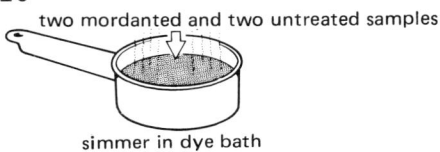

6 Rinse the samples under running cold water, then spin dry.

7 Wash two of your dyed samples, one mordanted and one not, in separate but equal amounts of hand-hot, soapy water. Rinse and spin dry.

Figure 20.11

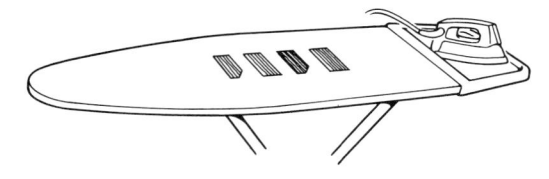

8 Iron all four dyed fabrics to finish off the drying. Compare all the samples carefully.

Q 1
Did the dye work on all the fabrics?

Q 2
Did the mordant affect the dyeing colour?

Q 3
Did the colour run when you washed the fabric?

Q 4
Did the mordant make any difference to how *fast* (non-fading) the dye was?

20.3 USING DIFFERENT MORDANTS

Here are some recipes for different mordants. What effect do they have on the dye colour?

Iron mordant:
1 g iron(II) sulphate
2 g cream of tartar
500 ml water

Alum mordant:
4 g alum
1 g cream of tartar
500 ml water

Try the next test to compare their results.

YOU WILL NEED:

Tin mordant and the mordant ingredients listed above
Dye used in section 20.2
Undyed woollen fabric

Enamelled saucepans (3 for class to share and one for each group)

Wooden spoon
5-ml (tea) spoon
Scissors
Measuring jug
Balance
Spin drier
Iron
Overall

1 Working in groups, make up alum, iron, and tin mordants. One saucepanful of each will do for everyone.

2 In each group, cut three 10 cm × 10 cm samples from the woollen cloth. Put each sample in a different mordant. Simmer for 10 minutes.

3 Remove the sample with a wooden spoon. Allow to cool, then squeeze out surplus mordant. Mark the samples with scissor cuts.

Figure 20.12

one sample from each group — alum mordant
one sample from each group — iron mordant
one sample from each group — tin mordant

Figure 20.13

iron mordant, alum mordant, tin mordant

4 Put the samples in the dye saved from section 20.2 and simmer for 10 minutes. Lift them out and rinse under cold running water. Spin dry and iron before comparing their colours.

Q 5
Does the mordant change the colour produced by the dye? Describe any differences carefully.

Save the fabrics to check whether the mordant used alters the rate of fading in sunlight.

20.4 CHOOSING YOUR DYE

Do dyes work equally well on all fibres? Today there are more textile fibres to choose from than ever before. But fibres can be very different in the ways they behave. How well do different fibres dye?

YOU WILL NEED:

Shop-bought dye (plus salt, washing soda, etc., as suggested by the manufacturer)
Samples of white cotton, wool, nylon, polyester, and acrylic fabrics
Scissors
Saucepan
Wooden spoon
15-ml (table) spoon
Measuring jug
Spin drier
Iron
Small knife or skewer (to pierce tin)
Overall
Rubber gloves

1 Make up the dye in a saucepan, following the manufacturer's instructions. Remember to add salt and washing soda if they say so.

2 Cut 10 cm × 10 cm samples from each fabric. Dye the samples, following the method suggested *exactly*.

3 When dyeing is finished, take out the specimens with the wooden spoon and rinse them three times under cold running water or until the water runs clear.

4 Dry the samples by spinning and ironing before comparing them.

Q 6
a Did each fabric dye to the same depth of colour?
b Did the fibre content make any difference?

Q 7
Did the manufacturers say which fibres would do best with the dye? If so, do you agree?

Different dyes suit different fibres. This can be a nuisance to industrial dyers, who have to make sure that a dye will work with the fibres to be coloured. But it can also be useful.

In cross-dyeing, for example, a fabric made from a mixture of fibres can be dyed in a variety of colours in a single bath. This is done by mixing a selection of dyes, each of which works with one particular type of fibre only.

Checks, plaids, and stripes are sometimes produced like this.

20.5
OVERDYEING

Can you always get the colour you want?

YOU WILL NEED:

Shop-bought cold water dye (plus salt, washing soda, etc., as suggested by the manufacturer)
Supply of hot water
Samples of cotton fabric of different colours
Washing powder

Scissors
Bowl or sink
Wooden spoon
15-ml (table) spoon
Measuring jug
Spin drier
Iron
Small knife or skewer (to pierce tin)
Overall
Rubber gloves

1 Cut two 10 cm × 10 cm samples from each of the fabrics you have chosen. Use one for dyeing, and keep one as the control, for comparing results later.

2 Make up the dye in the bowl, following the manufacturer's instructions. Don't forget the salt and washing soda, if you need them.

3 Dye your samples, carefully following the instructions. It is important to wet your samples first, if you want an even dyeing. (This is very important if you want to dye a whole garment.)

4 When you have finished dyeing, remove the samples and wash them in hot water. (You will need your rubber gloves for this, or you will find the water is too hot, as it needs to be about 60 °C.) Rinse them until the water is clear.

5 Dry the samples by spinning and ironing.

Q 8
Look at your dyed fabrics. Compare each one with its control fabric.
a Did the original colour of the fabric make any difference?
b Which fabrics showed the greatest colour changes — those which were light, or those which were dark? If you had a patterned fabric, look very carefully at the results.
c If they stayed almost the same colour after dyeing, why do you think this was?

If you want to be sure a fabric will dye the colour you want, the safest thing is to use a dye stripper first. This will remove any existing colour.

You must also make sure that there are no stains on your fabric. Stained parts of the material will just be stains of a different colour after dyeing. So most manufacturers make a stain remover, which you use before the dye on a stained article.

You could use a washing machine as your dye bath. This method is especially useful for larger articles such as sheets. See the special instructions on the manufacturer's packet.

As with cross-dyeing of fabrics made from a mixture of fibres, you can get different colours from a single dye bath. But this time you use a fabric made of the same fibres, but different colours.

20.6
DOES IT WASH OUT?

To be useful a dye must be fairly permanent. It should not rub off, come out in washing, or fade in sunlight. As a class experiment, make a collection of coloured cloths and try them out under warm and hot washing conditions. If you each use different fabrics, results can be pooled at the end of the test.

YOU WILL NEED:

Synthetic detergent powder
Coloured fabrics
White cotton fabric

Saucepan
Measuring jug
Thermometer
5-ml (tea) spoon

Scissors
Needle and white thread
Wooden spoon
Heatproof glass bowl
Spin drier
Iron

Warm wash
1 Cut out a 10 cm × 10 cm piece of coloured fabric, and a similar piece of white cotton. Tack them together along one edge. Keep a second piece of the coloured fabric for comparison.

Figure 20.14

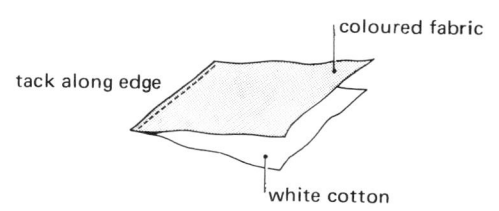

2 Heat 500 ml of water in a saucepan. Turn off the heat when the temperature reaches 40 °C. Sprinkle in a 5-ml (tea) spoonful of detergent.

3 Put your coloured fabric, with its attached piece of white cotton cloth, into the washing liquid. Stir with a wooden spoon for 5 minutes.

4 Pour the washing liquid into a transparent heatproof bowl.

Q 9
Has the washing water changed colour?

5 Tip away the water. Rinse, spin dry, and iron the test fabric and the cotton.

Q 10
a Has the white cotton picked up any colour?
b Does the washed specimen look any different from the piece of fabric kept for comparison?
c How do your results compare with those of the rest of the class?

Hot wash
6 Boil 500 ml of water in a saucepan. Turn down the heat to keep the water just simmering and add a 5-ml (tea) spoonful of detergent.

7 Make another 'booklet' of your coloured fabric and white cotton. Put it into the hot wash.

8 Stir the washing for 5 minutes. Then turn off the heat and allow to cool for 5 minutes longer.

9 Pour the washing into the heatproof bowl. Be careful — the water will still be very hot. ⚠

Q 11
Has any colour washed out of the fabric into the water?

10 Lift out the fabrics with the wooden spoon, then rinse and dry them as before.

Q 12
a Has the white cotton picked up any colour?
b Does the washed coloured fabric look any different from the unwashed piece kept for comparison?
c Is the test fabric colourfast to hot washing?
d What happened to the fabrics tested by the rest of the class?
(You must remember, of course, that many fabrics are never intended to be given a hot wash.)

Q 13
List three common-sense rules to be followed when washing coloured fabrics.

20.7
DOES IT FADE IN SUNLIGHT?

Some dyes fade if left for a long time in sunlight, but with modern dyes the loss of colour is usually very slow. Although it is easy to test for this type of fading, you may have to wait for the results. The experiment takes at least a month.

YOU WILL NEED:

Piece of stout card or hardboard
Coloured fabric specimens, including some dyed in sections 20.2 and 20.3
Glue
Cooking foil
Masking tape
Scissors

1 Cut two 5 cm × 5 cm samples from each fabric.

2 Mark out the card in matching halves and stick the fabric samples in matching positions on either side.

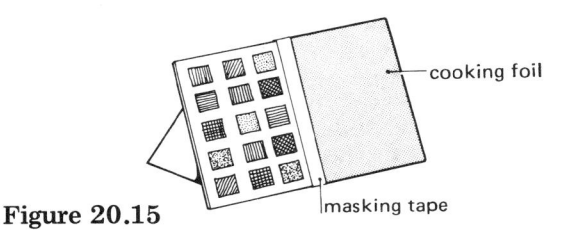

Figure 20.15

3 Cover the righthand side with cooking foil, smoothing it down carefully over the fabrics. Seal the open edge of the foil down the centre with masking tape, to keep out all light.

4 Prop up the cards in a sunny window, with the fabrics facing outwards. Leave for a month.

5 Take off all the foil and compare the samples. If you can see no fading, cover the card again and put it back for another month.

6 Keep the card in the window until you can see fading in several of the specimens. Make a table of your results like the one below.

Sample	After 1 month	After 2 months

Q 14
a How long did you have to wait before some faded?
b When would fading like this be particularly serious?
c Which faded first — the shop-bought coloured fabrics or the ones you dyed yourself?

CHAPTER 21
Fabrics for clothing

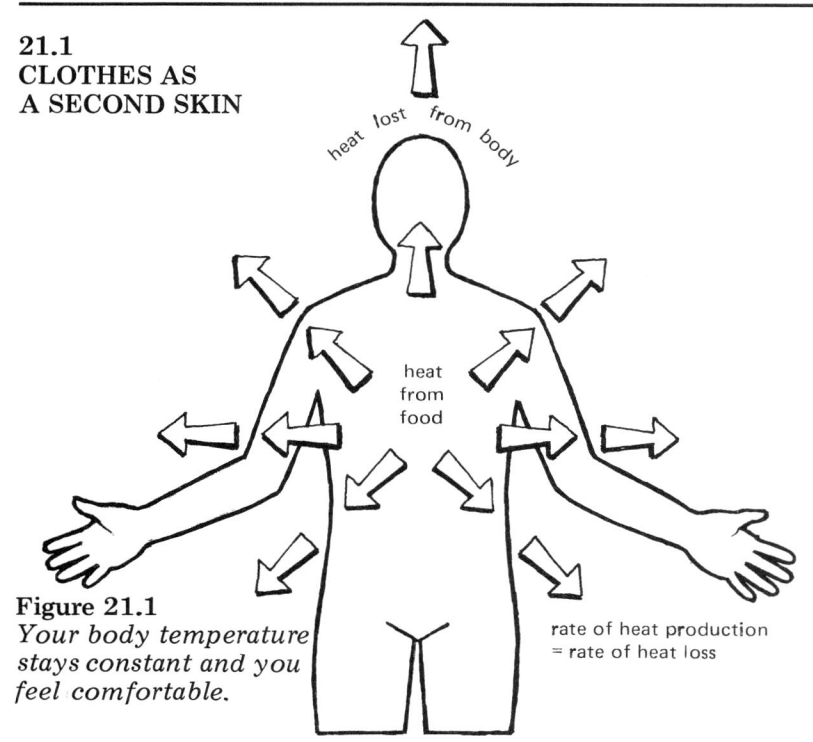

21.1 CLOTHES AS A SECOND SKIN

Figure 21.1
Your body temperature stays constant and you feel comfortable.

rate of heat production = rate of heat loss

Your skin is the frontier between you and the world outside. No matter how hot or cold the weather gets, you, inside your skin, have got to stay at about the same temperature. If your body temperature goes up or down by more than 5 °C on either side of the normal 37 °C, you will die.

Heat energy is being produced all the time inside your body from the food you have eaten. Unless this energy is lost in some way, your body temperature will rise. Most of the heat energy escapes through the skin.

Ideally, the rate at which heat is being produced inside your body should exactly equal the rate at which it is being lost.

There should not be any extra heat left over to force your temperature up and make you feel uncomfortable. But this balance can be upset. If you run about or take other vigorous exercise, heat production is stepped up. You begin to feel uncomfortably hot, and the body's defences have to come to the rescue.

Surface blood vessels enlarge, allowing the flow of blood just below your skin to increase. This brings more heat up to the body surface where it can escape. The increased blood flow may make you look flushed.

Figures 21.2a and b
The rate at which these men are producing body heat has increased because they are working hard.

Figure 21.3
This man's 'wetsuit' is essential for his survival in intensely cold water.

Figure 21.4
Dougal Haston wears a one-piece suit made of down, and Damart gloves, to stop his body losing heat too quickly in the intense cold on Mount Everest.

Figures 21.5a and b
A small baby can cool quickly. He needs to be wrapped up warmly.
Old people also need to be warmly wrapped.

There is a second way in which loss of heat is speeded up. The pores of your skin open, forcing sweat up to the surface. When sweat evaporates, it carries a lot of heat away with it.

But you can get too cold as well as too hot. If the outside temperature is low and you are not moving around very much, the rate at which you lose heat can be greater than the rate at which you produce it. Then the pores of your skin shut, giving you goose pimples; blood circulation to the skin is reduced; and shivering fits start your muscles working to release more heat.

Your body is cutting heat losses and stepping up heat production. Often this is not enough, and anyway, who wants to shiver? The body needs a second skin to give extra protection. This is where clothes come in.

In cold climates clothes are essential for comfort. They slow down the loss of heat, so that the body's protective mechanisms (shivering, etc.) do not need to be brought into play. Under really icy conditions, clothes can make the difference between life and death. Without them you would cool down more quickly than your body could produce heat.

Keeping warm is particularly important for babies. A small child has a larger surface area in comparison to his weight than an adult. (See worksheet M34.) This means that he cools down much more quickly and can easily die of exposure.

Even adults, especially old people, can die from over-cooling — this is called *hypothermia*. During cold weather the elderly should always wear extra clothes.

At night, when you are asleep and your body's rate of heat production falls to its lowest, the danger of over-cooling reaches its maximum. This is why you need warm bed-clothes in the winter.

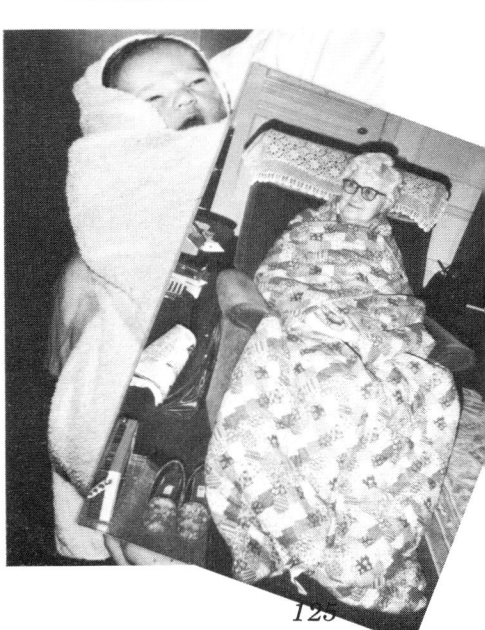

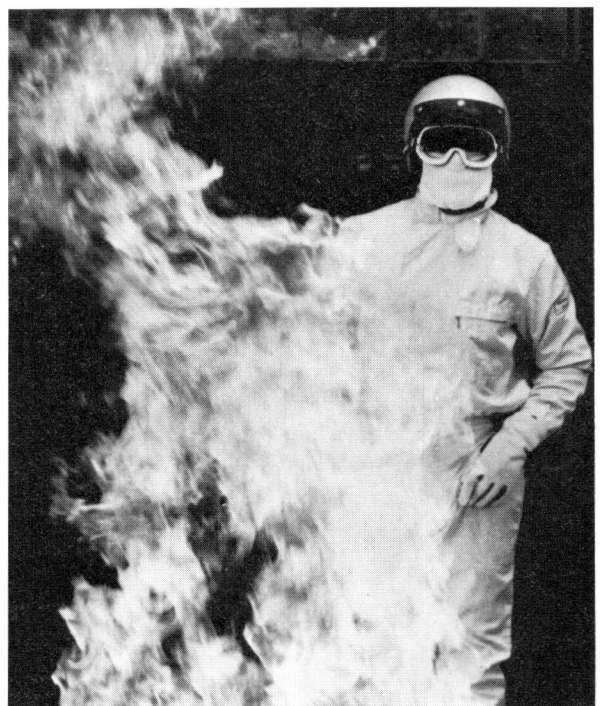

Figure 21.6a
A suit made of this material saved Nikki Lauda's life when his car caught fire.

Special clothes are used in industry and in rescue work. Heatproof suits are worn by people working in high temperatures.

Figure 21.6b
Steelworkers also wear protective clothing.

Living skin is incredibly flexible. Clothes cannot possibly compete in this respect, but at least they must not be too stiff. Would you like to be dressed in cardboard? Flexibility is particularly important in underclothes and sportswear, and for this reason a knitted structure is often chosen for such things.

Figure 21.7a
A knitted structure makes these casual clothes flexible and comfortable to wear.

Figure 21.7b
Underwear must be flexible.

Figure 21.8
Sportswear must be flexible too.

Figure 21.9

To help with the evaporation of perspiration, it is a good idea if underclothes are absorbent. They can then act as a second evaporating surface.

Because plastic raincoats will not let any water vapour from perspiration get through them, they can only be worn for a short time.

To summarize, clothes control the loss of heat from your body, and to be comfortable to wear must be flexible and able to let evaporating sweat escape.

21.2 LOSING HEAT THROUGH FABRICS

How do you slow down heat loss? Let's start off with an experiment.

YOU WILL NEED:

Thin but densely woven fabric
Open-textured dishcloth
Sticky tape
Electric kettle
Clock or watch
Scissors
Ruler
2 identical cans
Weighted polystyrene lids for the cans
2 thermometers (check that they read the same at room temperature)
Tray

1   Make a mark with a ball-point pen on the inside of each can, 1.5 cm down from the top. This is so that you can easily fill them to the same level.

Clothes must share another property with the skin. They must be able to let perspiration escape. Even when you are sitting still, about 10 per cent of the heat produced by your body is lost in the evaporation of sweat from your skin. When you start to move around, the proportion of heat lost in this way rises sharply.

If your clothes block this means of cooling, you will soon feel uncomfortably hot. Normal fabrics have plenty of gaps between the yarns through which the evaporating sweat can make its way, but the more layers of clothing, the more difficult the escape. This is one of the reasons why a fast bowler in cricket peels off his sweater as soon as he has 'warmed up'.

2 Fill the kettle with water, and put it on to boil.

3 Cut two strips from the tightly woven fabric as wide as the cans are tall. Cut a similar strip from the dishcloth. You are going to make these strips into jackets for the cans.

Figure 21.10
Cut off the overlap.

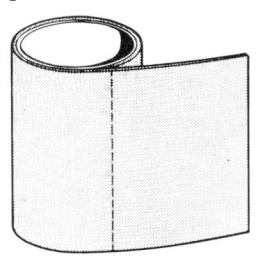

4 Wind the dishcloth strip around one of the cans, and mark where the overlap just begins. Cut along this line, so that the fabric wraps neatly round with no overlap. Join the edges together with short pieces of sticky tape.

Figure 21.11
Fasten the jacket with small pieces of sticky tape.

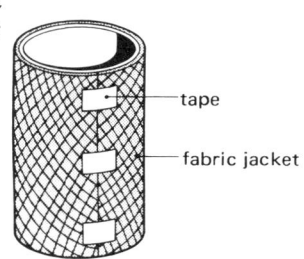

5 Wrap the tightly woven fabric over the first jacket, and trim and secure as before. Make sure that the tape-fastened seams do not come on top of one another. Make a single jacket for the second can from the remaining strip of densely woven fabric.

6 Put the jacketed tins on a tray, standing them at least 25 cm apart. Carefully pour hot water from the kettle into each of the cans, filling them exactly to the ink marks.

7 Take and note the water temperatures in the cans, then quickly put on the weighted lids.

8 Put the tray on a bench top near an open window. Make sure there is a good draught blowing onto the cans.

9 After half an hour take off the lids and read the temperatures again. Work out the drop in temperature for both cans.

Q 1
Was the fall in temperature the same in both the cans?

You probably found that the can with the open-weave jacket underneath the densely woven cloth cooled much more slowly. But why? After all, the second jacket was nearly all holes, so why should it have been so effective?

Well, strangely enough, the answer lies in the holes or, more accurately, in the air trapped in them. Remember that heat travels through air mainly by setting up currents of moving warm air (*convection*). If the air cannot move, not much heat can escape through it. So, although textile yarns are themselves good insulators, trapped air is even better. The more air pockets in a cloth, the more slowly will heat escape through it.

Figure 21.12
The yarns are the main paths for the escape of heat.

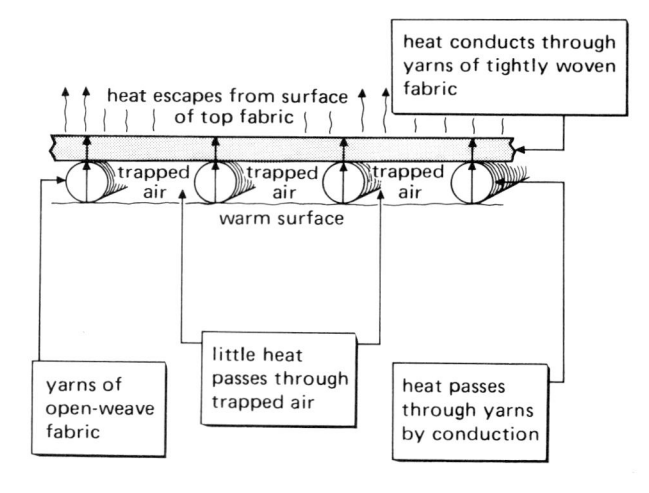

To keep you warm in winter, inner clothes should be made of thick, open-weave fabrics, capable of trapping lots of air. Outer clothes need to be very resistant to air penetration, so as to keep trapped air in and the cold winds out. If the wind manages to force its way right through your clothes down to your skin, it will carry away a great deal of heat.

Q 2
Explain how a string vest keeps you warm.

21.3 LETTING WATER VAPOUR THROUGH

Permeability is the property of letting something through. If a fabric has a high water-vapour permeability, it lets water vapour get through easily. A low water-vapour permeability means just the opposite.

Figure 21.13

Sportswear needs a particularly high permeability, because so much perspiration needs to evaporate during exercise. But even ordinary clothes must let some water vapour escape, if they are to be kept on for very long. Water-vapour permeabilities may be compared very easily, though the test takes a week to show results. The long time is because the surfaces used in the experiment are much smaller than your skin area and lose water vapour much more slowly.

YOU WILL NEED:

Identical plastic cups or yoghurt pots (one more than the number of fabrics to be compared)
Fabric samples
Elastic bands
100-ml measuring cylinder
Scissors

1 Pour 100 ml of water into each of the cups.

2 Leave one cup uncovered, but seal the rest with covers cut from the fabrics. Use the elastic bands to hold the covers in place.

Figure 21.14
Use an elastic band to hold the cover firmly in place.

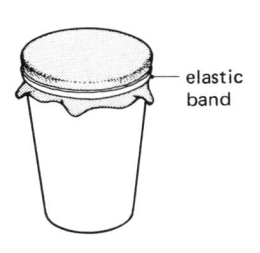

3 Place all the cups together in a corner of the room where they will be out of the way and protected from direct sunlight.

4 At the end of a week measure how much water is left in each container. To avoid confusion, take off only one cover at a time and note the volume of water in that cup before going on to the next. Don't forget the cup which was left uncovered.

5 Work out the volume of water lost from each container.

Q 3
a Which cup lost the most water, and which the least?
b List the fabrics in order of water-vapour permeability.
c Would any of the fabrics be unsuitable for clothes that had to be worn continuously for several hours?

You can go a stage further with the results from this experiment, and calculate a percentage water-vapour permeability for each fabric. If the volume of water lost from the uncovered cup is called U ml, and the volume lost from a covered container C ml, then

water-vapour permeability = $\frac{C}{U} \times 100$ %.

6 Calculate the percentage water-vapour permeability for each of the fabric samples. Put your results in a table like the one below.

Figure 21.15

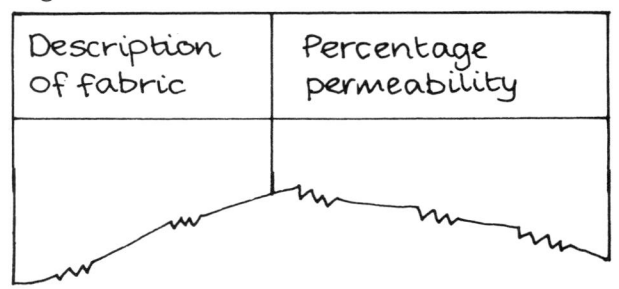

Description of fabric	Percentage permeability

CHAPTER 22
Soiling and cleaning

*Figure 22.1
Even without rolling in the mud, clothes get dirty in everyday use.*

22.1
THE SOILING OF FABRICS

Your clothes constantly get dirty. The air around you always contains tiny particles of mineral dust, and in towns there are sooty and tarry substances as well. All fabrics have lots of nooks and crannies in which dust particles can settle, so just leaving a cloth out in the air is enough to make it dirty.

Open-structure fabrics, such as nets, knits, and loose weaves, let air pass through them easily, so they are particularly liable to this type of soiling.

But dust-filled air is not the main cause of soiling. Sweat and grease from your body stain your clothes, and flakes of rubbed-off skin catch between threads in the cloth. If you are messy at meals, clothes can also get badly marked by spilt food and drink. Dust from the furniture you sit on or lean against is another source of dirt.

Figure 22.2
Grease on a polyester fabric magnified 600 times.

Figure 22.3
Cross-sections of a smooth fibre and a rough-surfaced fibre.

Q 1
From your own experience, which fibres have the most noticeable build-up of static electricity?

But textiles do not all get dirty at the same speed. Smooth fibres tend to stay cleaner for longer than rough-surfaced ones, because they have fewer places for the dirt to become trapped in.

Synthetic fibres build up charges of static electricity attracting dirt particles from the air and get dirty more quickly.

One of the few faults of polyester as a textile fibre is that it *adsorbs* (takes on to its surface and holds on to) oil and grease. If you have any polyester shirts or blouses, have a look at their collars.

Dirty clothes should be washed as soon as possible. The dirtier a fabric gets, the harder it is to clean. But there are other reasons for not letting clothes stay dirty for too long. Dirt and grease particles already on a fabric make good footholds for new deposits, so that the fabric soils more quickly. Dirty clothes also encourage the growth of bacteria. Some bacteria live on absorbed perspiration, decomposing it and producing a very unpleasant smell. It is important to know how to clean fabrics effectively.

22.2 USING DETERGENTS

Water used on its own is not very good at cleaning things. You must have realized this yourself, if you have ever tried washing your hands under the cold tap.

You can see from this sixteenth-century manuscript that clothes had to be rubbed and beaten to get them clean. To work properly, water needs the help of a cleaning agent or detergent.

The traditional cleaning agent is soap, but nowadays there are many synthetic detergents as well. Often only a tiny quantity is needed to make the water wash better. Carry out the following survey to see what concentrations the various detergent manufacturers suggest.

Figure 22.4

YOU WILL NEED:
A collection of different detergent packets

Most detergent boxes carry instructions on how much to use for both hand and machine washing. Where possible, note down what is suggested for hand washing in soft water. You might record your findings like this:

Name of detergent	Quantity of detergent (cups)	Volume of water (gallons)

Figure 22.5

Manufacturers usually give volumes of water in gallons and quantities of detergents in cups. However, it is quite easy to change this into metric units.

1 cup of detergent contains about 100 grams.
1 gallon is about 4.5 litres.

So to change cupfuls into grams you multiply by 100, and to change gallons into litres you multiply by 4.5. Let's look at an example. Suppose a manufacturer recommended 1½ cups of detergent per 5 gallons of water. This would be:
1.5 × 100 grams = 150 grams of detergent in 5 × 4.5 litres = 22.5 litres of water.

Therefore the concentration of detergent in water

$= \frac{150}{22.5}$ grams per litre

= 6.7 grams per litre.

But since a cup is not an exact measure, results are only approximate and should be rounded up or down to the nearest whole number. In the example above, the concentration should be rounded up to 7 grams per litre. Work out the concentrations for all the detergents under review, and tabulate them as below:

Figure 22.6

Name of detergent	Concentration for hand washing in soft water (grams per litre)

You will probably have discovered that most manufacturers suggest very similar washing concentrations.

Q 2
Was the concentration of detergent needed for hand washing high or low? (Remember when you answer that a litre of water weighs about 1000 grams.)

22.3
HOW DO DETERGENTS WORK?

The answer to this question lies in the nature of the detergent molecules, which have a sort of double personality. One end of each molecule behaves like oil and will not mix with water. The other end has a tendency to dissolve in water, like salt or sugar does. You can think of detergent molecules as being like tadpoles with water-repellent, oily tails, and water-soluble heads. The tails are said to be *hydrophobic* (water-hating), the heads *hydrophilic* (water-loving).

Figure 22.7a
A simplified picture of a detergent molecule.

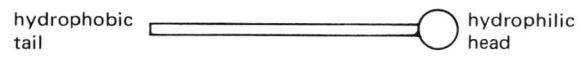

hydrophobic tail ⎯⎯⎯⎯⎯⎯ ◯ hydrophilic head

If put in water, detergent molecules gather on the surface with their hydrophobic tails sticking out.

Figure 22.7b
Detergent molecules in water.

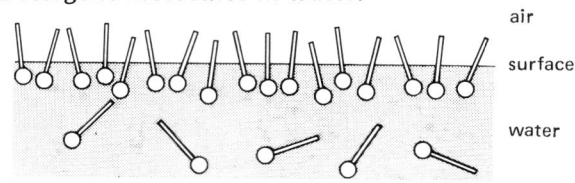

Left to themselves, water molecules have a strong attraction for one another. This is why water often gathers itself into droplets. But when detergent molecules get between the water molecules at the surface, the attraction is weakened, so that the water droplets collapse and spread out.

What happens when you add detergent to a drop of water? You can try this out for yourself.

YOU WILL NEED:

A small piece of water-repellent cloth, *e.g.* old mackintosh, felt, or tightly woven wool worsted
Washing-up liquid
Dropper
Thin glass rod

1 Lay the piece of cloth flat on a table and use your dropper to spot it with four separate drops of water.

2 Pick up a little detergent on the end of the glass rod and use it to touch two of the water drops. Leave the other two alone.

Figure 22.8
Touch two of the drops with the detergent-smeared rod.

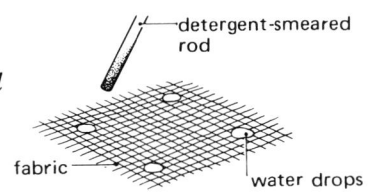

Q 3
Did the detergent make the water droplets collapse? What happened to the cloth just below these droplets?

One of the jobs of a detergent is to help water to wet soiled fabrics and sink into them. This lets the water get to grips with the dirt.

Once in contact with the dirt, the water quickly dissolves some of it, but the greasy and less soluble parts are harder to shift. This is where the detergent helps again. The hydrophobic tails of the detergent molecules try to escape from the water by pushing themselves into any greasy dirt they meet. They work their way under the edges of the grease, pushing it away from the fabric.

Figure 22.9a
This series of photographs shows how a detergent removes grease from a fibre.

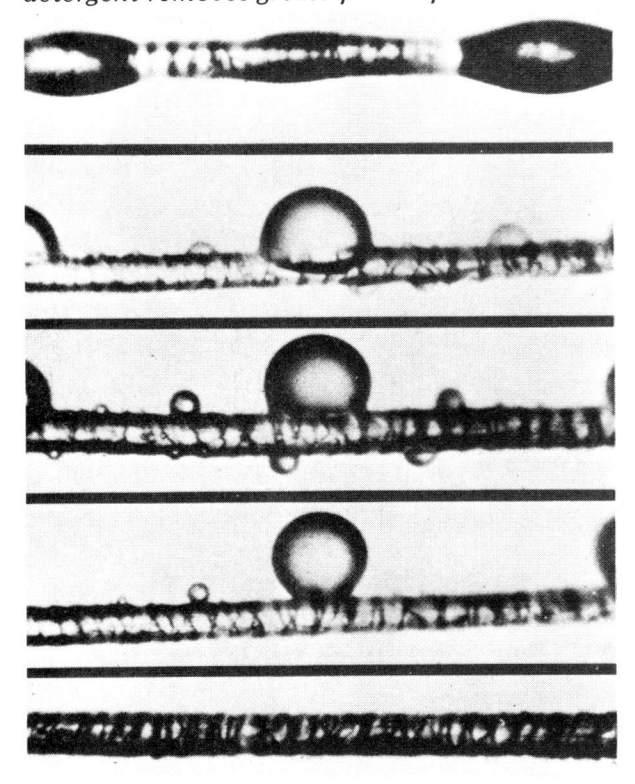

Figure 22.9b
The grip of the grease on the fabric is weakened.

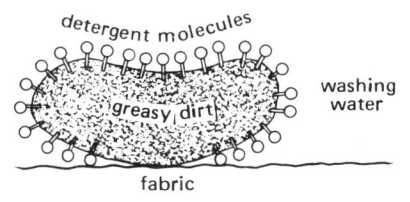

Now that the grip of the grease on the textile fibres has been weakened, the tumbling action of a washing machine can easily shake it free. Non-greasy, insoluble dirt particles can be removed in a similar way, though sometimes the process is more complicated.

But when all the dirt has been shaken off the fabric and into the washing water, it must be stopped from re-settling on the fabric. Some atoms inside the molecules of most common detergents are connected together by electrical forces. Water weakens the forces, so that each detergent molecule breaks into two *ions* (electrified pieces) with opposite charges. One ion is large and one small. The large ion consists of a hydrophobic (water-hating) tail and a hydrophilic (water-loving) head. It usually carries a negative charge. The small ion is positive. It is the large ion which is important in washing.

Figure 22.10
In water many detergent molecules break into two electrically charged pieces or ions.

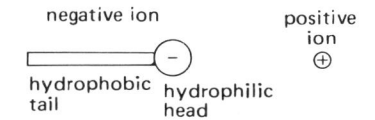

The charge of the negative ion is concentrated in its hydrophilic head. This means that grease or dirt particles that have become surrounded by detergent ions in the washing water carry haloes of negative electric charge.

Figure 22.11
Grease and dirt particles floating in the wash are surrounded by negative charge.

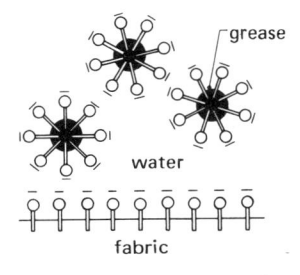

Any detergent ions that have settled on the fabric being washed have their hydrophobic tails pointing inwards to escape from the water. The heads point outwards, covering the fabric with a layer of negative charge. Because like charges of electricity repel one another, the grease particles are pushed away from the fabric. The dirt is kept in suspension.

Does a detergent help to keep oil or grease dispersed in water? You can test this very easily.

YOU WILL NEED:

Washing-up liquid
Cooking oil
2 test-tubes
Test-tube rack
Small measuring cylinder
Dropper

1 Half fill both the test-tubes with water. Then add 2 ml of cooking oil to each.

2 Put 2 drops of detergent in one of the tubes.

3 Shake both tubes vigorously to mix the oil and water. Put them in the stand to settle.

Q 4
In which tube did the oil and water separate faster? Does the detergent help to keep the oil dispersed?

In most ways soap and synthetic detergents are the same in their properties, but soap has one great disadvantage. It reacts with the dissolved minerals in hard water to give an unpleasant scum, and will only start to wash when all the hardness has been deposited. Synthetic detergents are much less affected than soap and go on working even in very hard water. But many people still like to use soap-based detergents, despite the problem of scum, because the soap gives a slightly better wash and has a softening effect on fabrics.

There are many different types of washing powder on sale — not all of them have the same washing properties. Some are more alkaline (pH above 7) and are good at removing grease; some are neutral, to allow them to be used with delicate fibres or special fabric finishes. Washing powders are quite complicated chemical mixtures. Ingredients may be added to:

loosen the dirt and break up the grease,
soften the water,
suspend the dirt,
make the clothes brighter and whiter (optical bleach),
break down protein stains,
perfume the clothes, and
protect the washing machine.

SYNTHETIC DETERGENTS AND SOAP increase 'wetting-power', loosen bond between fabric and dirt, and keep dirt in suspension

BUILDER (complex chemicals) helps cleaning process, softens water, and suspends dirt

ENZYMES break down protein stains (e.g. blood, gravy)

BRIGHTENING AGENTS make 'whites' whiter and coloureds brighter

PERFUME gives clothes a fresh, clean fragrance

BLUEING INGREDIENT gives a 'blue—white' hue to white fabrics

METAL PROTECTOR protects aluminium parts of washing machines

OXYGEN BLEACH removes stains such as black tea/coffee; gives added whiteness only at high temperatures and during long periods of soaking (so that at lower temperatures and short washes coloureds are not bleached)

Figure 22.12
Some of the ingredients in one brand of washing powder.

So there is a choice to be made, and manufacturers suggest what their products are best used for.

22.4
FABRIC CARE IN WASHING

Hot water is best at shifting most kinds of dirt, because it melts the greasy and fatty soil. But high temperatures can cause problems. Which fabrics are damaged by high temperatures?

YOU WILL NEED:

Cotton, wool, viscose, acetate, nylon, polyester, and acrylic fabrics — two pieces of each, cut into 10-cm squares (groups can share the washing)
Synthetic detergent washing powder

Saucepan
5-ml (tea) spoon
Measuring jug
Wooden spoon
Electric iron
Spin drier

1 Keep one set of fabrics for comparison with the set you wash.

2 Measure 500 ml of water into your saucepan. Add one 5-ml (tea) spoonful of detergent powder and bring to the boil. Then turn down the heat.

Figure 22.13
Sprinkle in a 5-ml (tea) spoonful of detergent and stir.

3 Drop your fabric samples into the wash and stir them gently for 5 minutes. Be careful not to splash the boiling water.

4 Lift out the fabrics with the wooden spoon. Rinse them thoroughly. Spin them dry. Iron, using a cool setting.

5 When your washed fabrics are dry, compare them with the ones you put aside.

Q 5
a Do any of the fabrics appear to have suffered in the boiling wash?
b Do you think some of the fabrics need a kinder treatment?

22.5
WASH OR DRY CLEAN?

Many fibres and blends and mixtures of fibres are used, making it difficult for you to know what will be the best way to wash each garment. If you choose the wrong way you might easily ruin something expensive. In fact, not every fabric can be washed.

To help you decide, textile, washing machine, and detergent manufacturers have agreed on a 'care labelling' scheme. This shows suitable washing temperatures, washing machine settings, and correct iron settings. You will find this information on boxes of detergents and on garment labels. If you keep to the instructions on the labels, you will not damage your clothes.

Figure 22.14
The international textile care labelling code.

	MACHINE	HAND WASH
[4/50]	Hand-hot medium wash	Hand-hot
	Cold rinse. Short spin or drip-dry	
[bleach crossed]	DO NOT USE CHLORINE BLEACH	
[iron]	WARM	
[P]	DRY CLEANABLE	
[O]	TUMBLE DRYING BENEFICIAL	

The labels use an international code which can be understood in any country.

Figure 22.15
The code consists of five basic symbols.

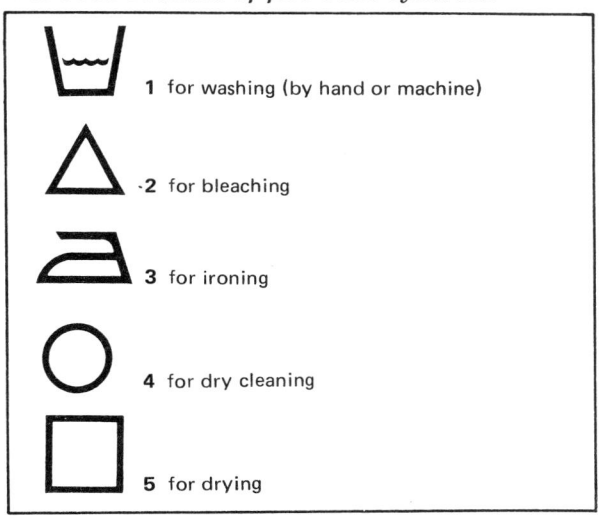

- [washtub] **1** for washing (by hand or machine)
- [triangle] **2** for bleaching
- [iron] **3** for ironing
- [circle] **4** for dry cleaning
- [square] **5** for drying

You might find dry cleaning symbols on your garment labels. These tell the dry cleaners what cleaning agents to use so that fabrics or fabric finishes, such as water proofing, are not damaged, and colours are not altered or removed. Some of these labels are shown on the next page.

135

Figure 22.16
Dry cleaning symbols. The letter in the circle refers to the solvent which may be used in the dry cleaning process.

Many dry cleaning agents must be used with care. Some are flammable; others have poisonous fumes. They have to be used in an enclosed machine which does not allow the fumes to escape. Because of the danger from these fumes, it is a good idea to let clothes hang in a well-ventilated room for several hours after they have been dry cleaned. You might have noticed the racks of clothes waiting to be collected in a dry cleaner's.

Figure 22.17

Warnings about fumes are also given in launderettes where there are coin-operated dry cleaning machines. It is dangerous to drive home in a car with the windows tightly shut with clothes that have just been taken out of the machine. The poisonous fumes could easily affect the driver and passengers.

Figure 22.18

Sometimes you need to remove stains from clothes yourself. Special *solvents* (dissolving agents) must be used.

For example, small marks or stains from ball-point pens or grass can only be removed by using a special solvent. Water is not effective because it cannot dissolve the special ink in the pen, or the *chlorophyll* (green pigment) in the grass.

Many solvents and cleaners are poisonous and should be used with care. There is a special danger when there are small children around. Toddlers want to taste everything. Bleach can kill.

Figure 22.19
This poster, produced by the Royal Society for the Prevention of Accidents (ROSPA), warns of the dangerous chemicals to be found in the home.

In *Fibres and fabrics* you have looked at the structure of fabrics and how they should be treated. You have learned some of the different things that can be done with different fabrics. Do you think about this when you go shopping?

People and homes is about you, your home, and about how many of the things in your home work. You will be looking at what *you* think a home is and also at what home is to all sorts of other people. Then you will look at the materials used in houses and at how to decide which material to use for which job.

By choosing the right equipment you can save yourself a lot of hard work in the home. However, labour-saving equipment, cooking, heating, and lighting all use energy. This is expensive to you and to the environment. *People and homes* will help you to understand how to use energy in your home safely and wisely.

People and homes

Chapter 23 Homes and houses *page 138*

Chapter 24 Windows, walls, and roofs *144*

Chapter 25 The materials game *150*

Chapter 26 Electricity: what it costs *154*

Chapter 27 Electricity: making it safe *160*

Chapter 28 Electricity: saving work *166*

Chapter 29 Lighting for living *170*

Chapter 30 Home heating and energy *178*

CHAPTER 23

Homes and houses

23.1
'A MACHINE FOR LIVING IN'
A famous architect, Le Corbusier, called a house 'a machine for living in'. Would you find this a strange way of thinking about your own home? Why?

Figure 23.1
Modern high-rise apartment and office buildings in Bombay tower over typical pavement squatter dwellings.

Figure 23.2
Putting the rubbish out. These two Skylab astronauts are forcing rubbish bags into a storage area. The bag on the left will float around until it is caught. Why?

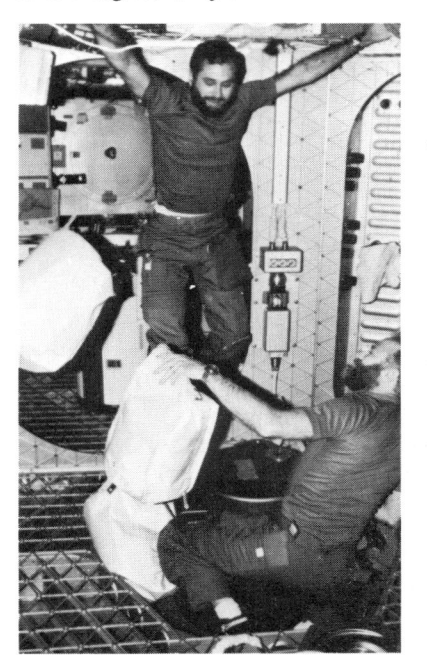

If you are poor in Bombay, home is just a space on the street. But at least it is never cold, and for nine months of the year it doesn't rain often. You may well be more comfortable than the American spacemen in their space station. To protect them from the hostile conditions of space — no air, no ground, no up, no down, bombarded by radiation and meteorites — they need a lot of expensive equipment.

Q 1
What do you think the effect on people might be of living
a on the street
b in a space capsule?

Inside your 'house machine' you have more machines to help you with the routine of living. Even the simplest home needs equipment for cooking and cleaning. Look at the equipment in figure 23.3.

Figure 23.3
A long house in Malaysia.

In Britain, the cold, wet climate and the complicated way of life in an industrial society demand a great deal of equipment. Equipment can be classified according to its function, *i.e.* movers, informers/controllers, suppliers of heat and light, and services. Services bring useful things into the house (gas, water, and electricity) or take out waste products (drains and chimneys). Some of this is shown on worksheet M37.

Q 2
What services can you see on worksheet M37? Make a list of them.

139

Figure 23.4
Bodiam Castle in Sussex. In the middle ages hundreds of castles were built to protect their owners and the lands around them. A castle is a home in which the needs of defence and attack are more important than any other need.

One of the main functions of the 'house machine' is to provide protection. This may be against the weather, insects, or other unwelcome visitors.

Q 3
List three other things that you might want to keep out of your home.

23.2 HOUSES TO SUIT THE CLIMATE

The kind of house that people need varies from country to country according to life-style and climate. Look at figures 23.5, 23.6, and 23.7. Think what the climate is like in the places shown in these photographs. Look at the figures in table 23.1. Try to find the places in an atlas.

Table 23.1
Average figures for temperature and rainfall in the months of January and July. (These figures are approximate.)

		Temperature (°C)	Rainfall (mm)
Bombay	January	23	5
	July	27	500
Malaysia	January	22	125
	July	27	350
Tunisia	January	13	5
	July	28	5
Sierra Leone (Guinea Highlands)	January	24	0
	July	24	350
London	January	4	60
	July	16	60

Figure 23.5
Traditional houses in Kairouan, Tunisia. These houses have thick walls, and are built around a shaded central courtyard.

Q 4
Why do you think the houses in figure 23.5 have
a thick walls
b small windows?

Figure 23.6 (left)
Thatched huts in Mabonto, Sierra Leone (West Africa). The people in this village are mostly farmers. Their houses are made of materials which they can find easily — a framework of saplings and branches covered with mud for the walls, and grass for the roof.

Q 5
Suggest two reasons why the houses shown in figure 23.7 on the next page would be unsuitable for the farmers in Mabonto.

Houses are also designed to suit different life-styles. Some people value their privacy and prefer to live in small family groups, as figure 23.7 shows.

Figure 23.7
Typical brick walls, tile roofs, and windows of British homes today.

23.3
WHAT MAKES A HOUSE INTO A HOME?

Everybody needs to feel loved and cared for and valued for him- or herself. People may enjoy being together, helping one another in times of trouble.

Q 6
Have you ever been away from home and felt homesick? What did you miss most?

Figure 23.8
A family in India.

Not all children live with both their mother and father, but most children do spend time with them inside and outside the home.

Figure 23.9
A one-parent family.

As you grow up you may begin to want to move away from your childhood home. At first you may have a bedsitter or a shared flat. Later on perhaps, you will live in a house or flat on your own or with friends of your choice.

So a home is
a place where people:

care for and about one another;
respect each others' differences;
accept the fact that each
person's needs change with
time (perhaps even at different
times of the same day);
share the chores as well as the
pleasant things.

These things make a home into
more than just a shelter.

Q 7
a   Make a class list of all the things that you think go towards making a happy home.
b   Are most of the important things goods which can be bought in a shop?

CHAPTER 24

Windows, walls, and roofs

24.1
WHAT DOES IT TAKE TO MAKE A HOUSE?

Most of today's new houses are built in large groups on so-called estates. Why do you think that is? How does it help the builder? How does it help the house-buyer?

How many people does it take to build a house? Have a guess. You can see some of them 'finishing off' a house in the picture. A tiler is working on the roof; painters are working inside and outside; an electrician is in the kitchen. The site foreman is talking to the new owners — perhaps they are choosing the colour of their floor tiles.

Other people have finished their work on the house and moved on to the next one.

Q 1
How many people will have worked on the house by the time it is finished? Make a list starting with the people in the picture. (Try to think of at least ten separate jobs that had to be done.)

A modern house uses many different materials: concrete tiles for the roof; brick for the walls; plastic sheet around the window frames to make them waterproof. Each of the materials is chosen to suit the job it has to do.

Figure 24.1

Q 2
How many different house-building materials can you think of? Try to list at least ten.

Q 3
Write down at least three reasons why wood is a good material for floors.

Q 4
Why *are* most of today's houses built on large estates? Try to write down three reasons.

145

24.2
DIFFERENT MATERIALS — SAME JOB!

One of the interesting things about British houses — especially the older ones — is that different parts of the country have different styles of house. Often this is because different materials have been used to do the same job. There are some examples in the pictures below. Look at the pictures and try to answer the questions.

Figure 24.2
A regency house made of London brick.

Just by looking at the bricks, you can tell that this house is more than ninety years old. Beneath the grime, the bricks are a yellowish-grey colour. They are rarely found outside the London area.

Q 5
How could the kind of bricks used tell you the age of the house? (Hint: the street sign comes from an area about three miles from the house.)

Figure 24.3
An East Anglian half-timbered house.

In East Anglia you can still see very old houses like the one in figure 24.3. Its walls are made from a wooden framework filled with plaster.

Q 6
Why wasn't stone or brick used to build the house?

Figure 24.4
Modern houses in East Anglia.

These houses have been designed to fit in with the local 'style'. In these modern houses, the black 'clapboarding' which covers part of the brickwork is only decorative. On very old wood-and-plaster houses it serves a useful purpose.

Q 7
Say what that useful purpose is.

Figure 24.5
Modern stone and thatch houses in Dorset.

Q 8
Why do you think the roofs have been thatched?

Q 9
Write down one advantage of a thatched roof and one disadvantage.

Discuss your answers to the questions with your teacher.

24.3
WHAT DOES IT COST?

There are at least three ways of reckoning the cost of a house. You can ask:

how much will it cost the people who are going to live in it?

how much did it cost the builder to build it?

how much has it cost the world in which we live (in other words our environment) to supply the materials?

Few people think about the third question, yet in the long term it could be the most important. The materials which are used to build a house have to come from somewhere; and removing them changes the place they come from.

Clay, for instance, is one of the most important building materials. It is used to make bricks and ceramic tiles. Cement is made by roasting a mixture of clay and powdered limestone.

Figure 24.6
Claypit in Lincolnshire.

Modern roof tiles, the mortar used to stick bricks together, and concrete for the foundations of houses are all made from cement.

Where does clay come from? One answer is in the picture (figure 24.6). It shows a clay pit in Lincolnshire. This enormous hole in the ground will get larger and larger until all the clay has been worked out. Then the clayworks will be moved to another area to make another giant hole in the ground.

Clay is said to be a *non-renewable resource*. That means that once the world's supplies have run out, we will have to manage without it.

Q 10
Find out where clay comes from in the British Isles. (Your geography teacher will be able to help you.)

Q 11
Find out what happens to disused clay and gravel pits. (Talk about this with your teacher.)

Wood is another important building material. It is used to make the framework of a house — which you can't see when the house is finished — and to do many other jobs.

Q 12
Write down three other ways in which wood is used in building and fitting out a house.

With careful planning, we can always have plenty of wood. We need to carry on planting trees to replace those we cut down. Wood is said to be a *renewable resource*. However, there are three problems to do with this:

Problem 1 Most trees grow very slowly, taking tens or even hundreds of years to reach useable size. If we use them more quickly than new ones can grow, we will never catch up.

Problem 2 Fast-growing conifers can be planted as the old broad-leaved trees (oak and ash for instance) are cut down. But, in doing this the community of animals, insects, and plants which live in broad-leaved woodland is destroyed.

Problem 3 Some kinds of soil will not grow new trees once the old ones have been removed. Already the great forests of South-East Asia and South America are disappearing. A wasteland is all that is left behind.

Figure 24.7

Surprising as it may seem, we in Great Britain do need to worry about the fate of forests in other countries. We import nine-tenths of the wood we use. For instance, most of our window frames are made from Keruing wood from South-East Asia. More serious is the fact that trees and forests are important to every human being on the planet Earth. We could not survive without them.

Q 13
What would happen to the Earth and all its living creatures if all the trees were to disappear? Try to find out.

24.4
WHY ARE OUR HOUSES SO COMPLICATED?

Our houses *are* very complicated. They use large amounts of many different materials. They need large teams of people to build them — at least one expert for each kind of material.

One way to get an idea why our houses need to be so complicated is to look at simpler kinds of house in different parts of the world.

Figure 24.8
A Bedu tent — the home of nomadic tribesmen in North Africa.

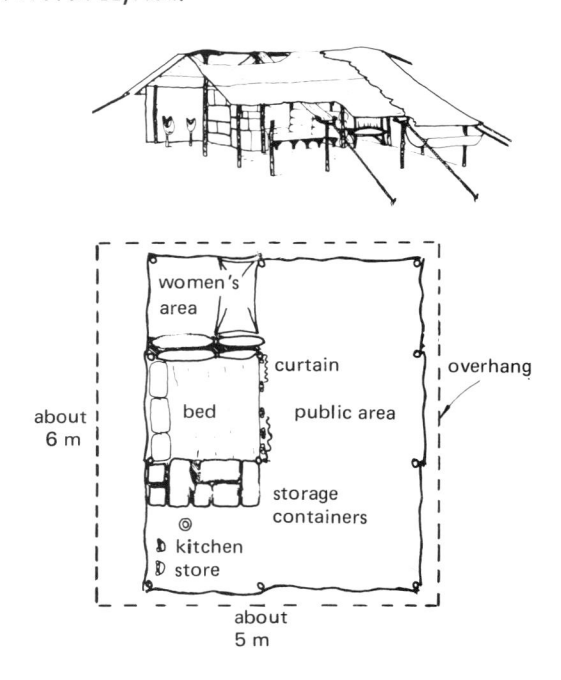

Here is a list of materials required to make a Bedu tent:

about 50 square metres of cloth
a few metres of webbing
a few metres of rope
about 12 poles
several wooden ridge-pieces.

Figure 24.9a
An igloo — the winter home of Algonquin indians (Eskimos) in Canada.

Figure 24.9b
A floor plan of an igloo.

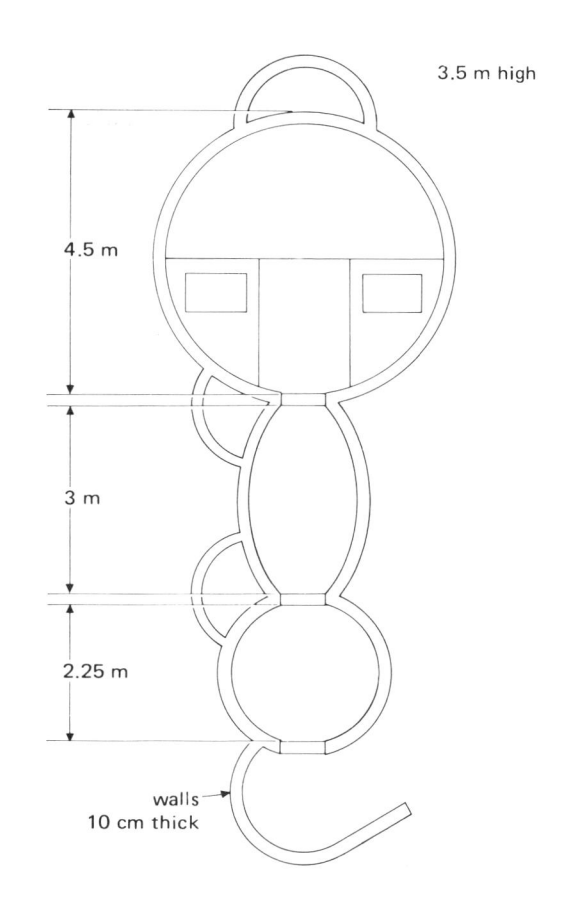

3.5 m high

4.5 m

3 m

2.25 m

walls 10 cm thick

These are the materials required:

about 5000 litres of water (frozen!).

Q 14
What is the floor area of the igloo? Try to work it out.

Q 15
What is the floor area of the Bedu tent?

Q 16
What is the floor area of your own house or flat? (Add up the floor areas of all your rooms.)

Get together with one of your friends and imagine that one of you is a Bedu and the other an Eskimo! Explain to each other the advantages of your kind of house. Score two points for each advantage you can think of.

Figure 24.10

WE NEVER NEED TO DECORATE—

NEITHER DO WE—AND WE DON'T NEED A DEEP FREEZE EITHER

Our homes provide us with warmth and shelter. If that was all they had to do, they could be much simpler and use far less materials of fewer kinds. But our houses do much more than that. For example, they provide us with space which we can decorate and furnish in ways to please us and lift our spirits. A house gives us space to entertain our friends and follow our hobbies. It gives us somewhere to keep our possessions. It can even be a place where we can work.

Our homes and possessions grow to match the kind of people we are. Perhaps we change to match the homes and possessions we have.

Q 17
Suppose you had to live in a much simpler house for a while, for instance in a tent on a camping holiday. How would your behaviour change to suit the different house?

CHAPTER 25

The materials game

25.1
WHICH MATERIAL?

In Chapter 24 you looked at the materials used in building a house and at some of the problems of using them. Here you will look at materials again, but this time you will be concentrating on their *properties*. That is, the special things about them which make them suitable for particular jobs.

To start with, look at the different materials found in a modern kitchen. Ten have been marked in the picture on the right (figure 25.2). Try to name each item and say what material it is made from. Then try to give at least one reason why the material is suitable for this job.

Draw up a table like the one below and fill in your ideas.

Figure 25.1

Item	Name of material	Advantages
Knife handles	wood	warm and comfortable to hold

All the materials in the picture have to stand up to pretty hard treatment. Later on in the chapter you will be taking a close look at one of these materials — the floor covering. Try to answer question 1 about kitchen floors now.

25.2
THE MATERIALS GAME

YOU WILL NEED:

A pack of 32 *property* cards made from worksheet M38.
(Trace two of each picture onto some white card.)
A sheet of *design jobs* (worksheet M39)
A pair of dice
One different-coloured counter for each player

Here are the rules of the Materials Game:

1 Each player in turn throws the dice. The number thrown gives the player a design job for the game. For instance, if a player throws a five (a two and a three) he will have to design a fishing rod. If you throw a twelve you have a choice of two jobs.

Each player puts his counter on his design job.

Q 1
Think of four different kinds of ill-treatment which a kitchen floor has to withstand.

2   The pack of cards is shuffled and put face down in the middle of the table.

Each of the cards has a *property word* on it. Each player has to collect a set of property cards to suit his design job. For example, to design a fishing rod he would want to collect the card with 'flexible' on it (and some others).

3   One player turns over the cards one by one. As the players see the cards they have to decide whether they want them for their design job. If a player does want a particular card he calls out 'Mine' to claim it.

4   The first player to call out gets the card. The other players can challenge the claimer. If they do, he has to explain how the property on the card suits his design job. If he cannot explain, he loses the card. If the challenger doesn't want it, it goes to the bottom of the pack.

5   As soon as any player has two or more property cards, he can stop the game and make everybody add up scores.

Scoring

Each player scores one point for each card he has collected, and two more points if he can name a material with the properties on the cards. For example, if he had collected 'brittle', 'stiff', and 'lets light through', and could name glass as a material with these properties, he would score five points in total.

6   When the scores have been added up, the dice are thrown again to give everybody a new design job. The game goes on until all the design jobs have been completed — or until time runs out!

Figure 25.2

Figure 25.3

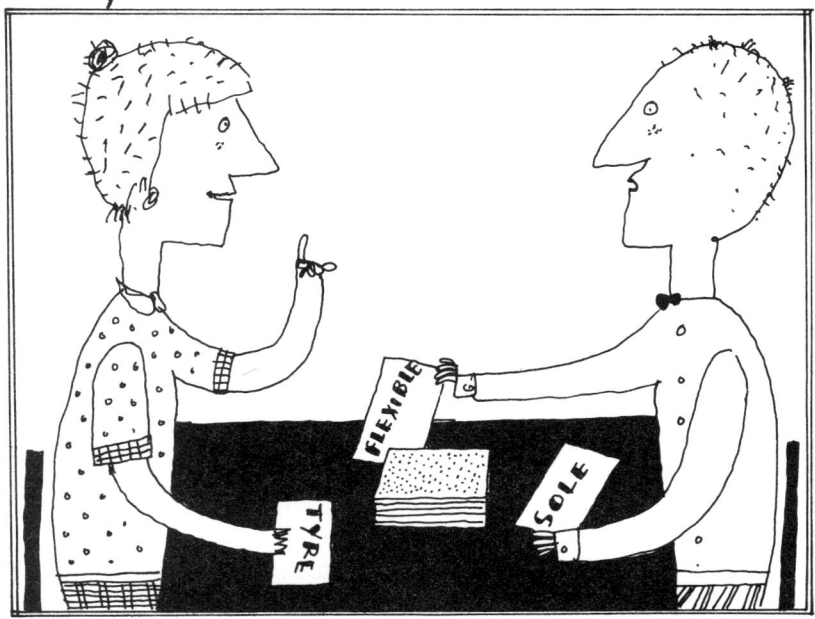

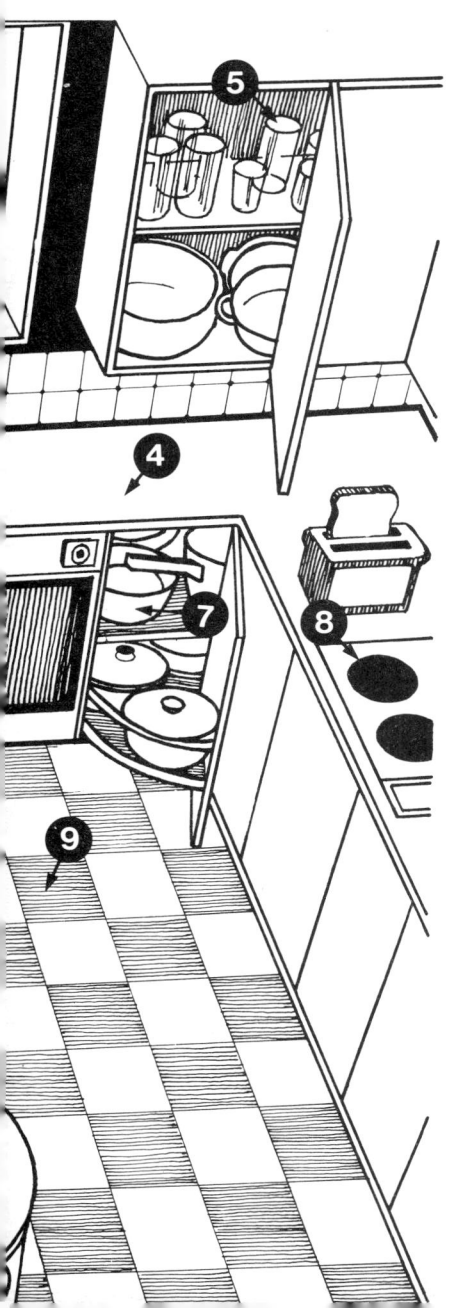

25.3
WHICH IS THE BEST MATERIAL?

Did you answer question 1 on the previous page? Could you think of four kinds of ill-treatment for floors? Did you get: attack by chemicals (bleach for instance); attack by food stains and hot liquids; frequent soaking with water; scratching; scuffing; and denting?

Everyone knows the kind of treatment handed out to kitchen floors. You might think that a list of properties could be drawn up and the perfect floor covering produced. But, as you know, it isn't as simple as that. There is great competition to sell floor coverings and there are dozens on the market.

Figure 25.4

The Consumers' Association (publishers of the *Which?* reports) is one organization which tests manufacturers' claims in a scientific way. You can carry out some *Which?*-type tests on kitchen floor materials.

You will need a good selection of samples of different kinds of floor-covering materials. It is probably best to stick to tiles of various kinds. Your teacher will help you with collecting some samples.

Whichever test you do, keep back a piece of untreated tile to compare with the piece you test. Scientists call such a separate sample a *control*.

Test A Bleach

YOU WILL NEED:

Household bleach in a small beaker
A plastic disposable syringe

1 Using the syringe, carefully put the same amount of bleach on each of your tile samples.

2 Leave the tiles for fifteen minutes.

3 Wipe off the bleach.

4 Compare with control samples.

Figure 25.5

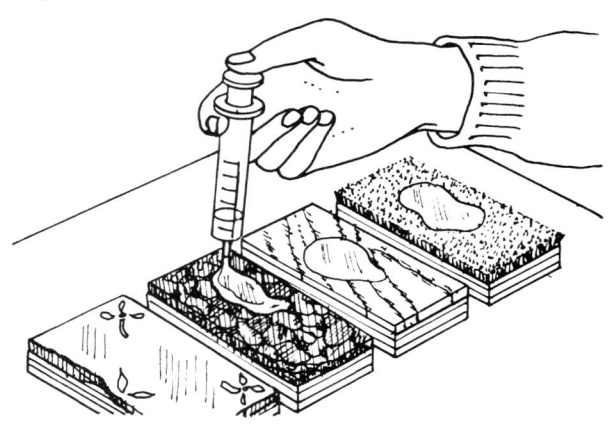

Q 2
Why is it important to treat each of the tiles at the same time? Why not finish a test on one and then go on to another?

Q 3
Why is the bleach left on for fifteen minutes? Is this treatment realistic?

Test B Staining

YOU WILL NEED:

Strong coffee or tea in a small beaker
Blackcurrant juice in a small beaker
A plastic disposable syringe

1 Using the syringe, carefully put the same amount of the two stains on each of your tile samples.

2 Leave the tiles for fifteen minutes.

3 Wipe off the stains.

4 Compare with the control samples.

Figure 25.6

Q 4
Why is it important to use two different kinds of staining substance?

Q 5
What other kinds of staining are likely to happen to a kitchen floor?

Q 6
How could you find out whether worn tiles stain more easily than new tiles?

Test C Soaking

YOU WILL NEED:
A small bowl of water
Tile adhesive and spreader

Figure 25.7

1 Glue two pieces of each of the tiles back-to-back with the recommended adhesive.

2 Allow to dry for the recommended time.

3 Soak overnight in cold water.

4 Dry off and compare with the control samples.

Q 7
Why is it important that kitchen floors should be able to stand up to being very wet?

Test D Scratching and scuffing

YOU WILL NEED:
A piece of wood a few centimetres larger than your tile samples and one or two centimetres thick
Long drawing pins or carpet tacks
A housebrick
Some string

1 Fix one of the tile samples to the piece of wood.

2 Arrange the brick so that you can pull it back and forth across the sample.

3 Pull it back and forth fifty times.

4 Repeat with the other samples.

5 Compare with the control samples.

Figure 25.8

Q 8
Why is it important to count the number of 'passes' of the brick across the tile?

Q 9
Is this a realistic test for a kitchen floor?

Q 10
Try to invent another apparatus for wear-testing.

153

CHAPTER 26
Electricity: what it costs

Figure 26.1

Figure 26.2

26.1
HOW MUCH ELECTRICITY DO YOU USE AT HOME?
Families use electricity to suit the way they live.

Some families are out all day and the house is only used in the evening. In this case very little electricity will be used during the day — it will be used mainly in the evenings.

Old people and mothers with young children may use the house all day. They may well have a lot of washing and cooking to do. So electricity will be in use throughout the day.

If your house is heated by electricity you will use a lot more than people who heat their houses in other ways. Some people cook by electricity and some by gas; so they will use different amounts of electricity.

Keep a record of the electricity you use at home in one week. Worksheet M40 will tell you how to do this.

154

Q 1
On which days of the week does your family use most electricity?

Q 2
Can you explain why you use more electricity on those days?

Q 3
Which appliances use most of the extra electricity on those days?

Q 4
On weekdays, when do you use most electricity? Why is this?

Compare your own survey with those done by friends.

Q 5
a In what ways are they similar? Explain why.
b In what ways are they different? Explain why.

This survey may help you to see how you can help save quite a lot of money for your parents. To do this you will need to know which appliances use most electricity. The following activities will help you to find this out.

26.2
LOOKING AT ELECTRICAL APPLIANCES
If you look at an electric iron, a kettle, a television set, or any other electrical appliance, you will find a plate like the ones in figures 26.3 and 26.4.

Appliances like those in figures 26.5 and 26.6 will have three important figures on the plate:

a number followed by the capital letter V

a number followed by the combination Hz

and a number followed by the letter W.

1 Find these on the two plates on the right.

2 Look for these figures on some of the electrical equipment you have at home and at school. The photographs in figures 26.5 and 26.6 will help you to find where the plates are.

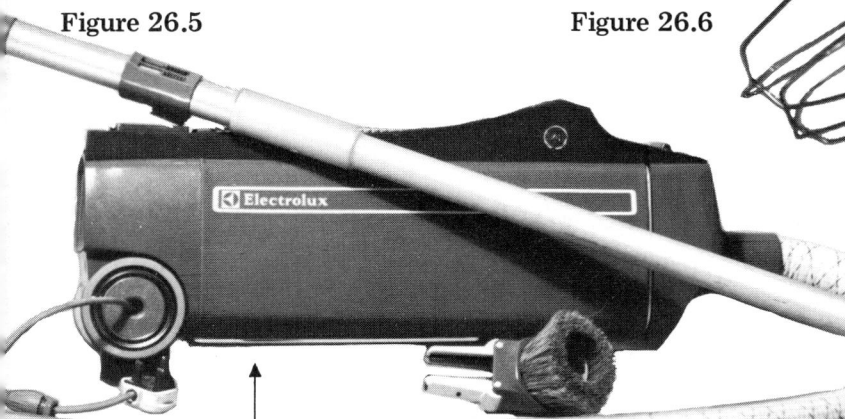

Figure 26.3

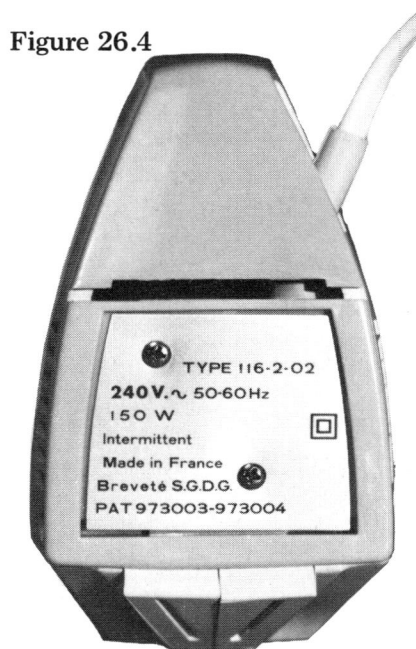

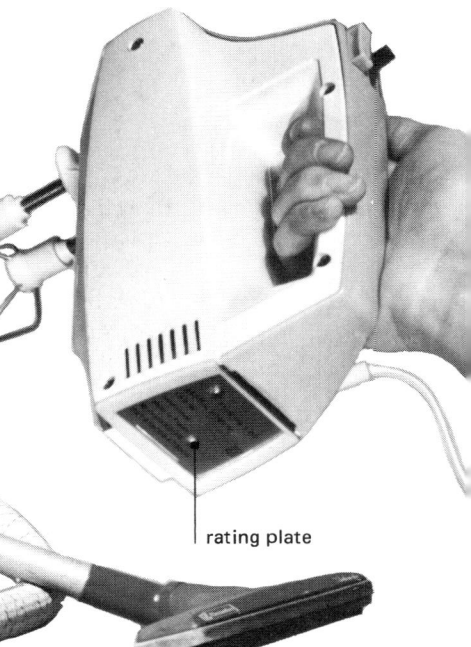

Figure 26.4

Figure 26.5

Figure 26.6

3   Draw a table like the one below and note down the numbers from the plates on some appliances. The first two results, taken from the mixer and vacuum cleaner shown in figures 26.5 and 26.6, have been filled in to help you.

Figure 26.7

Appliance	V	Hz	W
mixer	240	50–60	150
vacuum cleaner	240	50	750

4   Some appliances may not have an Hz number. If so, leave the space blank. Some appliances may quote the power in kilowatts (kW) rather than watts (W). For example, an electric kettle may have 2.4 kW stamped on the plate. If so, just multiply the kW figure by 1000 to get the W figure. For the kettle this would be 2.4 kW = 2400 W.

5   Think about the following questions so that you can discuss your answers in class.

Q 6
a   Look at the numbers in column V. What do you notice about them?
b   What about the numbers in column Hz?

Q 7
What do you notice about the numbers in column W?

The first two columns show what kind of electricity the appliance can use. They are all very similar numbers because all appliances have to use the same kind of electricity you get through the mains at home and at school. In Britain, mains electricity is 240 V at 50 Hz.

The figures in column W vary a lot from appliance to appliance, so they must tell us something about the appliance itself.

26.3
HOW MUCH CURRENT DOES IT TAKE?

YOU WILL NEED:
3 or 4 light bulbs of different wattages
Special ammeter
Bulb holder
Selection of appliances

1   Look at three or four light bulbs which have different wattages (W figures). Put them in order according to how much light they give.

2   Look at the W figure (wattage) printed on the end of each bulb. Put them in order of wattage: lowest first, highest last.

3   Now connect the bulbs to the meter to see how much electric current they take. Figure 26.8 shows you how to do this. Push plug P into the mains socket and plug the lamp or other appliance in at B. The ammeter (A) will show how much current is being used.

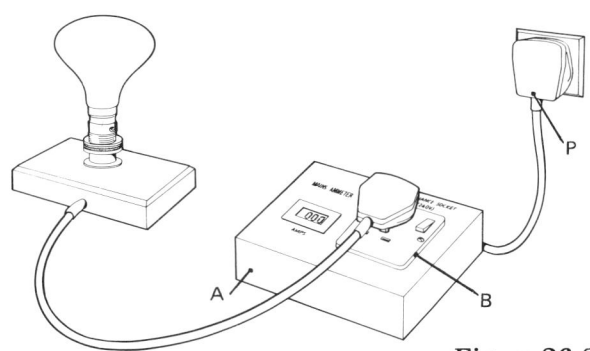

Figure 26.8

4   Make a table in your book like the one below. Write the figures in the table as you take them. You can then put other electrical appliances in place of the lamp and write the results in your table. One example, an electric kettle, has been filled in to help you. Don't copy these figures down. Use your own electric kettle. It may be different.

Figure 26.9

Appliance	W (watts)	A (amperes)
electric kettle	2400	10
lamp 1		
lamp 2		

5   Look carefully at columns W and A and compare them.

Q 8
Does the appliance with the largest wattage (W) marked on the plate use the most or the least electric current (A)?

Q 9
Which appliance used the smallest wattage? Did it use the most or the least current?

6 Plot a graph of the figures in your table set out like the one in figure 26.10 below. One point has been filled in for you as an example. It is the kettle shown in the table in figure 26.9 (2400 W, 10 A). Label each point neatly, just below and to the righthand side, like the example.

Figure 26.10

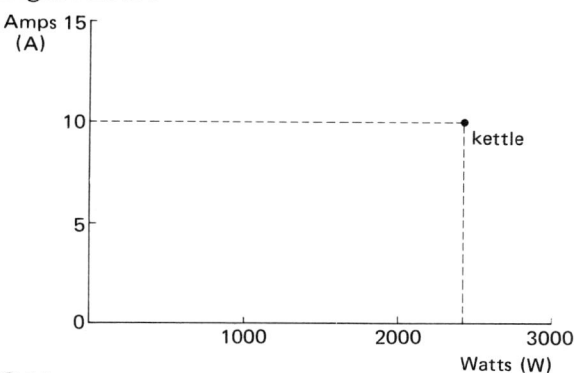

```
Amps 15
 (A)

     10 ----------------------•
                              | kettle
                              |
      5                       |
                              |
      0                       |
         1000    2000    3000
                          Watts (W)
```

Q 10
What do you notice about the points you have plotted on the graph? Do they make any pattern? Describe the pattern.

Keep this graph carefully. You will need to use it again later.

Figure 26.11

26.4
HOW MUCH DOES IT COST TO RUN?

You can use the wattage (W figure) stamped on electrical appliances to find out how much it costs to run them.

When you get an electricity bill (like figure 26.11 below), you will see that you have been charged for the number of 'units' you have used.

Q 11
In the bill below, how many units has the householder used?

What is a unit of electricity?

A unit of electricity is the amount you use when you run a 1000 watt (1 kilowatt) appliance for one hour. The first example in figure 26.12 (on the next page) shows this.

1 Copy figure 26.12 into your book. Try to fill in the missing figures in the blank spaces. Leave all the last column empty for the time being.

2 The bottom two lines of the table are for you to fill in with the appliances you have at home or at school.

An easy way to find the number of units used is

watts × hours used ÷ 1000.

| METER READING || UNITS USED | UNIT PRICE | V.A.T. | AMOUNT |
PRESENT	PREVIOUS		(pence)	code	£
39951 C	38751 E	200	5.0	0	10.00
		1000	4.0	0	40.00
E = Estimated reading C = Your own reading					
YOUR REFERENCE NUMBER	PHONE US ON	READING DATE	AMOUNT TO PAY		
113.1432.145.100	01–246 8011	25 JUL 81	£ 50.00		

157

Appliance	Watts	Hours switched on	Units used	Cost for one hour
Small electric fire	1000	1	1	
Large electric fire	2000	1	2	
Electric kettle	2500	1		
Television	175	1	0.175	
Light bulb	100	1		
Immersion heater		1	3	

Figure 26.12

What does it cost for one hour?

That will depend on how much you have to pay for one unit of electricity. If you look at the electricity bill shown in figure 26.11 you will see that the consumer paid 5.0p per unit for the first 200 units and then 4.0p for all the units on top of that.

3 Look at your own electricity bill at home and see how much your parents had to pay for each unit.

4 Now that you know the cost of a unit, you can work out how much it costs to run an appliance for an hour. Turn back to the last column of the table you have just drawn — the column you left empty. The first appliance, the small electric fire, is easy to calculate. It uses one unit in an hour, and that unit cost 5p. Put this in the table.

5 Now fill in the rest of the last column to see how much it costs to run each appliance for one hour. If you wish, you can use the actual cost of a unit from your own electricity bill instead of the example of 5p per unit.

26.5
HOW MUCH IS IT USED?

You have already found out how much it costs to run each appliance for one hour. To find the total cost of using each appliance, you will have to find out how many hours it is used.

The number of hours that any appliance is used will differ from family to family. It depends on how many people there are in the family, how they spend their time, and many other things.

It is useful to keep a check on how much you use each appliance at home for one week. Copy the following table (figure 26.13) into your book. Your teacher will tell you which pieces of equipment you should keep a record of. After the survey you will be able to compare your records with those of your friends.

Leave out the electricity used for lighting; you will make estimates of the cost of this later.

Q 12
Which appliances do you think are the greatest users of electricity over the course of a week?

Figure 26.13

| Appliance | Watts | Number of hours used ||||||| Total hours | Cost per hour | Total cost |
		Mon	Tues	Wed	Thur	Fri	Sat	Sun			
electric kettle											
electric fire											
toaster											
television											
vacuum cleaner											
cooker											

26.6
SAVING ELECTRICITY

YOU WILL NEED:

Electric kettle
Cup
Clock or watch with seconds hand

1 Imagine you are going to make coffee for two people. Put the water for this in an electric kettle.

2 Time carefully how long the kettle takes to boil. Write down the number of seconds it took.

3 Now empty the kettle into a sink. Measure into it 2½ cupfuls of water. Make sure this is sufficient to cover the heating element.

4 See how long this takes to boil.

You found out, in section 26.5, how much your electric kettle costs to run each week. You can now work out how much of this you can save by not overfilling your kettle.

Here is an example.

Imagine the water originally poured into the kettle took 150 seconds to boil and the water carefully measured into the kettle took 90 seconds.

So, when you used the kettle for 150 seconds, 60 seconds of this was wasted.

That is $\frac{60}{150}$ is wasted.

This is $\frac{2}{5}$ or 40 %.

If you normally used the kettle for a total of 2 hours per week (120 minutes), you would waste 40 per cent of 2 hours.

This is 120 minutes × $\frac{40}{100}$ = 48 minutes.

5 Do this calculation for your own figures to make an estimate of how much you might be able to save.

You may find that you would only save about 5 or 6 pence per week on your kettle by being careful only to heat up as much water as you need. But heating water is expensive, and you heat a lot of it each week for cooking, washing, and baths. If you were careful to use only as much water as you needed for all these things you might be able to save quite a lot of money. An immersion heater is really just like a big electric kettle element, but just think how much water you have to heat up for a bath. A little less water in a bath could save several kettles full. Showers use much less water than baths.

Q 13
How would you make a rough estimate of how much hot water you need
a for a bath?
b for a shower?

Figure 26.14

Discuss your ideas with your teacher. When you have decided on the best way to do it, you can estimate how much water you use at home when you have a bath. You will find that it amounts to an awful lot of cupfuls.

Some houses have special meters so that they can use electricity at off-peak times, when it is cheaper. If you have such a meter you can save money by having a time-switch to turn on your immersion heater at night.

Q 14
Find out how much electricity costs per unit, at
a the ordinary tariff
b the off-peak tariff.

CHAPTER 27
Electricity: making it safe

27.1
A NEWSPAPER STORY

When you read this tragic story taken from a newspaper, there will be several words and phrases you have seen or heard before. However, you may not be really sure what they mean or how the things they describe work.

Figure 27.1

Mower causes death
by Eric Robinson

A broken power lead, a faulty plug, and an unearthed appliance electrocuted a 39-year-old housewife and mother of two teenagers, Mrs Jenny Miller, as she mowed her lawn at 23 Acacia Drive.

The Newton coroner, Mr Thomas Hamilton, was told how Mrs Miller had been found by her 13-year-old daughter, Sally, lying beside their electric lawnmower, still holding onto the faulty plug in her hand.

Electricity board expert, Mr Michael Roberts, explained that Mrs Miller, mowing the lawn barefoot, had acted as an earth for the current from the broken wire. An inspection showed that the lead had snapped near the plug and that when Mrs Miller had touched the plug to see why the mower had stopped she received the fatal shock.

Fatal shock

'Normally', said Mr Roberts, 'the plug would have been completely safe, even with a broken wire inside. Unfortunately, in this case, the insulating cover of the plug was cracked and the broken live wire was touching a metal screw sticking through a crack in the insulation. If the earth connection from the mower to the mains plug had been complete', he continued, 'this fault would have blown the fuse, and all would have been safe.'

When he examined the flex, Mr Roberts found that 2-core non-earth cable had been used as an extension lead. The mower came with 3-core earthed-type cable. The use of two-core cable as an extension lead meant that the earth connection was not complete. Mr Roberts said that the double-insulated lawn mower was nearly new and in good condition. He said that millions of similar machines were in use and were quite safe provided they were used according to the instructions.

'Mrs Miller', he added, 'would have been insulated if she had been wearing rubber-soled shoes or wellington boots. This would probably have saved her life.'

A lesson to us all

Recording a verdict of accidental death, the coroner said 'This should be a lesson to us all. Let us hope that by knowing what happened in this tragic case we can prevent it happening again.'

Afterwards Mr Alan Miller said that his daughter Sally was extremely distressed.

Q 1
The following words are taken from the story in the newspaper: unearthed; two-core non-earthed cable; live lead; three-core earthed cable; double insulated; live bare wire; earth connection; fuse. Write them down the lefthand side of a page. Try to explain what each word or phrase means. Finding the word in the story may help you.

Clearly it is important to know something about these things; the newspaper cutting shows that it can be a matter of life or death.

27.2
LOOKING AT CABLES AND FLEXES

YOU WILL NEED:
Pieces of electrical cable of several different kinds

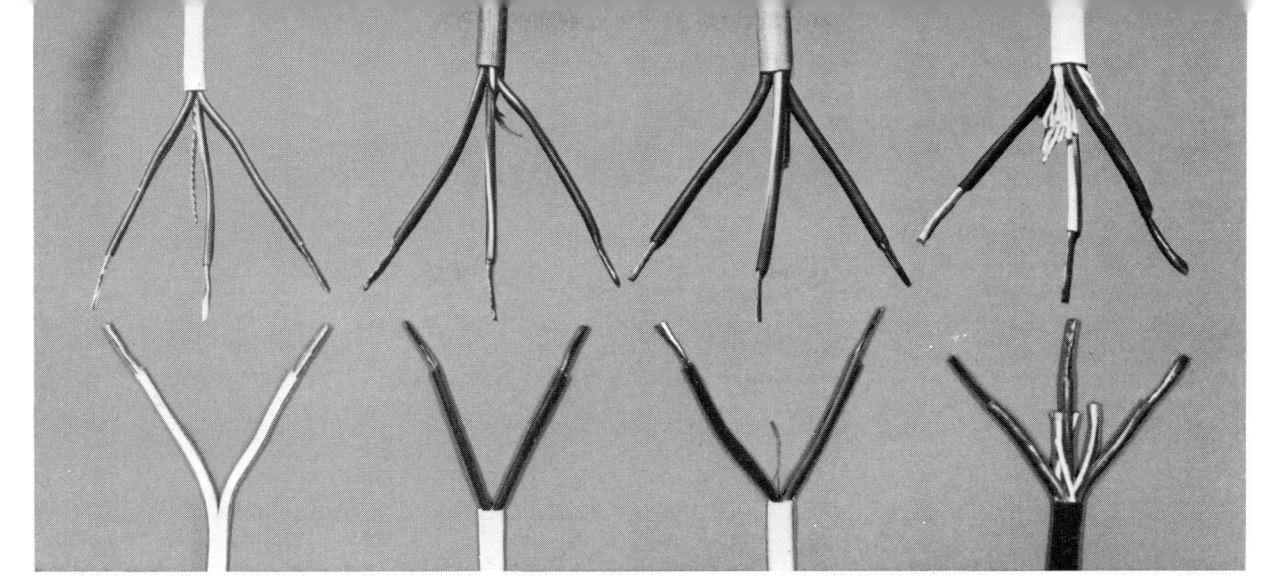

1   Look at the pieces of cable you have been given.

One important difference you will have spotted is that some wires are two-core and some are three-core, as shown in figure 27.2 above.

We sometimes use the word *flex* for some of these cables. This is because the cable is flexible.

As you can see, there are many different sorts of electrical cable. Some are very flexible, like the ones you use for table lamps, vacuum cleaners, and food mixers. Some don't need to bend much — like the ones built into the walls of your home to carry electricity to the sockets.

Some cables are two-core, some three-core.

27.3
WHICH CABLE FOR WHICH APPLIANCE?

YOU WILL NEED:
A range of domestic electrical appliances complete with their plugs and flexes

Look at as many electrical appliances as you can, and make a list showing whether each one uses a two-core or three-core cable. Look at the outer case of these appliances and see if you can tell what it is made from.

Write your results in a table like the one below. One example has been filled in to start you off.

Figure 27.3

Appliance	2- or 3-core cable	Material of outer case
electric kettle	3	metal with plastic handle

Figure 27.2

Q 2
Make a list of the ways in which the cables are different from each other. List as many ways as you can spot.

Q 3
Look back at the newspaper article. Write down one sentence from it which mentions *three-core cable* and one which mentions *two-core cable*.

Q 4
Can you spot any pattern about appliances which use two-core and which use three-core cables?

Q 5
Do most of the appliances with metal cases have three- or two-core cables? Make a list of any which have metal cases and two-core cables.

Q 6
Do all the appliances which use two-core cables have plastic cases? List any exceptions.

You probably know from your science lessons that to make an electric current flow you need a complete circuit. This means having a wire to take the current to the appliance and one to bring it back.

You can light a torch bulb using a dry cell (battery) if you use a two-core flex as in figure 27.4.

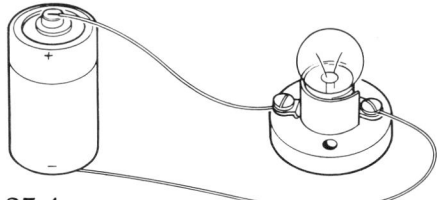

Figure 27.4

Many hair driers use two-core non-earth flexes. They have plastic cases. Notice how the two *cores* or wires in the flex are fastened to two of the pins in the plug. There is no wire connected to the third pin of the plug.

Figure 27.5

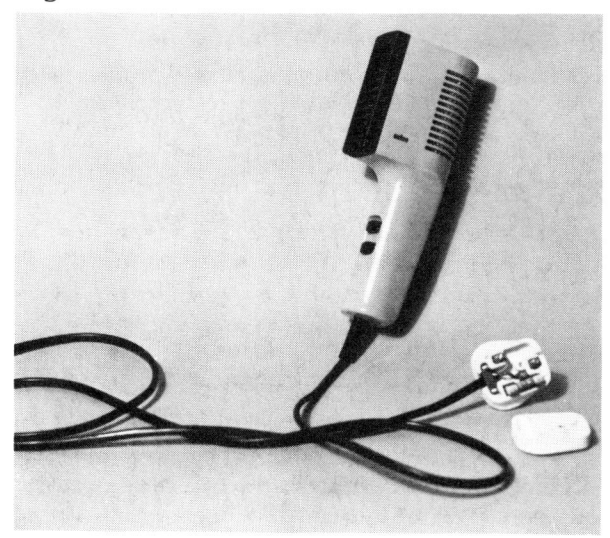

In figure 27.4 the electricity from the battery to the bulb always flows the same way round the circuit. We call this *direct current*. The food mixer uses *alternating current*. The live lead first becomes charged with positive (+) electricity, then with negative (−) electricity. This tries to escape to the neutral lead, which is neither positive (+) nor negative (−). The only way it can do this is through the motor in the mixer, and this makes the motor work.

Figure 27.6

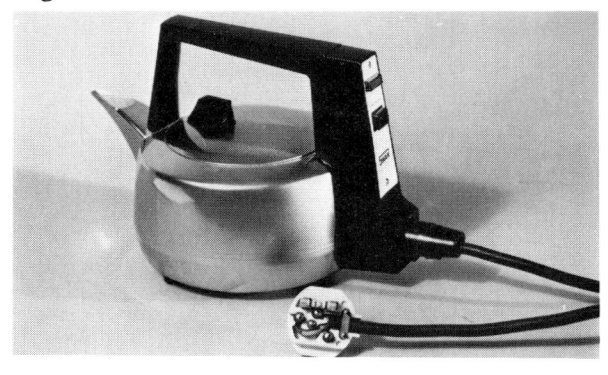

Most kettles use three-core cable. Only two are needed to make a circuit and carry the electricity. The third wire doesn't normally carry any electricity. It is the yellow and green wire connected to the centre pin. It is called the *earth* wire.

27.4
WHEN IS ELECTRICITY DANGEROUS?

Electricity in the brown (live) wire is at an effective voltage of 240 volts. You can think of this as the pressure behind the electricity. All the time this electricity is trying to escape to earth.

Usually, the only way it can 'escape' is through the appliance — which makes it work — and then back down the 'neutral' (blue) lead. This blue lead has connections right back to the power station, where it is connected to 'earth'.

Electricity will go to earth the easiest way it can. If you accidentally touched a live lead, it may go to earth through you. This is the danger! You may accidentally touch the live lead because the wire comes undone. If it touches a metal part of the appliance, this would become live.

Can electricity go through *you*?

YOU WILL NEED:
3 wire leads with crocodile clips
Electric kettle
Battery
Microammeter

To make it safe to find out if electricity can go through you, you will use a battery which is only 4.5 volts instead of mains electricity at 240 volts.

1 Connect the wires to a metal part of the kettle, the meter, and the battery as shown.

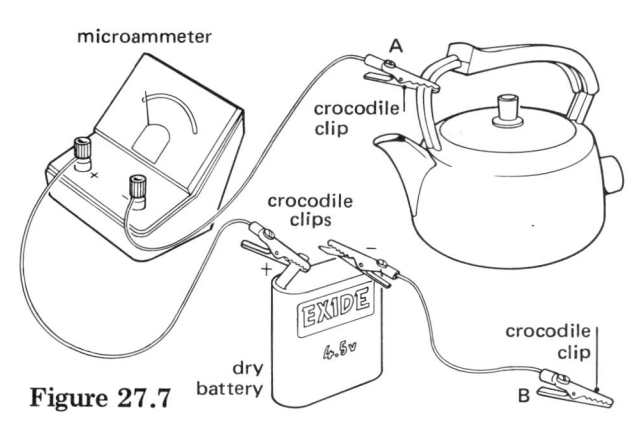

Figure 27.7

CAUTION: Crocodile clip B must not touch crocodile clip A or the kettle. This would make a large current pass through the microammeter which may damage it.

If you have made the connections correctly, the kettle is now 'live'. No current is flowing because there is no complete circuit.

2 Now take off one shoe and stand on crocodile clip B. This represents 'earth'.

3 Now hold the kettle and look at the microammeter. Write down the reading.

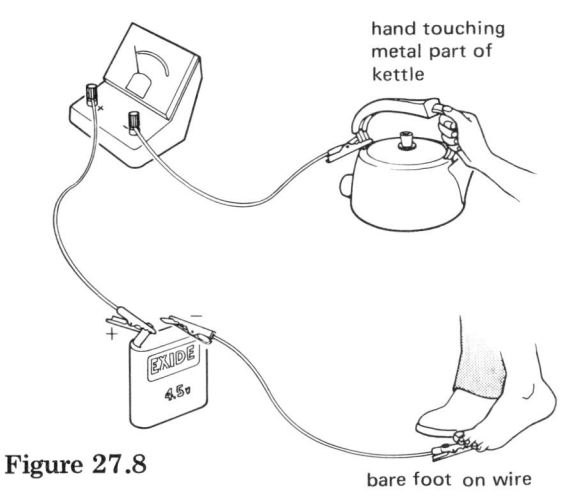

Figure 27.8

If there is a current shown on the meter, this is the current which is going through you, to earth.

4 Now put a wet cloth on the floor. Attach clip B to the cloth and put your bare foot on top of the clip. Is the current greater or less than your first reading?

Make a table like the one below.

Figure 27.9

Hand—wet or dry	Floor—wet or dry	Footwear	Current passed

5 Try the test with a dry hand on the kettle, then a wet one. Try it with a bare foot, a leather-soled shoe, a rubber-soled shoe, and a plastic-soled shoe. Try all these on dry and wet floors (using wet cloths again). Write the meter readings in your table.

When you have finished the table, look at your results for the current passed.

Q 7
What were you doing when the *biggest* current passed through you? This would be the *most* dangerous situation if you had been using mains electricity.

Q 8
What were you doing when the *smallest* current passed? This would be the *least* dangerous.

Wet hands or feet mean that your body is better connected to the kettle and the earth. This means that electricity can escape easier from the live lead, through you, to earth.

Now look back at the newspaper article in figure 27.1.

Q 9
What was the victim wearing on her feet at the time of the accident?

Q 10
Mr Roberts said that she might have been saved if she had been wearing a particular kind of footwear. What kind of footwear did he suggest?

The danger is that electricity might escape to earth through your body. You are safer if you make it harder for electricity to do this. One way to make it harder for electricity to pass to earth is to wear rubber or plastic footwear.

Electricity will not go through plastic or rubber. These materials are called *insulators*.

Q 11
Why do you think bathrooms are designed so that you cannot touch electrical appliances?

Q 12
Where is the light switch in your bathroom at home? What kind of switch is it?

Q 13
Have you any electric sockets in your bathroom? If you have,
a what are they like?
b what are they for?

Q 14
In Chapter 24 you saw that vinyl floor tiles in the kitchen have several valuable qualities. Can you now think of another advantage they have? (The table you have just completed should give you some clues.)

27.5
EARTHS AND FUSES

In section 27.3 you found that some appliances (electric kettles for example) use a three-core lead. Two of these cores (wires) carry the current to and from the kettle. These are called the 'live' and 'neutral' leads.

The third wire is called the 'earth' lead. It is coloured green and yellow and does not normally carry any electric current. It is there as a safety device.

One end of the earth wire connects to the outer metal case of the appliance. The other end is connected to the centre pin of the three-pin plug. When this plug is pushed into a wall socket, it is connected to the earth of the house wiring.

If, by accident, a live wire should come adrift and touch the metal case of the appliance, the case would become live too. If you touched it, the electricity may go to earth through you — especially if you haven't got your wellies on! The idea of the 'earth' wire is to provide a very easy path for the electricity to go to earth, much easier than going through you.

Because the earth wire makes such an easy path, a very large electric current goes to earth that way so much so that it blows the fuse. This shuts off the electricity and all is safe.

Your teacher may have a model to show you how a fuse works.

When electricity passes through a wire, the wire gets hot. A fuse is a thin piece of wire that gets hotter than the rest of the wire in a circuit. If too much electric current goes through it, the fuse melts. This makes a gap in the electric circuit and the current stops. To do this the fuse *must* be in the *live* lead.

Figure 27.10
A fuse is the weakest part of the circuit. It is a safety device.

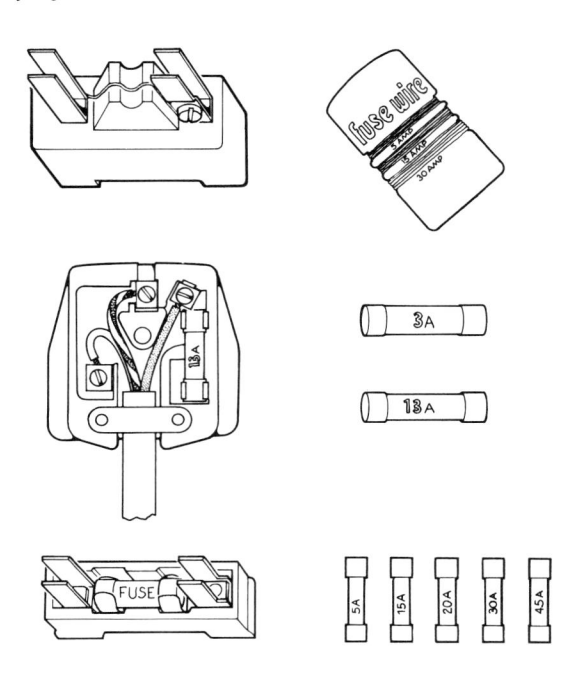

Figure 27.11
This diagram shows how the electricity would flow to earth if a live wire touched the metal case of the kettle.

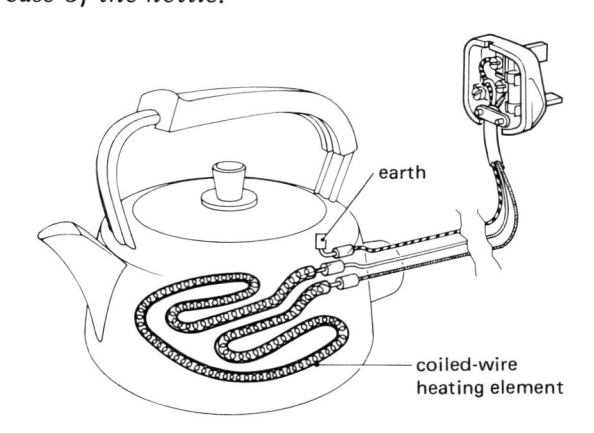

Why don't food mixers have earths?

Figure 27.12

These appliances are called *double insulated*. The parts carrying electricity inside are all insulated with plastic coverings which electricity cannot escape through. In addition, the outer case is plastic. There is no point in earthing a plastic outer case — it couldn't become live anyway, because electricity cannot pass through plastic.

27.6 WHAT SIZE OF FUSE?

Look back at the graph you drew in Chapter 26.

This shows how much current various appliances take.

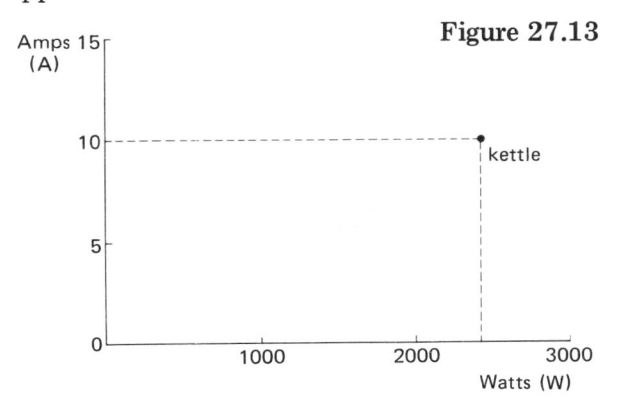

Figure 27.13

What size fuse should you fit in the plug on a toaster rated at 1200 watts? If you look at your graph you will see that 1200 watts corresponds to a current of about 5 amperes.

You want a fuse which will take 5 amps easily without melting, so you would choose the next size up which is 13 amps. This would not melt in normal use.

YOU WILL NEED:

Various electrical appliances
Your graph from Chapter 26

Draw up a table like the one below.

Figure 27.14

Appliance	Wattage	Current (amps)	Fuse rating (amps)
Toaster	1200	5	13

Look at the rating plates of the appliances and note down the wattage. Use your graph to find out the current they will need. If you have 1-amp, 3-amp, and 13-amp fuses, decide which you would use for each appliance.

It is important to fit the right size fuse. If the fuse is too big, the appliance could be ruined before the fuse burnt out and stopped the current. It could even be dangerous in certain circumstances.

On the other hand, if the fuse is too small it will be continually blowing, which could be a nuisance, although it would be harmless.

So there are four ways to protect yourself:

1 Make sure that wires don't come adrift. Don't tug on flexes; replace ones that get damaged or have worn insulation.

2 Make sure that there is no easy path to earth through you. Don't take electrical appliances into the bathroom; be careful anywhere there is water about; wear wellington boots or shoes with rubber or plastic soles if you use an electrical appliance outside.

3 Make sure the earth lead is properly connected if the appliance has a metal case.

4 Make sure appliances are fitted with the correct fuse.

CHAPTER 28

Electricity: saving work

28.1
'ENERGY SLAVES'
Your great-grandmother had to work much harder to prepare food and to keep her house clean than your mother does today. She had to lift rugs and carpets, carry them outside, and brush or beat them clean. Washing had to be scrubbed by hand. Coal for heating had to be carried to the stoves or boiler.

Today, electricity does the hard work in cleaning carpets, washing, and many other jobs. Heat comes at the touch of a switch or gas tap. It is almost like having a slave to do the hard physical work for you. Appliances which save people from this work are sometimes called 'energy slaves'.

28.2
APPLIANCES THAT SAVE TIME AND WORK
Most of the electricity used in your home is used either to heat things or to move things.

When electricity goes through a wire, it makes the wire hot. This is how electric kettles, toasters, light bulbs, and ovens work.

Electricity can also create a magnetic field. This is used to drive electric motors. These motors are used in many appliances in your home which have to move things.

Figure 28.1
In great-grandmother's day, 'energy slaves' were a science-fiction dream. This picture is from an American comic of the 1890s.

Q 1
Write down the names of the appliances in the picture in two groups. In the first group put those which use hot wires, and in the second put those with electric motors.

Appliance	Watts	Hours used in one week	Hours taken using hand tools	Time saved each week
Electric food mixer				
Vacuum cleaner				

Figure 28.2

Draw a table in your book like the one above.

The first column shows two appliances that you may have at home. They both have electric motors in them. These are 'energy slaves' or movers. But how hard do they really work?

The power of the motor tells you how fast it can do work. The faster it does work, the more energy it uses every second.

Write down the wattages in the second column of your table. This is the figure that tells you the power of the appliance. The number of watts tells you how many *joules* of electrical energy the appliance uses every second it is in use.

Q 2
Look at these two appliances at home and find their wattages. (This is the W figure you found in Chapter 26. Look again at figures 26.5 and 26.6 to remind you.)

Q 3
Think carefully how long you use these two appliances in one week at home. Check this guess if you can. You must count the whole of the time taken in using the appliance. Include time spent getting it out, setting it up, and putting it away after use.

Q 4
Work out how long you think it would take per week, if you had to mix the food or sweep the carpets by hand. If you have never tried to do these jobs by hand, make a guess. Check with your parents and see if their guess agrees with yours.

Figure 28.3

Q 5
In the last column, work out how much time you save each week by using the appliance.

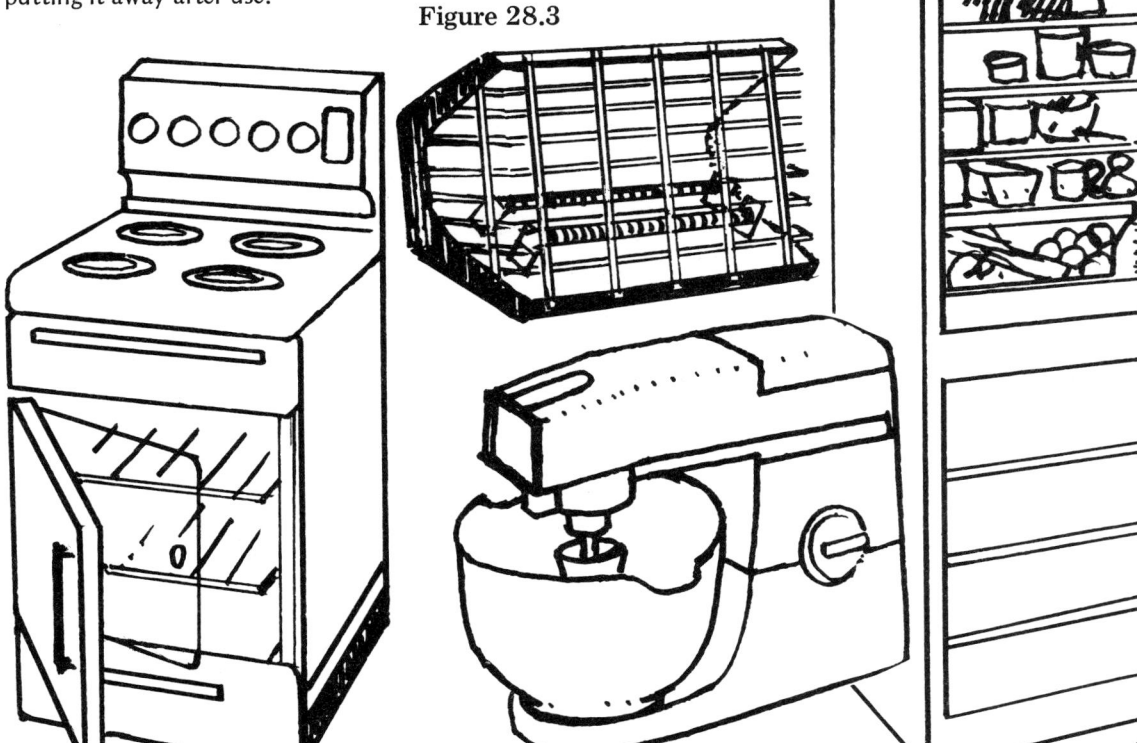

28.3
WHAT DOES SAVING TIME COST?

You can work out how much electricity the food mixer and vacuum cleaner use in a week by using columns 2 and 3 of your table (figure 28.2).

The number of units of electricity each appliance uses is

watts × hours used ÷ 1000.

For example, a vacuum cleaner of 500 watts used for 3 hours each week would use

500 × 3 ÷ 1000 = 1.5 units each week.

This, at 5p per unit, would cost 7½p.

Q 6
Do you think 7½p is a lot to pay for the energy you would have used in a week's carpet sweeping?

Q 7
How much would the electricity cost per week for your own food mixer or vacuum cleaner at home?

Q 8
The cost of electricity is not the only cost. What are the other costs involved in using the appliances?

Q 9
Try to estimate how much these other costs would add up to each week. For example, if a food mixer costs £20 and you think it should last 5 years, this would be £4 per year or about 8p per week.

28.4
GETTING THE SPEED RIGHT

Electric motors have to do all kinds of jobs. The motor in a washing machine uses a lot of force and a low speed when washing clothes. But it uses a high speed when spin-drying. The fan of a vacuum cleaner spins at a very high speed to create enough suction, but the force needed to drive the fan is not very great. A food mixer goes round much more slowly than the fan of a vacuum cleaner (otherwise food would fly out in all directions!), but the food mixer needs a greater force as it has to cut through food.

Your teacher may show you a mixer-blender in operation. Watch the demonstration and compare the speed of the blender attachment with that of the mixer. Which goes round faster? Compare this with the speed of a hand whisk.

Figure 28.4
An electric mixer with a dismantled motor beside it.

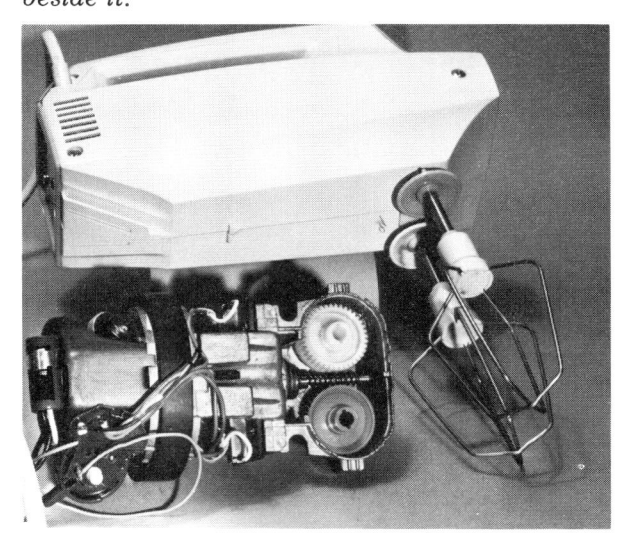

The electric motor inside the mixer-blender goes round at a very high speed. Electric motors work best when they go fast. Gears are used so that the attachments can go round more slowly than the motor. You can't see the gears because they are inside the case. This keeps the gears clean, and it is safer too.

A switch on the mixer is used to choose different speeds. This controls how much electricity goes to the motor, and makes it run faster or slower. You may know from experience how much better, or more quickly, you can do a whisking job if you have an appliance which works at the right speed.

28.5
GEARED HAND WHISKS

Your hands can't go round as fast as an electric motor. They work best going round fairly slowly. You can usually see the gears in a hand whisk. A large gear wheel is attached to the handle which drives smaller gear wheels connected to the blades.

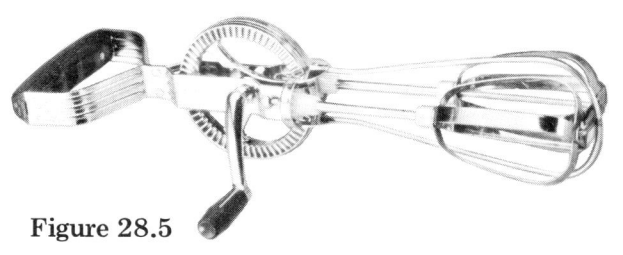

Figure 28.5

YOU WILL NEED:
Rotary hand whisk (or preferably two or three different models)
Felt-tipped pen

1 Steadily turn the handle of the hand whisk. See if the blades go round faster or more slowly than the handle. (Mark a dot on one blade of the whisk with a felt-tipped pen.)

2 Draw up a table like the one at the foot of this page ready to fill in your results. Don't copy the figures — they are just put in to help you work your own results out.

3 Turn the handle of the whisk exactly one full turn and count the number of times the blades go round. For greater accuracy, you can turn the handle exactly ten full turns, then divide the number of turns of the blades by ten. The example in the table (figure 28.6) shows you how to do this. Write down your results in the table.

4 Count the number of teeth on the large gear wheel on the handle. Now count the number of teeth on the gear wheel on the blade. If you mark a dot on one tooth with your felt tip it will help to avoid mistakes. Write down the number of teeth in your table.

5 Divide the number of teeth on the big gear wheel by the number on the small wheel. Put the answer in the table.

Remember, don't copy down these figures. They have just been made up to help you work out your own figures.

6 Repeat the measurements with any other geared hand whisks you can get. Fill in the figures in the next line of the table.

Q 10
What do you notice about the figures in column 3 and column 6?

Figure 28.6

When two gear wheels are connected together (like they are on the mixer), one will go round faster than the other. The *gear ratio* shows how many times one gear wheel turns while the wheel it is connected to turns once.

Q 11
If you couldn't make the gears of a machine go round so that you could count the turns, could you still tell the gear ratio? Explain how you could work it out by counting the teeth on each wheel.

An electric mixer uses a different kind of gear from the hand mixer. It is called a *worm* gear. The gear looks like a worm wound round a rod. It is really a kind of screw thread.

Figure 28.7

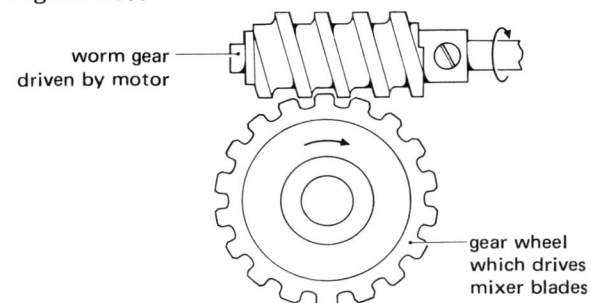

When the worm goes round once, the gear wheel only moves forward one tooth. The gear wheel shown has 18 teeth. This means that the motor has to make the worm gear go round 18 times for the gear wheel to go round once.

Q 12
If the motor goes round 18 times to make the blades of the mixer go round once, what is the gear ratio?

Worm gears are often convenient when such large gear ratios as this have to be used. They don't take up as much space as a very large gear wheel would.

Worm gears can only be used for *gear reductions*. A gear reduction is used when the appliance has to go round slower than the motor.

A No. of turns of handle	B No. of turns of the blades	B ÷ A Turns of blades per turn of handle	C No. of teeth on large gear wheel	D No. of teeth on small gear wheel	C ÷ D Teeth (large) ÷ teeth (small)
10	32	3.2	48	15	3.2

CHAPTER 29
Lighting for living

29.1
LIGHT FOR GOOD LIVING
It is not so very long ago that people had to live their lives according to the hours of daylight. When darkness fell, lighting was so poor that many activities became impossible. Streets were badly lit; there were no brightly lit shop windows to look at; reading or studying at home was difficult and tiring; and work in factories and offices was slow and inefficient.

Good lighting can extend your life in many ways. Today's cheap and efficient lighting means that you can use many more hours of your life doing things which are useful and enjoyable. Even though lighting nowadays is good and cheap, many homes, offices, and factories are still not making the most of it.

Figure 29.1
Modern lighting.

Figure 29.2 (left)
Vincent van Gogh's 'The potato eaters', painted in 1885. Notice the harsh contrast caused by the single lamp, and the darkness in the room away from the table.

29.2
HOW MUCH LIGHT DO YOU NEED?
This depends on what you are doing. If you just need light to find your way along a street or go from one room to another, you don't need a great deal. If you want to do some fine sewing or other delicate detailed work, you need much more light.

YOU WILL NEED:

A number of lamps of different powers (wattages)
Mixed bundle of blue and green threads
A sheet of black paper and a sheet of white paper
Stop clock (or wall clock with seconds hand)

1   Pick up a bundle of threads.

2   Work under one of the lamps and separate the threads into

piles of different colours. Work as quickly as you can and time how long it takes you.

3   Work with the threads resting either on a black sheet of paper or a white one — your teacher will tell you which.

Before you start, guess whether you think you will work more quickly on black paper or white paper.

4   Put your results into a table like the one below.

Figure 29.3

Lamp	Paper	Time taken by different people, in seconds								Average time, in seconds
15 watt	black	25	31	26	32	27	28	22	35	28
	white									
60 watt	black									
	white									

Q 1
Did the light make much difference?

5   When you have finished, carefully lay the threads together, nice and straight, into one bundle again. To do this, take one thread from each of your piles in turn so that the colours are all mixed up again.

6   Copy the graph (figure 29.4) into your book. Plot the points for those working on *white paper only*.

Figure 29.4

7   Draw in a smooth line joining the points.

8   Now plot the points, on the same graph, for those working on *black* paper.

9   Join these points to make a second line on your graph.

The graphs below (figures 29.5a and 29.5b) show the results of some scientific tests carried out in a factory. They were done on people who were sorting out six different types of screw. The tests were similar to the ones you have just done, though many more were carried out. The experts also had accurate instruments to measure the light falling on the work.

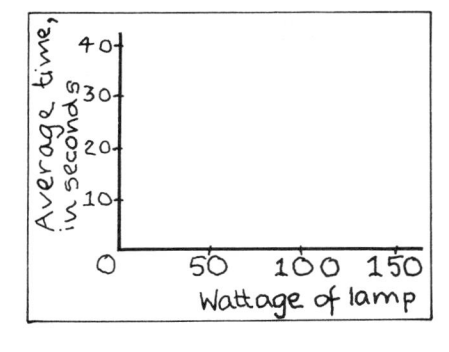

Figure 29.5a
This graph shows how sorting speeds up with better lighting.

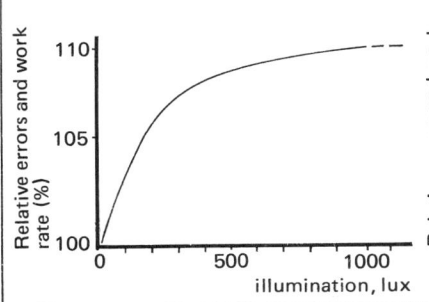

Figure 29.5b
This graph shows how the number of mistakes goes down with better lighting.

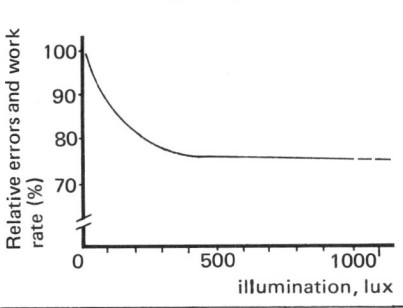

Q 2
Look at the line on the graph you drew (figure 29.4). Does the line show that more light makes you quicker or slower at doing a detailed job?

171

Experiments like these have been carried out by scientists in many countries. The table below gives some recommendations for some lighting levels.

Table 29.1
Recommended lighting levels.

Type of task	Examples	Amount of light needed (lux)
casual seeing	safe movement	100
large detail	washing up, laying the table	200
average detail	reading, writing	400
fairly detailed tasks	sewing, drawing	600
detailed and prolonged tasks	sewing with dark material	900

29.3
HOW MANY LAMPS? HOW POWERFUL?

When people are planning the lighting in their homes, they don't usually have the use of the experts' light meters. So how can you tell how many lamps you will need, and how powerful they should be?

Figure 29.6

The list below will give you a rough guide to lighting levels produced by two common types of lamp.

1 Outside in Britain on a dull day   *5000 lux*
2 Outside in Britain in bright sunshine   *100 000 lux*
3 Bedroom, 11 square metres, one filament lamp of 100 watts   *15 lux*
4 Kitchen, 11 square metres, one 4-foot long (1.2 metres) (40-watt) fluorescent tube   *50 lux*

In a small room, like examples 3 and 4 in the list, you will need for each 100 light units (lux) produced:

fluorescent: 10 to 15 watts per square metre
filament lamps: 35 to 40 watts per square metre.

29.4
ENOUGH LIGHT — IN THE RIGHT PLACE

The figures in the previous section are only average figures. The lighting level does not just depend on the lamps: it also depends on the colour of the walls, ceiling, and floor, the height of the room, and where the lamps are placed. Directly under one central lamp the light will be strong, but it will be much weaker round the edges of the room.

Turn back to your graph from figure 29.4. Compare your graph with those of your friends who used a different surface from yours.

Q 3
Was the task of separating threads quicker and easier on a black or a white background?

Most people expect it to be quicker on the white surface, so you may have been surprised. Good lighting puts light on to the thing you are looking at. Things are harder to see if light is shining in your face. The white background may hinder you because it reflects a lot of light back into your eyes. The glare may make it harder to see.

29.5
PLACING LAMPS AND FITTINGS

When you plan the lighting in your home, you try to get enough light in the places where you need it. The kind of lamps, and the fittings, shades, and diffusers you put them in, all help to do this.

Q 4
a In figure 29.7d, would the girl be able to look directly at the light from where she is standing?
b In figure 29.7g, would the boy be able to look directly at the light from where he is sitting?

Q 5
Copy the two sketches into your book. Draw dotted lines to show the areas where most of the light would fall.

Figure 29.7

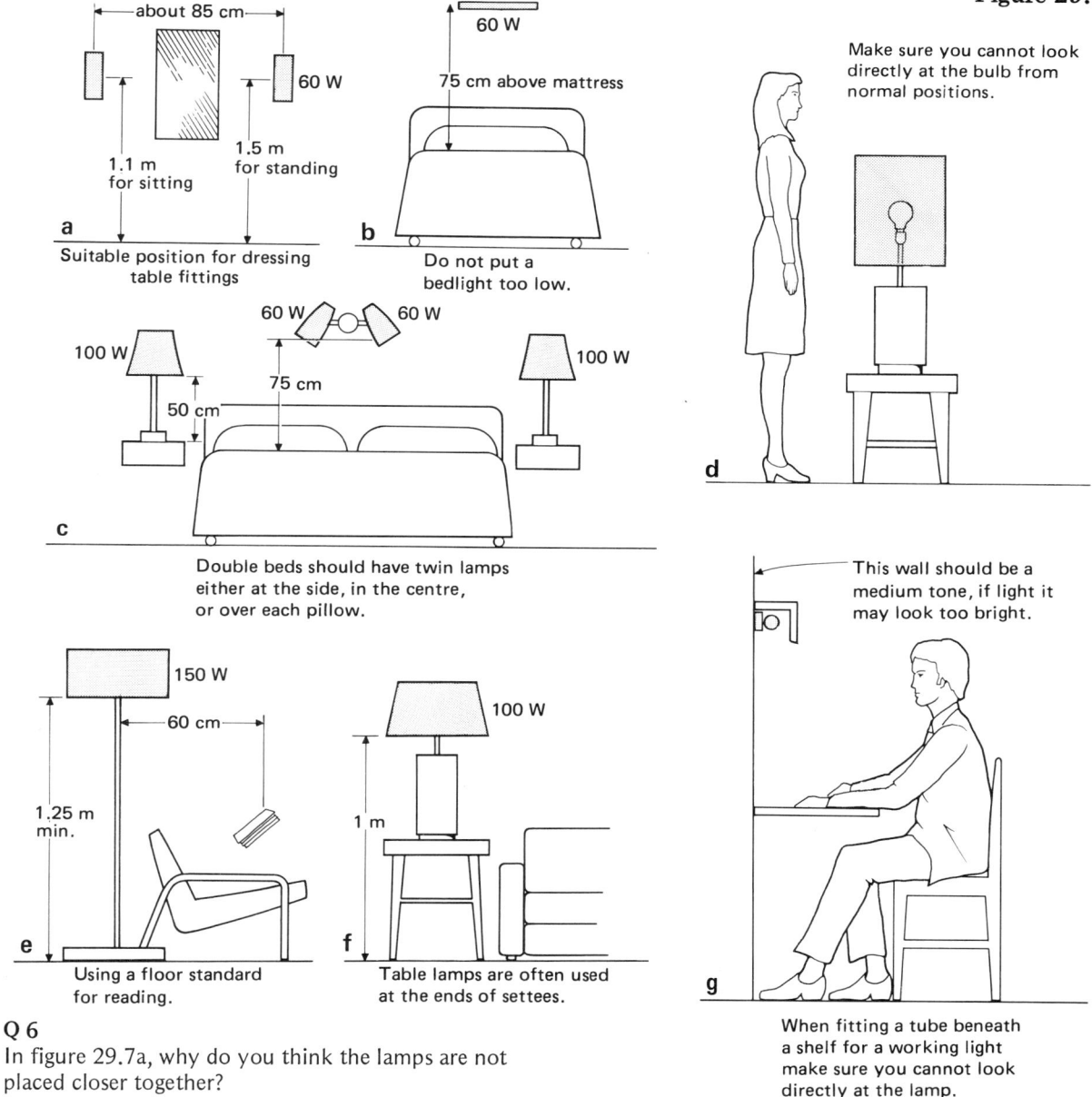

a Suitable position for dressing table fittings
- about 85 cm
- 60 W
- 1.1 m for sitting
- 1.5 m for standing

b Do not put a bedlight too low.
- 60 W
- 75 cm above mattress

c Double beds should have twin lamps either at the side, in the centre, or over each pillow.
- 60 W 60 W
- 100 W   100 W
- 75 cm
- 50 cm

d Make sure you cannot look directly at the bulb from normal positions.

e Using a floor standard for reading.
- 150 W
- 60 cm
- 1.25 m min.

f Table lamps are often used at the ends of settees.
- 100 W
- 1 m

g When fitting a tube beneath a shelf for a working light make sure you cannot look directly at the lamp.

This wall should be a medium tone, if light it may look too bright.

Q 6
In figure 29.7a, why do you think the lamps are not placed closer together?

Q 7
What is the total wattage of the lamps shown in each alternative layout in figure 29.7c?

Q 8
This would give enough light around the bed, but the lamps are all near one wall. What do you think the light would be like in other parts of the bedroom?

Q 9
If you were planning this bedroom, where else would you put lights? Say why.

29.6
LIGHTING YOUR KITCHEN

The kitchen is a place where you work. When using appliances and preparing food you need good even lighting, without shadows in the working areas. You should always arrange lighting so that shadows don't fall on surfaces (usually around the walls) where you may be working. The diagrams on the next page suggest some ways of doing this.

173

Figure 29.8

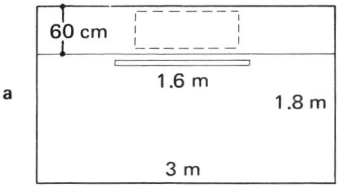

a

A small kitchen. One 65 W fluorescent fitting may be enough and should be positioned over the front edge of the sink.

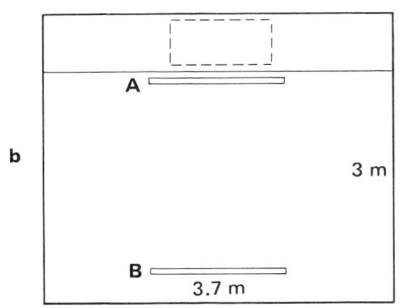

b

Medium size kitchen. Use two fittings as indicated.

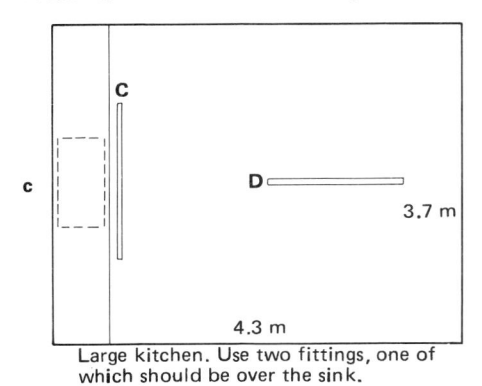

c

Large kitchen. Use two fittings, one of which should be over the sink.

A kitchen with light-coloured decoration, lit by fluorescent tubes, needs about 10 watts of lamp power for each square metre (one watt for each square foot) of floor area.

To get the right amount of light, you can choose from the following fluorescent tubes.

Table 29.2

length	4 foot	5 foot	6 foot	8 foot
wattage	40	65 or 80	85	85 or 125

If more light is needed you can get fittings which hold two tubes side by side.

Q 10
Which size of lamp (or lamps) would you use at A and B in figure 29.8b and at C and D in figure 29.8c?

Figure 29.9

Q 11
Imagine that the two lamps in the kitchen shown in figure 29.9 were replaced by a single lamp in the centre of the room. Why would this not be as good — even if the single lamp gave as much light as the total of those shown?

Q 12
a Do you think the lighting shown in figure 29.9 could be improved?
b If you could fit one more lamp, where would you place it? Explain why.

29.7
LIGHTING FOR EFFECT

Figure 29.10

Figure 29.11

When you are working in a kitchen or in a classroom, too much contrast in lighting is bad. However, in rooms where you relax, more contrast can help to create a more attractive appearance and 'atmosphere'. It can help to create different areas of the room for different activities. It can also be used to focus attention upon attractive features of the decoration.

29.8
LIGHTING AFFECTS COLOUR

You may have bought an item of clothing in a shop and then found, when you got it home, that it wasn't quite the colour you wanted. Sometimes, people take clothing to the door or window of a shop to get a better idea of the colour.

The colour you see doesn't only depend on the colour of the material: it also depends on the kind of light you use to see it. This applies to the colour of walls, curtains, carpets, and furniture, as well as to clothing.

How does light affect colour?

YOU WILL NEED:
Simple light boxes with coloured plastic windows
Samples of coloured materials
An electric lamp

1 Look through the opening in the boxes at the paint and fabric samples under different colours of light.

Figure 29.12
The lamp and light box set up.

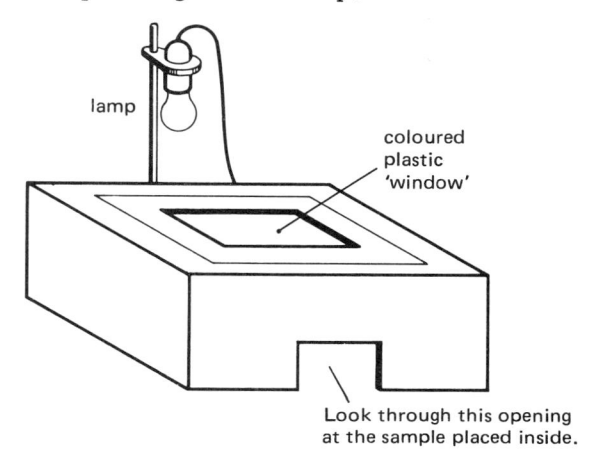

2 Draw a table in your book like the one below and fill it in.

3 Wait until the end of the experiment to fill in column 1.

Figure 29.13

Sample Number	Colour of material in daylight	Colour of light	Colour the sample appears
1			
2			
3			
4			

The colour you see depends on both the colour of the material and the colour of the light.

Q 13
Can you see any pattern in the results which will help you to predict how a colour will appear under different coloured lights?

You can't always take things home and see how they look before you buy them. It is useful to be able to predict their appearance while you are still in the shop.

175

29.9 DIFFERENT KINDS OF LAMP

Everyone is familiar with the two main kinds of lamp we use in homes, schools, and shops. They are the tungsten filament lamp and the fluorescent tube.

Which is 'best' depends on what you want to use it for.

Q 14
a Make a list of the places where you would expect fluorescent tubes to be used most.
b Make a list of places where you would expect to find tungsten filament lamps used most.

You have seen that fluorescent lamps are useful where good, shadow-free lighting is needed for working, and that tungsten filament lamps are used more when contrast and 'atmosphere' are needed.

Which lamp gives most light?

To be a fair test, you will have to compare two lamps which use the same amount of electricity.

YOU WILL NEED:
A room lit by one fluorescent lamp
A filament lamp of the same wattage as the room's fluorescent lamp
One photographers' light meter (optional but useful)

You can do this experiment at school or at home. If you do it at school, draw the blinds to shut out the daylight.

1 Turn off all the lights except one fluorescent tube. Look at the lamp and then look about the room to see how well lit it is.

2 If you have a light meter, make a note of its reading when pointed at different surfaces in the room.

3 Now replace the fluorescent tube with an ordinary filament lamp bulb of about the same wattage. This will use the same amount of electricity as the fluorescent tube.

4 Repeat your tests by looking at the lamp, about the room, and using the light meter.

Q 15
Which of these lamps gives more light?

You probably found in the last activity that you get more light from a fluorescent tube than from a tungsten filament lamp which uses the same amount of electricity.

The cost of electricity is not the only cost though. You also have to know how much the lamps themselves cost, how long they last, and how much they cost to install.

Using the table below, you can compare the cost of running a 150-watt filament lamp with a 40-watt fluorescent lamp. These two are compared because they give about the same amount of light.

Q 16
Copy the table into your book. Some of it has been filled in for you. Fill in the other spaces yourself.

Figure 29.14

	Filament lamp	Fluorescent lamp
a) Wattage	150	40
b) electricity used in 1000 hours	150 kWh (units)	
c) cost of each unit	5 p	5 p
d) total cost of electricity (b × c)	£7.50	

If you wish, you can put in the actual cost from your own electricity bill.

Lamp replacement costs are roughly the same: fluorescent tubes cost more but they will last longer. If this estimate is accurate, you would save £5.50 every 1000 hours.

Q 17
If a fluorescent tube fitting costs an *extra* £20 to install, how many hours would you have to use the lamp before you saved that £20?

Q 18
Estimate how many hours per year you use the lights in your kitchen at home. Discuss with your teacher how to make this estimate.

Q 19
a At a saving of £5.50 every 1000 hours, how long would it take you to recover the cost of the fluorescent fitting?
b Is the cost the only thing to think about?

29.10 TUNGSTEN FILAMENT LAMPS

Can you get more light out of a tungsten filament lamp? How can you make these lamps last longer?

Many people have asked this question. The Consumers' Association has investigated it and published a report in *Which?* magazine. Lamp manufacturers are always carrying out research into this. You can do a simple test yourself.

YOU WILL NEED:
A cell holder or circuit board
3 dry cells (batteries) type U2
An ammeter, reading up to 1 ampere
3 torch bulbs labelled A, B, and C
Lampholder for torch bulbs
Connecting wires
Hand lens

1 Connect up the batteries, ammeter, and lampholder as shown below in figure 29.15. Do not put the torch bulbs in the lampholder yet.

Figure 29.15

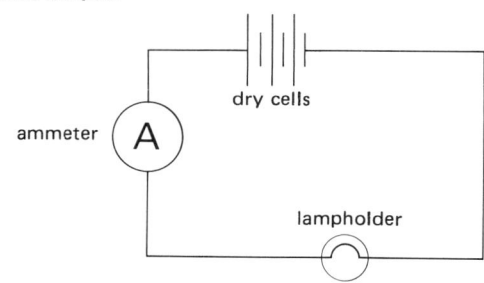

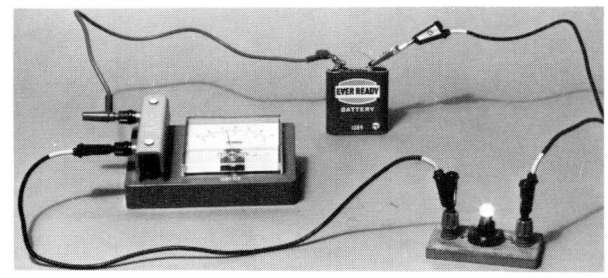

2 Draw up a table, like the one below, in your book.

Figure 29.16

3 Look at the filaments using your hand lens. Write in the second column of the table which is longest, shortest, thickest, and thinnest.

4 Screw each of the lamps into the lampholder in turn. Leave each one switched on for a few minutes while you fill in the rest of the table.

Q 20
What did you notice about the amount of electricity the lamps used?

Q 21
Did they all give the same amount of light?

Q 22
Which lamp was the most efficient at turning the energy of electricity into light? Which was least efficient?

Q 23
What happened to the most efficient lamp after a few minutes? Why do you think this happened?

This shows you that filament lamps can be made to give a lot of light. The way to do it is to make the lamps so that their filaments get very hot.

Tungsten is used to make the filaments because it can get hotter than other metals before it melts. The hotter the filament gets, the more light it gives.

There is a snag though. The hotter the filament gets, the sooner it burns out.

So there is a choice. You can have lamps that give a lot of light, but don't last long. Or, you can have lamps that will last for ever, but won't give much light.

Manufacturers strike a balance between the two. Lamps which last about 1000 hours are generally the best compromise. There are some 2000 hour lamps made. They don't give as much light for the electricity they use. They may be a good thing though if they save you having to change lamps in awkward places.

Lamp	Description of filament	Current filament takes	Brightness of light	Brightness after a few minutes
A				
B				

CHAPTER 30

Home heating and energy

30.1
HEATING YOUR HOME

In the last chapter, you saw how people's lives have been improved by good and cheap lighting. Modern heating has done the same — although it is not so cheap.

Good lighting means that you can use more hours of your life — the hours when it is dark. It's like living longer!

Good heating means that you can use more of the space in your home. Not many years ago, most homes in Britain had just one coal fire in the living room. In cold weather, the whole family would be together in that one room. Today, with central heating, the whole house is heated so the family can do different things in different rooms.

Figure 30.1   Figure 30.2

In January 1965, about 2¼ million homes were centrally heated in Britain out of a total of about 19 million homes. This is less than one-eighth of all the homes. By January 1979, this figure had grown to 47 per cent — nearly half.

As standards of living rise, more and more energy is needed, so more and more fuel is used. The fuels we use are getting both scarcer and more expensive.

Nearly one-third (about 30 per cent) of the energy used in Britain is used in homes. Most of this is used for heating.

Is it possible to use less fuel and still be warm enough?

30.2
HOW MUCH HEAT? HOW POWERFUL SHOULD HEATERS BE?

Set up the box and the other apparatus as in figures 30.4 and 30.5. You will use it to find out how different powered heaters affect the temperature inside a house. The box represents the house and the 24-watt lamp represents its heaters. You will also use it to find out how different insulating materials affect the way a house heats up. Your teacher will tell you what to put on top of the box.

YOU WILL NEED:
Box to represent a model home
Piece of cardboard
Pieces of building materials and home insulating materials
12-volt lamp (car headlight type) and lampholder
Thermometer, −10 °C to 110 °C
12-volt power supply

Figure 30.4

1 Connect the wires from the bulb to a 12-volt power supply and switch on.

2 Note the temperature reading of the thermometer at the start and at every half minute thereafter.

3 Make a table of the time and temperature readings in your book as shown in figure 30.3.

Figure 30.5

Figure 30.3

Time (minutes)	0	½	1	1½	2	
Temperature (°C)	20	24				

Your teacher will tell you how long to go on doing this. Don't copy down the temperature readings shown in figure 30.3. Use your own figures.

4 You will have some spare time while waiting to take temperature readings. Use it to draw a graph on rough paper like the one on the right (figure 30.6). Plot the points on the graph as you write them into your table.

Figure 30.6

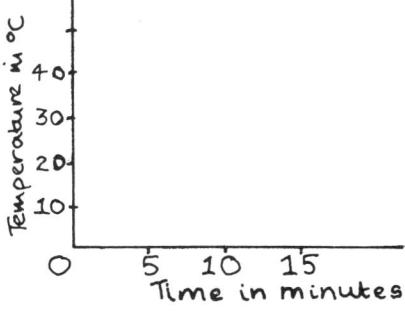

Q 1
Look at your graph. When is the temperature rising fastest? Is it when the house is coldest or later when it has warmed up a bit?

Q 2
a If the 'heater' was left on for a long time, roughly what temperature do you think the 'house' would reach?
b Describe what you think would happen to the temperature after this.

5 Switch off the lamp when your teacher tells you to. Continue to note the temperature every half minute. Make a table and draw a graph as you did before. (This time the 'house' will be cooling down instead of heating up.)

Q 3
Describe what happened to the temperature after you switched off the heater. Look at your answers to questions 1 and 2 on the previous page and try to use similar sentences to describe cooling down.

Compare your results and graphs with somebody else's whose experiment was different from yours. (You should compare two experiments, one with the 'house' roof insulated and one without insulation.) The boxes and heaters should be exactly the same to make it a fair test.

Q 4
Which 'house' heated up quicker, the one with the insulation or the one without?

Q 5
a Estimate the temperatures at which the insulated 'house' and the uninsulated 'house' would finally settle if the heater were left on for a long time.
b Which would be warmer?

Q 6
How long did it take the insulated 'house' and the uninsulated 'house' to warm up from 20 °C to 30 °C? Use your graph to find out.

Q 7
Which house warmed up more quickly?

Your experiment will probably have shown that an insulated house:

warms up more quickly;
gets warmer;
and cools down more slowly

than an uninsulated house. So, you could have turned down the heater on the insulated 'house' and still made it heat up as quickly as the uninsulated one. In a real house this would have saved fuel.

30.3
WHERE DOES THE HEAT GO?

In figure 30.7, the figures show typical heat losses for a semi-detached house which has no added insulation. It gives you some idea of where most saving can be made.

Q 8
Write down *one* thing you could do to cut down the heat a house loses by each of these ways.

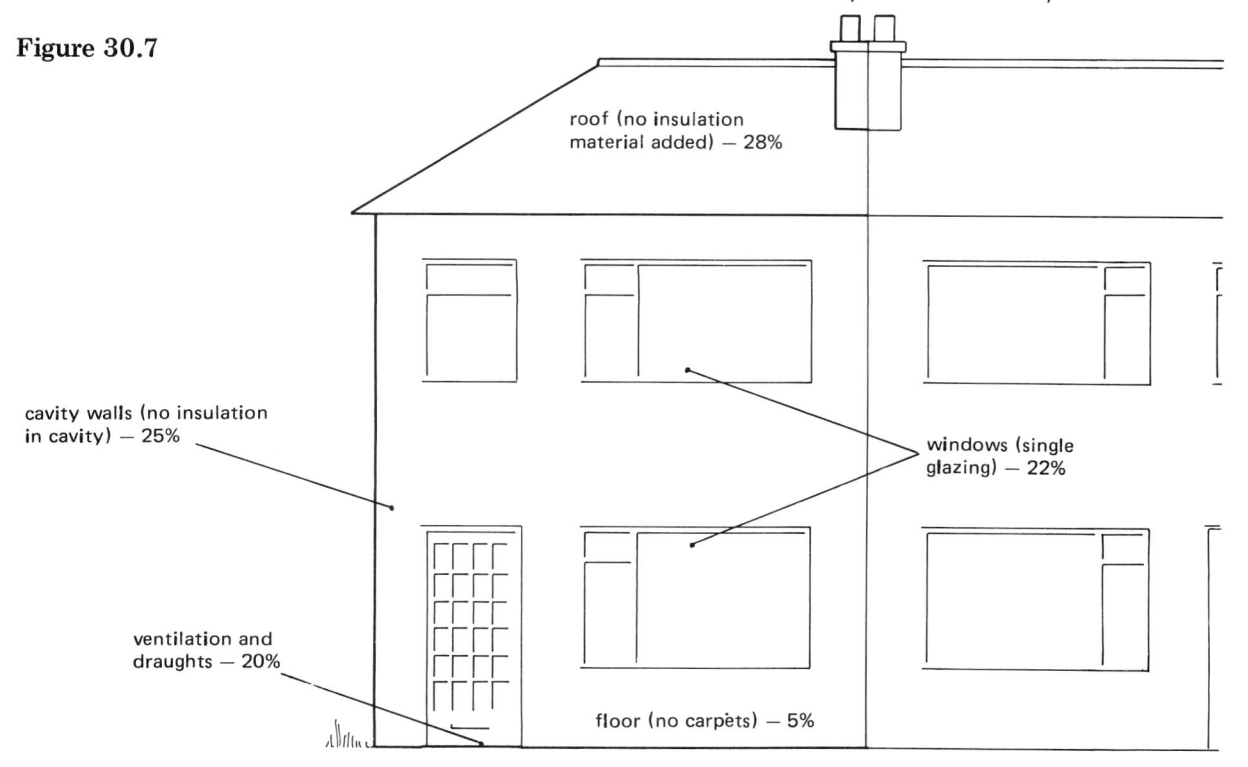

Figure 30.7

roof (no insulation material added) — 28%

cavity walls (no insulation in cavity) — 25%

windows (single glazing) — 22%

ventilation and draughts — 20%

floor (no carpets) — 5%

30.4
THE CHOICE OF FUELS FOR HEATING

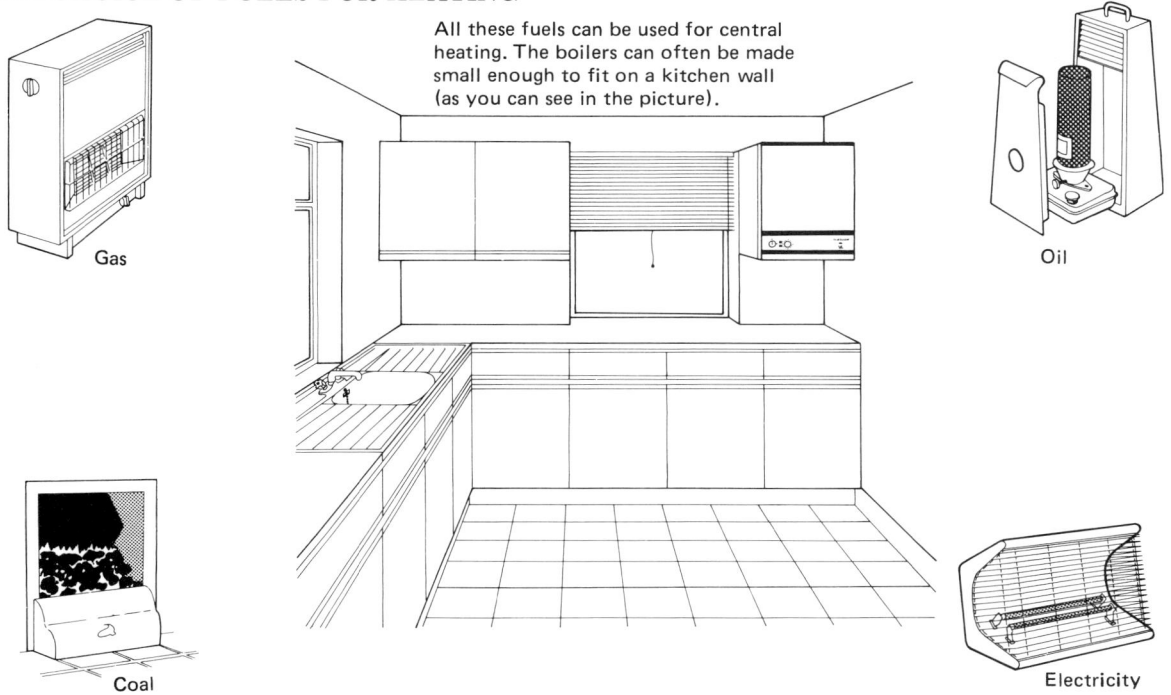

All these fuels can be used for central heating. The boilers can often be made small enough to fit on a kitchen wall (as you can see in the picture).

Gas

Oil

Coal

Electricity

Q 9
Which of these ways of heating is the odd one out? Discuss your ideas with your teacher.

You can choose from a number of different fuels and heating systems. Each has its advantages and disadvantages. These make each type suit some people and not others. For example, having to carry fuel to stoke a solid-fuel boiler or fire may not be a serious disadvantage if you are fit and healthy, but it could be for someone who is old or disabled.

Some qualities you might have to think about in deciding on which heating system and fuel to use are:

cost;
convenience;
controllability;
the space needed for the heaters, radiators, and flues;
fuel storage.

There are many others.

Q 10
Make a list of as many other qualities as you can think of to add to the list above. Put your ideas together with your teacher to make as long a list as you can.

Figure 30.8
Different sources of energy and appliances for home heating.

In figure 30.8, electricity is the odd one out. All the others are fuels which you can burn. This turns their chemical energy into heat. Usually when you use electricity, the fuel has been burnt at the power station. The heat it gives is used to raise steam which drives the turbines. These turbines drive the generators which make electricity.

Figure 30.9
Turbines at a power station.

30.5 HEAT FROM ELECTRICITY

Q 11
In your model 'house', you used a 24-watt lamp as a heater. Would the 'house' have warmed up quicker if you had used a 24-watt heater instead of a 24-watt lamp? Discuss this question with your teacher.

When an appliance is rated at 24 watts, it means that it changes 24 joules of electrical energy into other sorts of energy every second. Eventually, all this energy turns into heat. So it would not matter what sort of electrical appliance you used because, in the end, you would always get 24 joules of heat every second.

Where does energy go?

Figure 30.10
This is what happens to the energy put into a 500-watt vacuum cleaner.

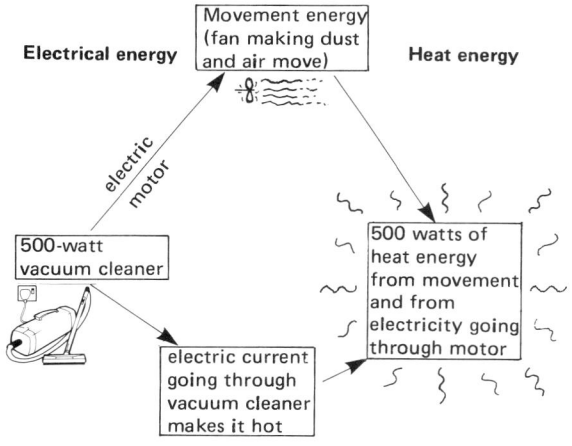

Figure 30.11
This is what happens to the energy put into five 100-watt light bulbs.

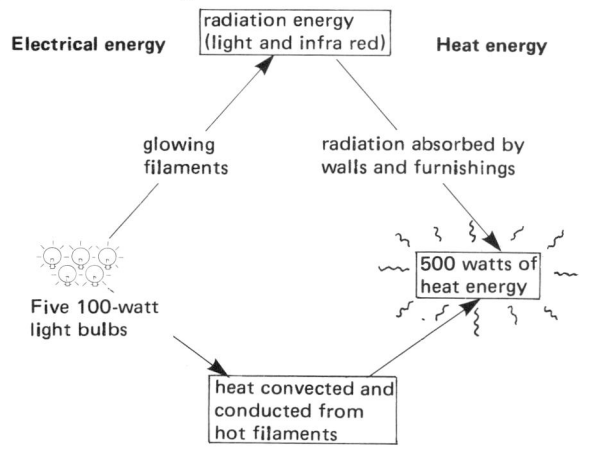

Whichever way you use the electricity, you get 500 watts of heat energy out of it. That is 500 joules every second. An electric heater of 500 watts; a vacuum cleaner of 500 watts; or electric lamps totalling 500 watts, all end up giving exactly the same amount of heat every second.

It is really wasting electricity just to use it in a heater — you may just as well use it for something else first — like running a food mixer, a vacuum cleaner, or some lights. You still get the same amount of heat. Of course, usually it isn't all that convenient to use a vacuum cleaner as a heater!

However, you should not forget the contribution to heating that electrical equipment makes: especially things like lamps, fridges, freezers, and television sets which are used for long periods.

Figure 30.12

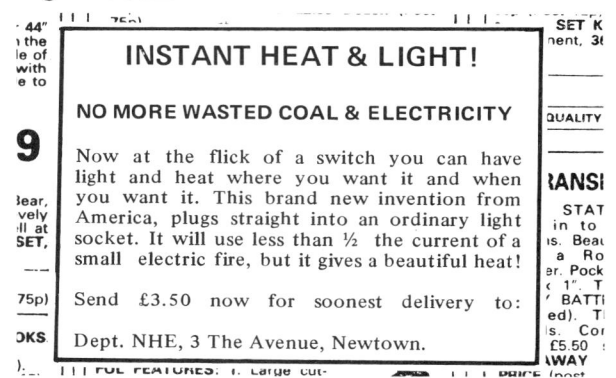

> **INSTANT HEAT & LIGHT!**
>
> **NO MORE WASTED COAL & ELECTRICITY**
>
> Now at the flick of a switch you can have light and heat where you want it and when you want it. This brand new invention from America, plugs straight into an ordinary light socket. It will use less than ½ the current of a small electric fire, but it gives a beautiful heat!
>
> Send £3.50 now for soonest delivery to:
>
> Dept. NHE, 3 The Avenue, Newtown.

Look at the advertisement in figure 30.12.

Q 12
What do you think the advertisement means when it says 'gives beautiful heat'? Does it tell you how much heat it gives?

Q 13
The advertisement says 'it uses less than half the current of the smallest electric fire'. How much heat will it give compared with that electric fire — more, slightly less, or less than half?

You may have read that electricity is 100 per cent efficient when used for heating. It is true that all the electricity you use turns into heat. Refrigerators, food mixers, lamps, and heaters all give out heat to the room.

You may wonder why electricity is generally more expensive than other fuels for home heating. The reason is that only about one-third of the energy from the fuel burned at the power station is actually turned into electricity. Two-thirds of the fuel is wasted. Most of the wasted heat is in the steam after it has driven the turbines. It is still quite hot, but not hot enough to drive the turbines. One idea is to have many small power stations near people's homes. The waste steam could then be piped into homes for central heating. It is still quite hot enough to be used to heat a house.

30.6
ENERGY CONSUMPTION IN HOMES

Heating homes does use up a lot of energy. About 30 per cent of Britain's energy is used in homes and heating accounts for nearly two-thirds of this. All this heat eventually leaks away and warms the air outside. By insulating your home, you can make the heat leak away more slowly so you don't have to use so much fuel to keep the house warm.

In other sections of this book, you will have seen how important energy really is.

In *Food science* Chapter 4, you will have learned that in cooking heat reaches food by conduction, convection, and radiation. This energy changes the food, and makes it more pleasant to eat or easier to digest.

Cooking uses about 10 per cent of the energy used in homes. So, if you think about what you have learned in that section, you can save some energy as well as time.

In *Nutrition* Chapter 10, you learned that your body needs energy, and that it gets it from food. This energy is needed to keep your body warm, keep all its parts working, and let you move about.

Anything that moves — cars, ships, planes, or trains — needs fuel for energy. Food provides that fuel to give your body energy.

Fibres and fabrics help to keep you warm. This can be as clothes or bedclothes, but remember that carpets, curtains, and glassfibre matting in your roof all help to keep your house warm. By cutting down heat loss they both save fuel and make life more comfortable.

In *People and homes*, you have seen how people's lives have been changed by having supplies of energy which are easily available and can be controlled. Everybody would live poorer lives without energy for heating, lighting, and running the many appliances used in modern homes.

Figure 30.13
The first experimental windmill to be connected to the National Grid. It could provide 30kW.

Energy is one of the most important ideas there is in home economics, in science, and in the whole world. Without it all life and movement would stop.

The planet Earth is using up many of its sources of energy. Once all the oil, natural gas, and coal are used up, there won't be any more for future generations. The only answer will be to find other sources of energy.

Q 14
a   Write down some other ways we could get energy for homes apart from burning fuels.
b   What are their advantages and disadvantages? Discuss your ideas with your teacher.

It makes sense to understand about energy so that you can save fuel and your own money, and still live comfortably.

Index

A
acid and tooth decay, 81—2
additives, 53
alimentary canal, 72
amino acids, 76
amps, 156—7
appliances, electrical, *see* electrical appliances
appliances, kitchen, 10—13
Arab houses, 141
astronauts, 139

B
babies, and food, 66—7, 92
bacteria, 41
baked beans, 1—7; canned, 2—7; home cooked, 6—7
balanced diet, 69
batik, 118
beans: baked, varieties of, 1—7; navy, 1
Bedu tent, 148—9
bicarbonate of soda, 29, 31—2
bile, 73
blender, 10—11
blends and mixtures (fabrics), 110
blood, 75
Bodiam castle, 140
boiling water, different methods of, 17
Bombay, 139
bones, 75
bread: cooking, 28—31; or flour, 69; nutrients in, 86; mould on, 44; protein in, 70
breast feeding, 66—7, 92
building materials, 144—8; properties of, 150—3

C
cables, electric, 160—2; three-core, 160—2; two-core, 160—2
calcium, 54—5, 76, 82—3
calories, 60
carbohydrates, 48; structure of, 72
care labelling, 135—6
carrot-juice addict, 76
central heating, 179—83
chocolate sauce, 34—5
chromatography, 56
clay, as building material, 147
cleaning of fabrics, 130—5
Clinistix test for glucose, 56
clothes: and body temperature, 124—8; flexibility of, 126—7; heat loss through, 127—8; permeability of, 129
cobalt chloride test, 43
coeliac disease, 91
coleslaw, making, 10—11
colon, 73
conduction of heat, 20, 23—4, 128

convection, 20, 24—5, 128
convenience foods, 3, 8—10
conversion scales, metric/imperial, volume, temperature, 38
cookers, 14—19; costs, 15; design of, 14; testing, 18—19
cooking: basic processes, 14, 20, 24—5; choosing methods, 16—18; cost of, 15; time of, 20; utensils, 22—4
cotton, 112—3
crease recovery, 117
'Crispometer', 43—4
cucumber, effect of freezing, 42—3
culture, and food choice, 65
curry, 46

D
DCPIP test for vitamin C, 32—3, 56
detergents, 131—4
diet: choosing a, 84—9; problems, 90—2
dietary fibre, 77
dietary survey, 78—9
digestion, 72—7
digestive system, 73
Dorset houses, 146
dry cleaning, 135—6
dyes, 118—123; natural, 119—121; synthetic, 119, 121—123

E
earth wire, 162, 164—5
East Anglian houses, 146
egg separator, 11
electric current, 156—7; alternating, 162; direct, 162
electric motor, 166—9
electrical appliances: cost to run, 157—8; safety, 160—5; wattage, 155—8; work saving, 166—9
electricity: cost, 154—9; for heating, 181—3; safety, 160—5; saving work, 166—9
energy: and exercise, 60—1; and fat, 58—9; in food, 48, 51, 53, 55, 61—3; in peanuts, 62—3; measurement, 60—1
energy consumption in homes, 183
'energy slaves', 166
enzymes: digestive, 72—5; in food, 40—1
epidemiology, 79

F
fabrics: and clothes, 124—7; cleaning, 130—6; different uses of, 94—9; dyeing, 118—23; effect of heat on, 115, 134—5; flammability, 116—7; heat loss through, 127—8; knitted, 103, 104—5; non-woven, 101; structure of, 100—5, 114; water loss through, 129; wear testing, 114—5; woven, 102; yarns in, 106—11
fatness, testing, 58—9
fats, 48
fatty acids, 76
felt, 101—2
fibres: continuous filament, 109; creasing, 117; in fabrics, 100—3, 114; flammability of, 116—7; man-made, 112; natural, 112; staple, 109; textile, 112—3; in yarns, 106—11
flammability of fibres, 116—7
flex, 160—2
fluorescent tubes, 172, 174, 176
food: and age, 66—7, 91—2; changes on cooking, 26—33; choice of, 64—71; choice of cooker, 14—19; digesting, 72—7; energy in, 58—63; foreign, 46—9, 64—6; and health, 51, 78—83; labelling, 40; measuring, 37—9; methods of cooking, 20—5; and nutritious diet, 84—9; nutrients in, 52—7, 86—7; preparation, 8—13; recipes, 34—7; and slimming, 90; storing, 40—4; take-away, 8, 10; tests, 55
food industry, 68, 84
food processor, 13
'Foofoo', 47
freezers, 41—3
frozen food: and ice crystals, 42; popularity of, 8—9; storage of, 41—3
fuels for heating, 181—3
fuses, 164—5
'Foofoo', 47
freezers, 41—3
frozen food: and ice crystals, 42; popularity of, 8—9; storage of, 41—3
fuels for heating, 181—3
fuses, 164—5

G
gadgets, kitchen, 10—13
gears, on appliances, 168—9
glucose, 65, 76; test for, 74
gluten: in bread making, 30; and coeliac disease, 91
grease spot test for fat, 56
green vegetables, cooking, 31—3, 71
grilling, 16, 20

H
hamburgers, 46
heart attack, 80

heat: effect on fabrics, 115, 134—5; effect on food, 27—33; in homes, 178—83; transport in cooking, 20—5
histograms, 38, 49, 81
homes, 142—3
house building, 144—9; cost of, 146—7; local styles, 146—7; materials, 150—3
houses, 138—43; and climate, 140—2; electricity in, 154—69; heating, 178—83; lighting in, 170—7
hypothermia, 125

I
igloo, 149
insulation, 128, 179—80
insulators, electrical, 163
intestine, 73
intravenous feeding, 74
iodine, 76
iodine test for starch, 30, 56, 74
iron in diet, 55, 76, 88, 92
ironing, 115

J
joules, 60

K
kilocalories, 60—3
kilojoules, 60—3
kitchen: floors, 150, 152—3; gadgets, 10—13; lighting, 173—5
knitted fabrics, 103—5

L
lamps, 172, 174—7
Le Corbusier, 138
lemon chiffon, 11—13
light boxes, 175
lighting: in homes, 170—7; kitchen, 173—5; levels, 172
looms, 102—3

M
Malaysian long house, 139
malnutrition, 47—9, 80, 82—3
materials game, 150—1
mauveine, 119
measuring equipment, 37—9
microbes (micro-organisms), 41
microwaves, 20, 22
milk, 69
mixer-blender, 168
models of solids, liquids, and gases, 23
mordants, 119—121
mould, 41, 44
mower, fatal accident, 160
muscles, 75

N
nerves, 75
newton, 60
nomograms, metric/imperial conversion, 38
nutrients: bar charts of, 86—7; in diet, 84—9; digestion of, 72—6;
in foods, 48, 52—7, 70—1; storage in body, 76

O
onions, cooking, 31
orange drink experiment, 62
oven: testing temperatures in, 17—19; usage, 16
overdyeing, 122

P
'peanut power', 62—3
people, differences in size, 49—51
Perkin, W.H., 119
plaque, 81
ply, yarns and, 106—7, 110
potassium in diet, 54
potatoes, cooking, 25, 28, 63
protective clothing, 125—6
proteins, 27, 30, 47, 48, 53—7, 70, 72—6, 86—87; test for, 56
pygmies, 50

Q
quality control: of clothes, 114—5; in food, 4—5

R
R.D.A., 55, 86—9
R.D.I., 55, 86—9
radiation of heat, 20—2
raising agents, 28—30
rating plate, 155—6, 165
refrigerator, 41—3
religion, and food, 65
rice, 64
rickets, 82—3

S
saliva, 73
scones, 19
shelf-life of foods, 43
shortcrust pastry, 35—7
silk, 112—3
slimming, 63, 90
slow cooker, 25
small cakes, 19
Smartie: energy in, 61; test, 56
smoking, 51
snacks, 8, 85
sodium in diet, 54—5
soiling of fabrics, 130—6
spaghetti, 46
spices, 3
sport, fabrics for, 96—7, 109, 129
stairs, work in climbing, 60—1
starch, 27, 30, 74—5; structure of, 72; test for, 30, 56, 74
'stuffer box', 109
stomach, 73
sucrose, 55
sugar and tooth decay, 51, 81—2
sugar cane and beet, 2

T
taste panel, 5
thatched huts, 141
thermostat, 17
therms, of gas, 15
thiamin, 76, 87
tiles, for floors, 152—3
toast experiment, 21
tooth decay, 51, 81—2
tungsten filament lamps, 172, 176—7
Tutsi, 50

U
unit, electrical, 15, 157—9

V
vegetables, cooking, 31—3, 71
vegetarianism, 89
Victoria sandwich, 19
Victorian menus, 68
vinegar, 3, 31—2
vitamin A, 54—5, 76
vitamin B, 54—5, 76
vitamin C, 54—5, 76, 92; in vegetables, 32—3; test for, 32—3
vitamin D, 54—5, 82
vitamin K, 54—5
vitamins, 48
volts, 155—6, 162

W
warp and weft, 103—4
water: in diet, 48, 55; food test for, 43
watts, 155—8, 165
wear-testing, 114—5, 153
weight, people's, 58, 80, 90
Which? reports, 152, 177
whisk: electric, 12—13; gears of, 168—9; hand, 12—13
wood, as building material, 147—8
wool, 112—3
work, calculation of, 60; saving, 166—9
working women, 9
wrapping materials, 43—4

Y
yarns, 100—111; blended, 110—1 bulked, 109—110; continuous filament, 108—9; in different fabrics, 102—5; special effect, 111; spun, 108—9
yeast, 29—30, 41